Esther Baldwin, Martin Curley

Managing Innovation in the Digital World

Esther Baldwin, Martin Curley

Managing Innovation in the Digital World

DE GRUYTER

ISBN 978-1-5015-1578-1
e-ISBN (PDF) 978-1-5015-0733-5
e-ISBN (EPUB) 978-1-5015-0723-6

Library of Congress Control Number: 2025940833

Bibliographic information published by the Deutsche Nationalbibliothek
The Deutsche Nationalbibliothek lists this publication in the Deutsche Nationalbibliografie; detailed bibliographic data are available on the internet at http://dnb.dnb.de.

Cover image: Jackie Niam / iStock / Getty Images Plus
Typesetting: Integra Software Services Pvt. Ltd.

www.degruyterbrill.com
Questions about General Product Safety Regulation:
productsafety@degruyterbrill.com

Foreword

It is my pleasure to introduce *Managing Innovation in a Digital World*, a book that arrives at a critical time when navigating and harnessing digital technologies is more important than ever for driving innovation. This work is particularly relevant for anyone involved in leading change within today's complex environments.

As President of Maynooth University in Ireland, and through my experience in higher education leadership across different countries, I've seen firsthand the challenges and opportunities that come with innovation. Digital innovation has transformed every sector, including higher education, from how we operate to how we teach and learn. While I value steady progress, I'm also a strong advocate for taking bold, transformative steps when the moment calls for it. The challenge is not just knowing when to act but how to do so effectively, building on our strengths while moving forward. This book offers practical insights into managing these complexities and understanding when—and how—to seize opportunities for real impact.

At Maynooth University, innovation and digital transformation are central to our strategy and vision. I've had the pleasure of working with Professor Martin Curley who exemplifies our commitment to these areas. Through his work at the Innovation Value Institute, Martin has made Maynooth University a hub for thought leadership and practical solutions, especially in healthcare. His ability to bridge academia and industry has led to impactful collaborations, reinforcing our university's role as a leader in innovation.

Esther Baldwin, an AI strategist at Intel, brings a wealth of experience to this book. Intel, renowned for its pioneering approach to innovation, has been at the forefront of technological advancement for decades. Esther's work in artificial intelligence is shaping the technologies that influence our world today. Our strategic partnership with Intel has allowed Maynooth University to collaborate closely with leaders like Esther, advancing our shared goals in research, innovation, and nurturing future talent. Together, Esther and Martin offer a powerful combination of academic insight and practical expertise, making this book a comprehensive guide to managing innovation in the digital age.

This book addresses a pressing need: how to innovate effectively in a fast-evolving digital landscape. The strategies and methodologies Martin and Esther share, supported by real world examples from sectors such as healthcare, retail, and manufacturing, are designed to help organisations increase their success rates and achieve greater impact. They explore how innovation can become a systematic capability within organisations, introducing tools and frameworks that guide improvement.

https://doi.org/10.1515/9781501507335-202

A highlight of the book is its exploration of the evolution of innovation, particularly the emergence of Open Innovation 2.0 (OI2). This approach, built on open collaborative ecosystems, is illustrated with case studies showing how OI2 delivers exponential outcomes. The Innovation Value Institute at Maynooth University is featured as a key example, demonstrating how organizations across multiple industries collaborate to drive advancements using the practices outlined in this book. Additionally, the Innovation Value Institute hosts a vast repository of research on OI2, supported by the European Commission, Intel, and Maynooth University, offering further resources for those interested.

Central to these strategies is the understanding that innovation thrives in a culture of creativity and collaboration. The 4E Leadership philosophy—Envision, Enable, Empower to Excel—captures this connection between leadership and innovation, providing practical guidance for those leading change today. As Martin and Esther demonstrate, the right blend of culture and innovation practices can lead to better solutions, sustainable progress, and long-term impact.

Managing Innovation in a Digital World is an essential guide for anyone navigating the challenges of innovation today. The insights, examples, and methodologies provided will empower you to drive successful innovation initiatives and make a lasting impact.

I hope you find this book as enlightening and thought-provoking as I did. May it guide and inspire you on your journey to innovate and make a difference.

Professor Eeva Leinonen
President
Maynooth University

Contents

Chapter 1
Introduction

Innovation is the specific instrument of entrepreneurship. It is the act that endows resources with a new capacity to create wealth. — Peter F. Drucker

Innovating while living in a world that has become increasingly digital has moved innovation tools and practices into virtual spaces. The COVID-19 pandemic required a rapid migration to working digitally and accelerated innovation and adoption everywhere. Where once people could meet and practice innovation face-to-face, working from home has forced the use of digital tools and practices in order to foster innovation in a digital world.

We need to recognize the centrality of innovation to all our lives and collective human progress. Former US President Barack Obama once said, "Innovation just doesn't change our lives, it is how we make a living" emphasizing innovation is the engine of progress.

Marc Andreesen famously said software is eating the world and industry after industry is succumbing to digital innovation with giants of the past being replaced by new companies, which are disrupting and creating waves of new value. Take, for example, the retail industry where in the United States, giants such as Sears and JCPenney saw their market capitalization fall by more than 80 percent in the decade from 2006 to 2016 (to bankruptcy in ensuing years) while Amazon, which has pioneered digital innovation in retail, has seen its market capitalization grow by over 1900 percent even by 2016.

Hans Vestberg, CEO of Ericsson, is credited with saying, "The pace of change will never be this slow again." According to Professor Mark Perry of the University of Michigan, "75% of the current S&P 500 will be replaced within 10 years." This is an unprecedented level of change. How do and should companies respond to this phenomenon?

Kurzweil's Law of Accelerating Returns predicts that the pace of digital innovation will continue to accelerate as new innovations quickly become infrastructure to underpin future innovations. The new Open Innovation 2.0 (OI2) Digital Innovation paradigm illuminates key broad patterns to improve the success of digital innovations. The rapid rise of digital infrastructure during the COVID-19 pandemic has become foundational to support working from home, shopping from home and home delivery of every kind. It is the Zoom and Windows Teams platforms, partnered with innovation-specific tools like Miro, that have allowed innovation to continue during the world's largest "shutdown" in history. COVID-

https://doi.org/10.1515/9781501507335-001

19 indeed acted as a big bang disruptor for the global health industry, rapidly accelerating both innovation and innovation adoption to meet very specific needs.

This book discusses how to manage innovation in a corporate environment in this new digital world. We believe that innovation is something that can be measured and managed and we share best practice and experience, from our corporate experience, to provide patterns others can follow and improve upon to deliver innovation results, which are more predictable, probable, and profitable.

In the book, information technology (IT) innovation and digital innovation are seen as synonymous. We define digital as the innovation with, and the use of, both information and technology to drive improved individual, organizational, and ecosystem performance.

Digital innovation is closely related to digital transformation and Vial's (2019) definition of digital transformation is powerful: "a process that aims to improve an entity by triggering significant changes to its properties through combinations of information, computing, communication, and connectivity technologies."

We define innovation as the creation and adoption of something new that creates value for the organization that adopts it. When narrowly defined, the primary goal of innovation is new product development. When defined more broadly, as it is in this book, opportunities to innovate and create business value permeate the organization. Indeed, it is a mistake to only focus on product innovation. Opportunities to build innovative IT or digital solutions methodically and to deploy these solutions quickly are especially attractive, and that is one focus of this book. The second focus is on IT systems that support innovation across the enterprise. We describe *innovation-enabling service environments* with examples and case studies from leading companies such as Intel, Ireland's Health Service Executive (HSE), and others.

For some, innovation necessarily implies that an entirely new idea is required, as if innovation were entirely equivalent to invention. We believe that innovation also includes the reapplication of existing ideas in different contexts. Across the organizations at companies like Intel, MasterCard, HSE and fellow travellers, we seek out best-known methods (BKMs) or design patterns to share.

Michael Schrage of MIT has written, "Innovation is not innovators innovating, it is customer's adopting." New ideas with the potential to create value can fail to do so, usually because of problems with adoption. New ideas, clever products, and helpful IT solutions that do not find their way into usage, for whatever reason, cannot deliver business value. Innovation theorists, such as Everett Rogers (2003), believe adoption is driven by *diffusion*, which they believe to be primarily a social process. We will discuss diffusion later in the book.

Table 1.1: Impact of Maturity in Innovation Capability.

Maturity level	**Who sees the innovations?**	**Who benefits from the innovations?**	**How do they benefit?**
Optimizing	Industry	Shareholders	Increased shareholder value, stock appreciation, higher dividends, willingness to invest, societal value
Advanced	Executives	Customers	Needs are met, customers are satisfied, loyal, and committed
Intermediate	Managers	Company	Growth, new markets open, image and reputation enhanced, increased revenues and markets, higher retention of employees and customers, greater longevity
Basic	All employees	All employees	New job opportunities, greater job satisfaction, recognition and rewards, creative workspace, higher energy, and a sense of ownership
Initial	Individuals and managers responsible for R&D and incubation	R&D's individuals and managers	Big wins, which occur occasionally in unstructured environments, receive recognition and rewards

Source: Intel IT

The Importance of Innovation

Innovation is a capability that can help companies, organizations and indeed ecosystems stay ahead of their competition and exceed their customers' and stockholders' expectations. Executed poorly or not at all, IT innovation or digital innovation can cause a company to fall behind as the pace of business change quickens every year. There is a certain minimum pace of innovation required just to maintain an organization's current competitive position.

IT and digital innovation are especially important because they are a pervasive enabler of business processes and new products and services. Thus, innovative IT capabilities fuel the agility and efficiency of the entire company. The ability to quickly adapt and adopt new digital innovation was never more important than during the COVID-19 pandemic. Companies that were not already innovating in this space began to fail due to the dramatic change in our working and living environment.

We are also seeing a shift in the focus of innovation from being about just creating shareholder value to the new economy of mutuality where innovation raises all boats and there is a genuine attempt to create value for all stakeholders in the ecosystem. For example, in the health industry where many people, according to Harvard's Prof. Michael Porter, were paid more to do the wrong things, there is a shift to an Accountable Care Ecosystem (ACE) model where all ecosystem participants innovate and work to maximize value and efficiency for all particularly the patients.

In addition to traditional IT systems, such as enterprise resource planning, innovative IT systems now reach out to customers to provide services and to extend strategy – "Power by the Hour" – enabled by substantial IT and digital innovation. The development of advanced telematics that tracked and measured aircraft engine usage and performance allowed Rolls Royce the opportunity to create a whole new business model whereby instead of selling aircraft engines, Rolls Royce sells hours of flight time. This annuity-based model provides more stable revenues and is often favored by shareholders. Today almost 50 percent of Rolls Royce revenues come from services. In addition, both Rolls Royce and GE Aircraft Engines have created digital twins of their engines and the average aircraft such as a Boeing 737 generates 20TB of data per hour per engine which enables predictive maintenance and data driven innovation. The estimated cost of an hour of downtime is $10,000, so optimizing flying time using data has a high return on investment (ROI).

Innovation is increasingly visible as it matures, and the importance of innovation increases in proportion to how different audiences value it. Like quality and safety, innovation is becoming a new standard with which employees, company executives, customers, and shareholders evaluate the company.

As Table 1.1 shows, the audience expands in scope as innovation capability matures, that is, as companies progress from basic innovation capabilities to optimizing ones. The same is true when innovation capability becomes a competitive advantage. Table 1.1 also identifies who sees and benefits from innovation and how benefits take form. Benefits can be tangible, such as a monetary reward, or intangible when emotional or perceived. People are motivated by different benefits, so understanding and providing different motivations helps to create a well-rounded, inclusive innovation system people want to engage with. For an innovation to be sustainable multiple entities need to receive value, including the provider and the adopters, and increasingly the innovation is delivered by an innovation ecosystem so there has to be shared value.

Innovation's Virtuous Circle

Innovation is a key ingredient to longevity and survival, according to Arie de Geus (2002). Innovation is indeed about delivering value and, more importantly, innovation capabilities enable companies to build the future and adapt to change. New ideas need to be cultivated constantly, to mitigate or counter economic, political, competitive, and industry risks. When innovation capabilities mature, they foster a virtuous circle, as shown in Figure 1.1. Satisfied customers remain loyal, stockholders are rewarded, the company is successful, and employees are energetic and capable innovators. Intel founder Robert Noyce said, "Optimism is an essential ingredient for innovation and the culture of the company is crucial in creating the opportunity for a virtuous cycle of innovation."

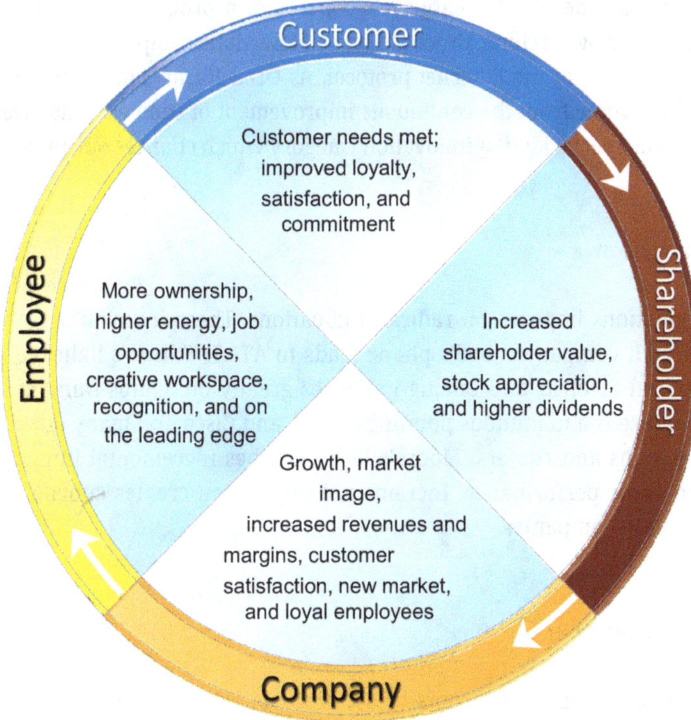

Figure 1.1: Innovation's Virtuous Circle.
Source: Intel

Four Types of Innovation

To sharpen your thinking about innovation, consider the following categories: radical innovation, incremental innovation, innovation by reapplication and finally architectural innovation.

Radical Innovation

Radical innovations fundamentally change an industry and our daily lives. These innovations define entirely new categories of devices and processes. Radical innovations are often closely associated with the innovator. Examples include Edison's light bulb, Alberto Santos- Dumont's airplane, and Lin Yutang's typewriter. In IT, radical innovations include Charles Babbage's concept of a programmable computer, Alan Turing's Turing machine, Grace Hopper's Flow-Matic compiler, and Robert Metcalfe's co-invention of the Ethernet protocol. As Oren Harari famously said, "Electric light did not come from the continuous improvement of candles." Thus we need to recognize this special kind of innovation category which changes our lives.

Incremental Innovation

Incremental innovations improve on radical innovations. These innovations are often associated with companies. Bell's phone leads to AT&T, Edison's light bulb morphs into General Electric, and Boeing improves greatly on Santos-Dumont's plane. In IT the mouse is a ubiquitous pointing device, and Cisco and many others provide Ethernet hubs and routers. Moore's law describes incremental innovation of microprocessor performance. Incremental innovation creates enormous benefits for successful companies.

Innovation by Reapplication

Other innovations are existing concepts or solutions operating in one domain that are applied to new domains. An example is the modification of *Super Glue* chemistry to make a liquid stitch for medicine. Digital examples in IT frequently see software being re-applied to different areas. Computer aided design software first designed for three-dimensional architectural design has been reapplied to other three-dimensional design needs, such as mechanical design or semiconductor design. A knowledge management system constructed to manage product documentation can also be used to track market data. A version-control system designed for software development can be repurposed for engineering and documentation version control. Especially in IT, the opportunity to reapply applications is common, and because reapplied innovations reuse existing applications, they are far less expensive to deliver and the ROI is higher. Innovation can be achieved through a recombination of existing, new and emerging components to achieve a better result.

Architectural Innovation

Architectural Innovation happens when new, emerging and existing components and knowledge are configured and connected in a different way. The creation of Apple of a whole new way of listening to music through the creation of the iPOD and the linking with iTunes resulted in a whole new architecture and growth for the music industry. Intel shut down its MP3 player factory two weeks before Apple launched their first iPOD. Why was it that Intel, who were in the market far ahead of Apple with their MP3 player, failed while Apple succeeded. The answer lies in architectural innovation and courage, with Apple conceiving a totally new architecture for music delivery and also have the courage to bring that about.

Innovation Need Not be Wholescale Invention

While radical innovations are inventions, incremental innovations and innovations that reapply known solutions to new problems are not, (however, they are both a source of patents to be discussed later). Especially in business, incremental innovations are highly valued because they add value on top of a sunk cost. Companies that can create new and improved products stand on the shoulders of prior investment. As Newton once said, “If I can see so clearly, it is because I stand on the shoulders of giants.”

We believe that reuse and thoughtful recombination of available technologies are powerful ways to innovate. At a fundamental level, IT or digital solutions are based on storing, searching, sorting, calculating, and presenting information to users. And, with the advent of artificial intelligence, taking action on behalf of users a whole new opportunity of generative innovation could be possible. Radical inventions such as the relational database model and the graphical user interface are highly generalizable. Assembling these ingredients to address a business problem or streamline a business process will deliver significant value.

Table 1.2: The Ten Types of Innovation.

Innovation category	Innovation type	Description of type	Intel examples
Finance	Business	How you make	Intel: Not processors, but platforms
	model	Money	Intel IT: 100% ebusiness
	Networks	How you join forces	Intel: Founder of Sematech, member of Supplier
	and	with other companies	Network
	alliances	for mutual benefit	Intel IT: Active with the Innovation Value Institute ivi.ie
Process	Enabling	How you support the	Intel: Support global standards, for example, 5G
	process	company's core processes and workers	Intel IT: Global standardized IT infrastructure to support distant collaboration
	Core	How you create and	Intel: 300 mm wafers reduce cost by 30%
	processes	add value to your offerings	Intel IT: Move processor design to Intel Architecture and Open Source to save $1B
Offerings	Product	How you design your	Intel: Shift to multicore design for low power and
	performance	core offering	high performance
			Intel IT: Provide idea capture and management to
			strategic planning team. Intel Unite® Solution
	Product	How you link or	Intel: Same cores support different processors
	system	provide a platform for multiple products	Intel IT: Uniform handling of knowledge management
	Service	How you provide	Intel: Account representatives aimed at
		value to customers	customers beyond the products
		and customers beyond and around your products	Intel IT: Demonstration systems such as skoool™ content delivery technology reach beyond typical customers. Innovation Training curricula.

Table 1.2 (continued)

Innovation category	Innovation type	Description of type	Intel examples
Delivery	Channel	How you get your	Intel: Multichannel, differentiation by channel
		offerings to market	Intel IT: Early access to IT innovations at IT
			Innovation Zone intranet site
	Brand	How you	Intel: Intel Inside® brand
		communicate your offerings	Intel IT: Showcase IT Innovation Centers. IT@Intel White Papers, IT Annual Report
	Customer	How your customers	Intel: Online demonstration of multicore
	experience	feel when they	processing to invoke confidence in the
		interact with your company and its offerings	Technology Intel IT: Ethnographic study and user experience design to guide innovation

Source: Category, Type and Description, the Doblin Group; Intel Examples, Intel.

Innovation is Not Just About Products and Services

Larry Keeley is cofounder and president of the Doblin Group, a Chicago-based consulting company specializing in innovation. Keeley has identified ten different types of innovation, which are grouped under four broad classes of business functions, as shown in Table 1.2. Those who focus innovation narrowly on product performance, which is common in some companies, miss nine other opportunities to put new ideas to work.

Using Keeley's framework, we sorted through our Intel and Intel IT experiences to provide examples for each of the ten types. As the examples demonstrate, innovation is pervasive, and the opportunity to improve business practices with IT systems can occur for all ten types. We encourage our readers to ponder Keeley's types and generate opportunities at their own companies.

Over a six-year period, Keeley and his colleagues at Doblin studied more than 400 firms in more than sixty industries. Using the ten types, they surveyed investments and cumulative payback. Their findings are shown in Figures 1.2 and 1.3. An interesting pattern emerged.

Investment in Innovation

According to Keeley, innovation could be applied to the finance function by developing new business models or by improving networking with trading partners, but as Figure 1.2 shows, innovation effort is not typically high for these business processes. Similarly, innovation effort is relatively low for seeking improvements to a company's enabling and core processes. Effort expended to improve delivery components such as the sales channel, brand equity, and to improve the customer's experience is also typically low.

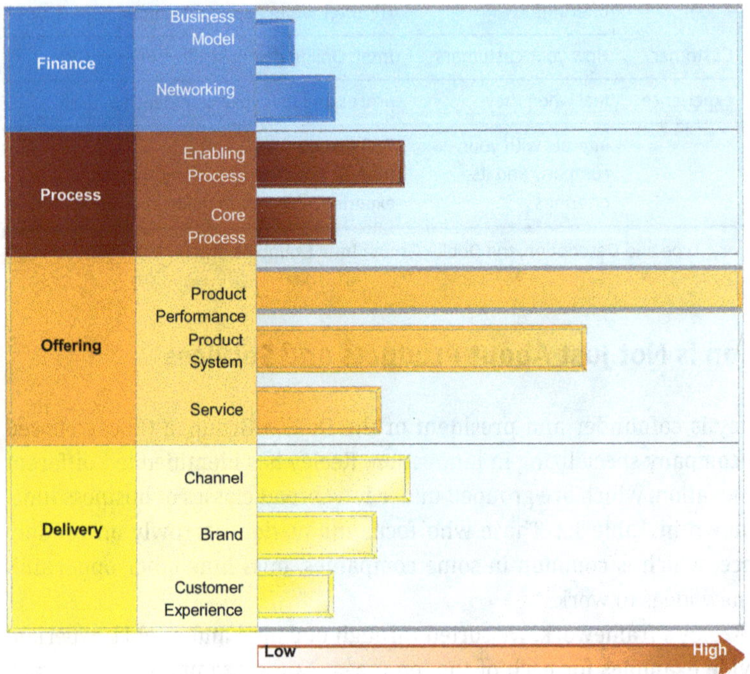

Figure 1.2: Investment in Innovation for Ten Opportunities.
Source: Adapted from the Doblin Group (presentation in 2006), Larry Keely, Helen Walters, Ryan Pikkel, Brian Quinn, 2013, *Ten Types of Innovation,* John Wiley, NY.

Innovation is most typically identified as a critical feature for product development and, more specifically, for product performance. Enterprises invest most heavily in finding new ideas about the capacity, speed, strength, or durability of their products. Performance will manifest itself in different ways for different industries. For printing engines, dots-per-inch resolution might emerge as a performance indicator, while agricultural equipment performance will likely be judged on reliability and durability. New adjacent products or iterations would fit here and are where most new investment occurs.

Value Creation Opportunities

Keeley and the Doblin Group surveyed these same companies and classified cumulative payback by innovation type. The results of this research are shown in Figure 1.3. A dramatically different picture emerges.

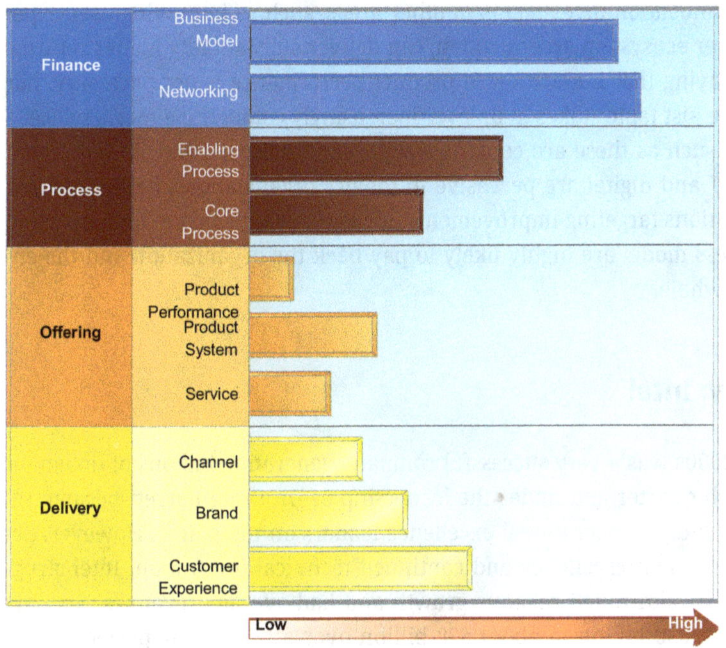

Figure 1.3: Cumulative Value Creation over Ten Years.
Source: Adapted from the Doblin Group (2006)

One major finding is that innovative effort in the finance functions can lead to dramatic returns. A new business model, which is a new way to make money, can pay back handsomely. Improvements in the company's networking and alliances also pay back significantly. Dell is arguably a great exemplar of this. The transformation of their business to enable customers to customize and buy products directly supported by a sophisticated cash management cycle made them a world leader in PC systems with superior profitability compared to their competitors. While household PC names such as Compaq have disappeared, Dell continues to prosper as one of the largest privately held IT companies. Intel founder Andy Grove was quoted as saying, "Don't fall in love with the technology, fall in love with the business model" and Dell is perhaps a great exemplar of this. Great technology, but an even better business model. Alexander Osterwalder's Business Model Canvas is a very useful tool in collaboratively co-designing a business model for successful introduction of a cross ecosystem designed and delivered innovation.

The second major finding is that improvements in product performance lead to the lowest cumulative ROI. This has a very significant implication for where to allocate innovation budget. Companies such as Intel and BMW invested heavily in improving microprocessor and engine performance, respectively, but this data tells us that innovation investments in other areas, such as improving user experience or better ecosystem orchestration, can deliver substantially higher returns. We are not saying that innovation in product performance is not necessary, but often it can be just table stakes in an ever increasingly competitive marketplace.

Findings such as these are consistent with our thinking about IT and digital innovation. IT and digital are pervasive in today's organizations, both large and small. Innovations targeting improvements in customer satisfaction or supporting a new business model are highly likely to pay back the organization and the enterprise as a whole.

Case Study: Intel

Intel in the 2000s was a very successful company generating billions of dollars in free cash each quarter and under the leadership of Dr. Craig Barrett became renowned as one of the operational excellence leaders on the planet. However, despite the operational excellence and continued technical innovation, Intel struggled to drive breakthrough revenue growth and had average revenues per year spanning from $30 billion to about $38 billion over a seven-year period. In the same period Intel was one of the highest spenders in R&D with an average R&D intensity of about 15.5% and was also a leader in patent generation and filing. But still revenue stubbornly refused to budge out of the $30–38B range. In 2005 Paul Otellini became the new CEO of Intel and introduced the concept of a platform strategy. One of the authors (Martin) and Herman D'Hooge convened two global innovation conferences in 2006 and 2008 to address Intel's perceived innovation problem in terms of converting high R&D spending into significant revenue growth. Many key Intel executives and leaders contributed to the working conferences, including then Intel CFO Andy Bryant, head of sales Sean Maloney and then CTO and future CEO Pat Gelsinger. Gelsinger made a very insightful observation when he said, "Intel can do anything it wants, it just can't do everything" meaning Intel had to prioritize and pick its big bets. The star of the 2006 conference was Larry Keeley who gave a spellbinding three-hour lecture on the ten types of innovation which was very influential in Intel's future innovation strategy. It takes time for strategy changes to take effect, but between 2009 to 2011 Intel's annual revenue grew by a remarkable 54%, an amazing innovation result.

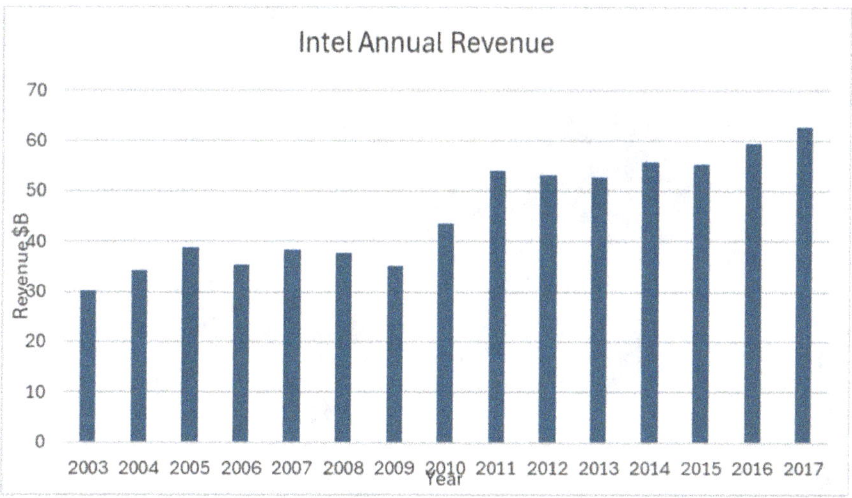

Figure 1.4: Intel Revenue Growth 2003–2017.
Source: Dazeinfo.com

There were many innovation interventions which were helpful in achieving this breakthrough growth. One of the key infrastructure interventions was the establishment of a global network of IT innovation centers led by Martin (Esther set up the IT innovation centers in Pudong, Shanghai and Beijing) which focused on both internal and external IT and digital innovation as seen in Figure 1.5. A special focus of the innovation centers was on innovating with Intel's customers' customers, co-innovating new usage models which would create demand for new and emerging Intel products. The IT innovation centers focussed on multiple domains such as education, health, automotive, manufacturing and others. A team led by Martin won a coveted Intel Achievement Award for working with and accelerating the adoption of eLearning with European governments. A collaboration with the UK Health Sales Team led by Roy Simpson led to a special Sales and Marketing Development group award for the then largest PC sales order in Intel history with the UK's National Health Service (NHS).

The network of innovation centers interacted with multiple diverse firms such as Statoil (now Equinor), and L'Oreal.

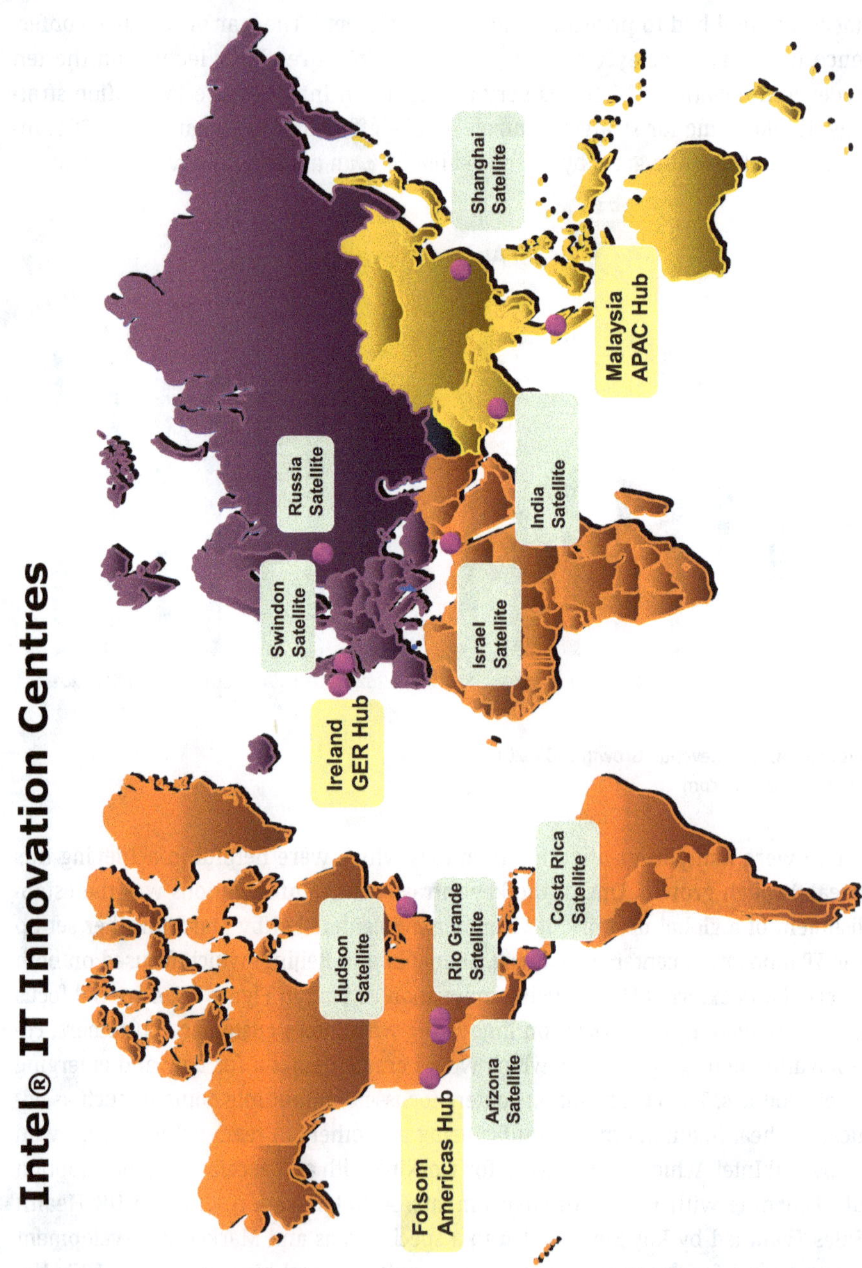

Figure 1.5: Network of IT Innovation Centers – 2007.
Source: Martin Curley

Open Innovation and the Drive for Best End Value

Henry Chesbrough (2017) provides another important perspective on innovations of any kind. The traditional lifecycle model is ordinarily portrayed as a funnel with fuzzy ideas arriving from research activities at universities and industrial laboratories. Within the walls of the enterprise, the R&D group studies how these ideas might be used to create new or improved products for the company. As these ideas mature, some are set aside and others are combined into useful components, processes, methods, devices, etc. Innovation managers draw the line, narrow the funnel, and make the necessary investment decisions as research hands off demonstrated results to the development team.

Chesbrough's major contribution, shown in Figure 1.6, is illustrated by the wire-form funnel. It is Chesbrough's contention that ideas can also enter the product development lifecycle from outside the company. In fact, he would argue, successful companies are those that actively pursue intellectual property and innovative component technologies from outside the enterprise walls.

Customer and User Experience

When thinking about content to support the rise of customer and user experience as a critical component to adoption, one of the authors reflected back on an experience that really stood out.

I was flying on Virgin Atlantic Airways from the USA to London, long before customer experience was a widely known imperative, and noticed that the stewards and stewardesses were all wearing thick black rimmed glasses reminiscent of the old UK National Health glasses that no one who could afford to pay for their own glasses would EVER wear. It piqued my interest. The bag of toiletries and personal care items were bright purple and yellow clear plastic in rounded lines with a very 1960's feel. So unique that I had to keep them. I thought, "Something is definitely different about this flight!" Then the crew treated us to an Austin Powers show in the aisles! "How entertaining! Now I get the glasses."

As we were deplaning I could hear a buzz coming from the front of the plane then it came closer and I could hear, "it's him, he's here", "he's on the plane". It was electrifying. Sure enough Richard Branson was standing by the door greeting everyone, smiling and shaking hands with every passenger as we got off the plane. I shook his hand! The entire flight was a new experience and something I never forgot. This was the earliest exposure I had of a novel customer experience designed to entertain and of course build loyalty. It made the long hours of the flight go quickly. Oh and I still have my purple comb.

The primary determinant of successful innovation is best end value. This is often achieved by harvesting ideas from others, identifying valuable end states, and establishing exit points. Licensing innovative components from others relatively late in their lifecycle can accelerate the development process as well.

When focusing only on products as an end value, what happens to all the other good unused ideas? Are they bad ideas? Might they have value? Instead of managing ideas in the pipeline to a single end state, Chesbrough suggests managing them to end values, some of which will be outside the enterprise. As part of the vetting process in pipeline management, all possible end values should be considered. A company can license or sell an innovation, or it can create a simulation for use as a sales tool, for example.

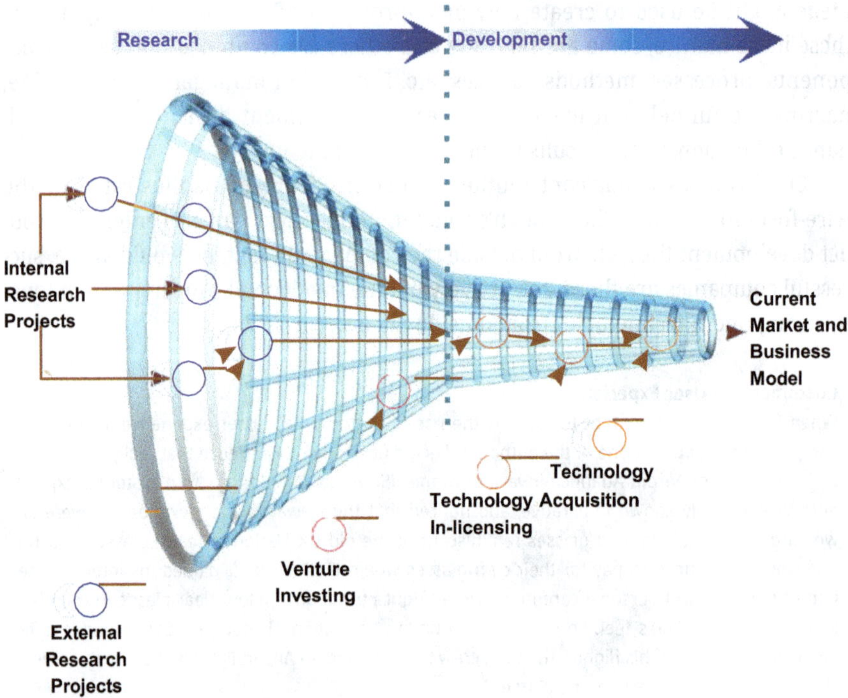

Figure 1.6: Chesbrough's Open Innovation Model.
Source: Adapted from Chesbrough (2006)

While Chesbrough's model applies to all kinds of innovation, it has some interesting implications for digital innovation. Namely, licensing and assembling digital components in innovative ways is far more practical than engaging in research or foundation development. The point is obvious with respect to hardware; few companies would ever consider manufacturing special-purpose servers, for example. (Google and Facebook are interesting and very notable exceptions.) The implication for software is more profound. Coding solutions from scratch is rarely a good idea. To see why, read *Innovative eSupport at Intel.* The case study can be found in Appendix A.

We also believe that the open innovation model requires IT support; that is, IT is uniquely positioned to build systems that track innovations throughout the company, monitor their development, and provide the information necessary to decide which is the best end value.

A new mode of innovation has evolved, one which is called Open Innovation 2.0 (OI2). Promoted as a concept and launched in a joint whitepaper published by Intel, Maynooth University and the European Commission during the Irish presidency of the European Union in 2013, OI2 is about deep collaboration across an ecosystem, often with users and customers involved. OI2 recognizes that the unit of competition and performance is shifting from the organization to the ecosystem and from the product to the platform. An open collaborative ecosystem (OCE) is at the core of OI2 initiatives and Gastaldi et al (2015) describes OCE's as a fundamental mutation in the business competitive landscape. A more evolved form of an OCE is a Directed-Open Collaborative Ecosystem (D-OCE) with the Innovation Value Institute's OCE for Digital Health, which is directed by the Stay Left, Shift Left-10X paradigm being an excellent example of this. We will discuss these new forms of cross ecosystem innovation in Chapter 8 and readers can find further information in the following references (Curley, 2016) and (Curley and Salmelin, 2017).

Innovation Shifts in Business Models

Highly successful enterprises often thrive on shifts in an industry's underlying business model. A business model, as Keeley defines it, is how a company earns its money. In the United States, Southwest Airlines demonstrated that offering lower-cost, no-frills, direct flights to secondary metropolitan airports was a viable business model. Ticketing need not require seat assignments, thus saving time as passengers more quickly board the planes. Internet access to create boarding passes further streamlines the departure process. Less expensive, classless passenger service without meals was found to be acceptable to a wide audience of travelers. Building incrementally on Southwest's experience, Ireland's airline, Ryanair, found other ways to change the business model. Rather than paying landing fees at smaller airports in Europe, Ryanair asks for and receives a fee. The airport and the ecosystem of stores, restaurants, and transportation services gain a steady stream of customers, thus justifying an investment that supports Ryanair's model. Ryanair, in turn, can lower the cost of tickets even further, making the no-frills choice difficult for customers to ignore. Re-applying and extending the Southwest airlines business model was so successful that Ryanair grew from a very small regional airline to become the largest airline in Europe, bigger than the traditional giants such as Lufthansa and British Airways. And, Ryanair's growth was enabled by increasing levels of IT innovation for example through adoption of internet reservation and yield management systems.

In the PC market, Dell Corporation's business model collects payment before delivery and relies heavily on IT to do so. IT systems provide sophisticated infrastructure and modeling tools that allow market planners to identify buying trends, simulate changes to operations, and prepare for the short product lifecycles prevalent in the PC industry. Dell also allows and encourages customers to suggest new features and to vote and prioritize features for new products.

In China most real estate is purchased in a similar way, before construction has started. Buyers looks at building renderings and floor plans, purchase their apartment and funds flow to the developers long before construction.

Digital Innovation: A Two-Part Process

At a macro-level, a successful digital innovative effort has two distinct phases. First, new solutions must be created for supporting enterprise strategies and objectives. Second, these new solutions must be adopted and diffused throughout the user community.

Creation

There is much to know about the systemic creation of new digital solutions. Successful companies develop ways to methodically identify inefficiencies and weaknesses in enterprise functioning and then to seek innovative digital solutions. Areas such as customer experience and satisfaction provide rich opportunities to explore how IT systems might improve a company's reputation and streamline problem solving (e.g., product support and the help desk function). Agile methods, including techniques such as prototyping, are crucial to ensure that a potential improvement can, in fact, be fielded successfully. Agile methods allow iterative and fast development to minimize risk and help ensure that the right solution is developed to meet customer and market needs.

Adoption and Diffusion

It is our belief that adoption and diffusion of innovative digital solutions is the more challenging half of the overall process. Value only is accrued when solutions are adopted and often there can be significant resistance to the adoption of new solutions. A key design pattern from OI2 which can help with this is "Designing for Adoption" which we will discuss in the last chapter. By making a solution so compelling, offering breakthroughs in performance, functionality or usability, the normal barriers to adoption melt away. Additionally there is also a fundamental tension when IT organizations are the gatekeeper to adoption between the need to make IT efficient and to make IT better, which is illustrated in Figure 1.7. However, the introduction of application stores such as Apple's App store or Google Play have dramatically lowered the barrier to adoption for independent software vendors as these App stores immediately provide access and a software distribution mechanism to millions of customers.

IT Efficiency and IT Innovation

It is widely and correctly believed that new, innovative IT systems require investment, carry a measure of risk, and only become efficient over time. It is less widely appreciated that legacy systems also require investments, carry risk, and become more efficient over time when efficiency is measured year after year with the same technology in place. These understandings naturally lead to a tension among IT staff and IT managers assigned to address different goals. Unfortunately, some of this tension can also disrupt and confuse the investment decision-making process when business and financial managers view these tensions and puzzle over them.

What is needed is a sense of balance. As Figure 1.8, shows, the balance is unlikely to be fifty-fifty. For organizations with ongoing core business systems, then the balance point will place greater resources in support of efficiency. We would argue, however, that some percentage of IT investment ought to be dedicated to accelerating the deployment of innovative IT solutions.

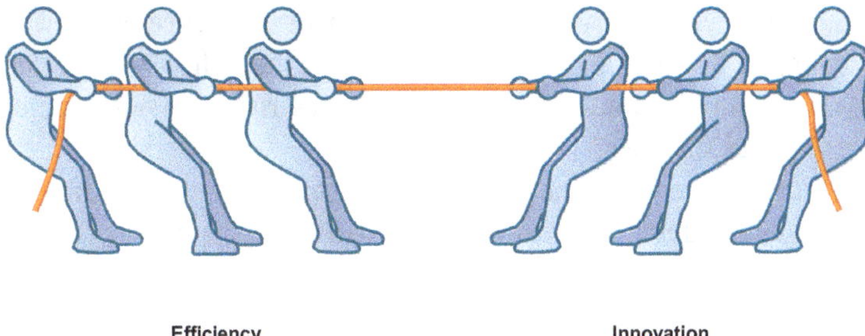

Efficiency

Innovation

Figure 1.7: IT Efficiency Versus IT Innovation.
Source: Intel Corporation

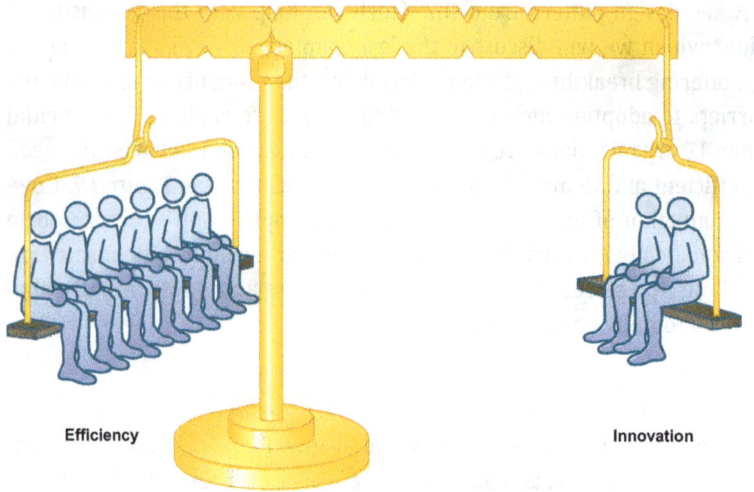

Figure 1.8: IT Efficiency Balanced with Innovation.
Source: Intel Corporation

The balance point is affected by variables that may be different from company to company, such as the tolerance of the IT leadership for change and risk, the ratio of IT investment to corporate revenue, or the level at which competitors are using IT innovation as a strategic weapon.

IT Efficiency and IT Obsolescence

Innovation is particularly critical to IT organizations because of the high rate of change in IT capabilities. There is no practical way to maintain state-of-the-art technologies when next year's server will offer higher performance at a lower total cost of ownership. The critical question is, "What are the right 'lag times' for your IT systems?" and a related question is, "What are the risks and opportunity costs associated with the lag times?"

In the late 1980s, using the Internet for electronic commerce was an innovation that reshaped some industries. A year or two of lag time left some companies with smaller market share. The risk that a competitor would leverage this new medium was significant and the opportunity cost was appreciable.

We stand at that same point today when considering the adoption and use of artificial intelligence. It is already disrupting many areas such as using individuals' preference prediction for advertising and sales. The accuracy of medical imaging analysis now exceeds that of a human. The opportunity cost must be considered and the risk of competitors adopting more quickly and gaining an early market advantage from the innovations it can deliver must be considered by every decision maker for their respective businesses.

Today, technologies such as radio frequency identification, the internet of things or artificial intelligence offer potential, and innovators are finding ways to put this technology to work to completely disrupt industries. The deployment of contactless payment solutions at London Underground stations is a great example of this providing an easier and more seamless traveler experience and providing lower cost solutions to the London Underground. Artificial intelligence has reached a point where it is more efficient than a human for some tasks such as identity verification or medical image analysis and is steadily transforming tasks in every industry.

Copy-Exactly

One important way to leverage innovations is to diffuse them actively with a process we call *copy-exactly*. The idea grew out of Intel's manufacturing strategy. When we issue laptop computers, for example, we standardize the hardware, operating environment, and software so that an entire group of people have identical systems. Copy-exactly accelerates the diffusion process and, at the same time, it simplifies system maintenance and user training.

Identical Fabs at Intel

When Intel develops its next-generation fab, it is engineered to speci- fication, put into operation, and tested thoroughly. This fab becomes the standard for new fabs in other parts of the world.

After the first fab is running successfully, exact replicates of the first fab are built at other locations. Intel engineers and business managers monitor key indicators including yield, spend on mate- rials, and excursion avoidance to measure success.

When *copy-exactly* succeeded for the fab, the technique was used to deploy assembly-and-test facilities, and then to the overall construction of the factory. When copy-exactly was reapplied to construction at Intel, for second and subsequent fab facilities, the cost per square foot was reduced by half.

The main point about copy-exactly is not simply that an innovation is copied to everyone. What is important is that production systems harvest research investments in every way. When research systems are engineered to meet the high standards needed for production, exact copies will be easier and faster to distribute. Distribution is more likely to be to be successful and maintenance more efficient.

The cost of customization goes down when we identify users with similar needs. At Intel, for example, engineering requirements are supported separately from employees at large, but they still copy-exactly within the engineering community.

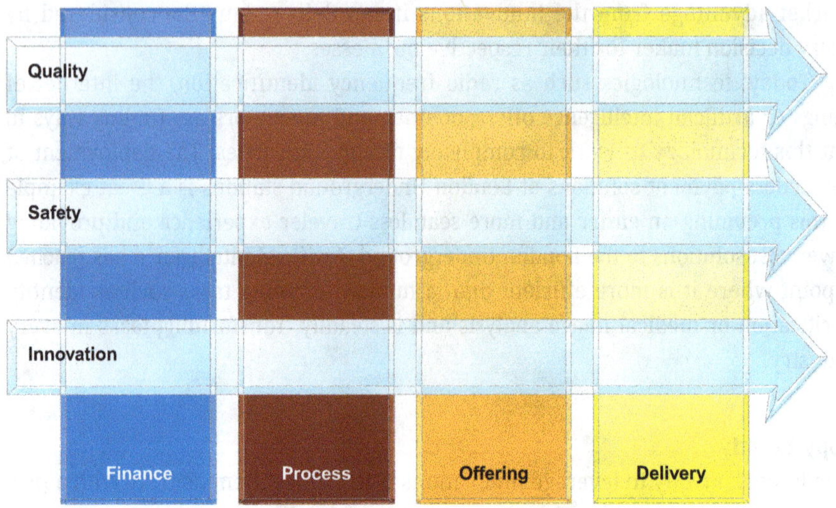

Figure 1.9: Quality, Safety, and Innovation as Lateral Processes.
Source: Intel Corporation

Innovation as a Lateral Process

Innovation can be managed as a lateral process that reaches across all business functions and a portfolio of IT solutions. Without lateral management, pockets of activity are poorly supported and innovation may or may not align with enterprise objectives.

As Figure 1.9 illustrates, innovation can be managed just as quality and safety are managed in well-run organizations.

In earlier days, corporations managed quality haphazardly until they realized that an enterprise-wide approach was needed. To use Keeley's dimensions, quality was not just about the company's *offerings*, but also about *finance, process*, and *delivery*. All systems, IT and otherwise, need to reflect quality. When managing quality enterprise-wide, quality becomes an intrinsic part of the business. In a similar manner, and for the same reasons, safety has emerged as a lateral process as well.

When planning our management strategies for Intel IT, we studied quality and safety management. We believe that innovation and diffusion will be far more effective when managed in a similar way. Haphazard innovation can quickly turn into tinkering, especially in an IT department filled with clever engineers. We also believe that lateral management will lead to systemic innovation, which, like quality and safety, will become an integral part of the company's culture and values.

At MasterCard, innovation is managed as a systematic and lateral process, supported by sophisticated and integrated processes and tools. Indeed Innovation with the finance SME ecosystem was managed by a Lateral process in a program called Startpath led by Senior Vice President Amy Neale. In Ireland's HSE we managed Innovation as a lateral process and implemented a sophisticated software solution, Innovation Pipeline Manager' to manage, harvest and diffuse digital health innovations being tested and iterated across a network of living labs in Ireland. Both HSE Digital Transformation and Mastercard Startpath were awarded global innovation awards by the International Chambers of Commerce and Mind the Bridge for these exciting developments in managing innovation as a lateral process for promising startups in the health and finance fields respectively.

Innovation Versus Tinkering

Copy-exactly and lateral management are methods to avoid tinkering. At its best, tinkering is inefficient, and at its worst, it presents a risk, especially in the IT environment. Small improvements to applications applied locally and without documentation can and do raise the cost of maintenance and can even cause system outages.

Communicating the importance of copy-exactly can be a management challenge. Users need to understand the boundaries within which they must remain. IT personnel need to understand the purposes and benefits of the approach. And finally, places are needed where innovation is allowed and where new ideas can be stored and evaluated.

Barriers to Innovation

The barriers to innovation comprise a familiar list of concerns. While innovation is not necessarily expensive, many managers begin with the assumption that it is. Finding a place in the budget can be difficult in the best of times, and defending the commitment to IT or digital innovation will be even harder when times are tough.

Another inhibitor to innovation is risk aversion, and, like cost, it is often underestimated, especially by non-IT or digital managers. Using agile methods, IT or product organizations will often need to work through demonstrations and prototypes that show how risk is mitigated. Finally, it is important to weigh the consequences of not taking enough risk in a competitive environment.

Cultural norms embedded in everyday speech can form an innovation barrier. Chic Thompson (2016) provides a top ten collection of familiar innovation killers, such as: *We tried that before*, *It's not in the budget*, *It's out of scope*, and the venerable preface, *Yes, but . . .*

In the case of IT, a significant barrier to innovation is undivided attention focused on IT operating efficiency. As we discussed earlier, enterprises need to set and revisit a balance point when allocating resources to improve operating efficiencies and cultivating innovation.

In This Book . . .

In designing our book, we aimed to provide the reader with a smooth path from basic IT business value concepts to the intricacies of building an IT or digital innovation program. While experienced readers may choose to sample, here is our primary path.

Business Value Management

The foundation to our thinking about IT is that its success should be measured in business value terms. A full discussion of our thinking is in Curley (2004) and this chapter provides a nutshell explanation.

IT and Digital Innovation

IT and innovation are separate disciplines that intersect. In this chapter we share our basic strategies when managing innovative projects. A case study illustrates each of the six key vectors for adoption, which we believe are best managed concurrently, not sequentially. While this book focuses on IT and digital innovation, much of the content can be applied generically to manage innovation.

Systemic Innovation

We believe that innovation should be pervasive in enterprises and that growth over time is well described by a capability maturity framework. This chapter identifies four components of IT innovation management, provides growth curves for each component, and describes the sequence of capabilities that emerge at each maturity level.

Innovation Capability

Our innovation capability chapter describes our ideas infrastructure and identifies the tools and methods we use at different stages in the IT innovation process. The survey is not exhaustive, but rather provides a sample that we have found useful.

Innovation Assessment

We created an innovation assessment method. It is used by teams to develop innovation capability and move teams up the innovation maturity framework using action plans over time. We once again use a capability maturity framework to describe the increasing competence of a single team or a sampling from a larger organization. Appendix B provides additional details and stands as a model that could be tailored to fit the needs of other companies. An innovation assessment leads to explicitly-stated goals that are a part of both an organizational action plan and an individual employee's performance appraisal.

Innovation Pipeline Management

We manage digital innovation projects with the same pipeline that oversees traditional projects, but we use different criteria to make decisions. We discuss stage-gate management and treat emerging innovations like financial options.

For example, while traditional systems progress at a predictable rate, digital innovation projects explore new ideas and occasionally encounter difficult obstacles. We are willing to selectively speed up and slow down projects in our innovation portfolio.

Diffusion of Innovation

Accelerating the adoption of new IT and digital capabilities is one of our key principles of innovation management. While, historically, diffusion was described as a social process, we push our capabilities by marketing them actively. In some cases, innovations can be wrapped into the IT refresh process and moved rapidly through the company.

Launching Systemic Innovation

This chapter brings together all the themes in our book and lays out a plan for building an innovation program in the IT or labs organization and across a company or organization. Much of the innovation activity will result in better IT systems for the company and better products and services offered by the company. Some of the innovation activity will support innovation excellence across the company.

Innovation Culture

Culture is determined and evolves largely based on leadership behavior and agendas. As the innovation self-assessment shows, management commitment is the forcing function that drives innovation as a culture – this chapter shares more about the importance of culture and the key role of an innovation pacemaker. It outlines the 4E philosophy and the contrasting 4C philosophy. May we all work in a 4E environment and be able to vote with our feet if we find ourselves under the thumb of 4E's.

Open Innovation 2.0 – A New Digital Innovation Paradigm

The consequence of Moore's Law is that the unit of competition and indeed performance has moved from the organization to the ecosystem. This had led to the birth of a new paradigm Open Innovation 2.0 (Curley and Salmelin, 2013). We define Open Innovation 2.0 (OI2) as a new paradigm based on principles of integrated collaboration, co-created shared value, cultivated innovation ecosystems, unleashed exponential technologies, and extraordinarily rapid adoption. Based on a decade of research curated by the European Commission, Intel and Maynooth University core design patterns to enable success ecosystem innovation have emerged and these are described in Chapter 10.

As IT innovation and indeed digital innovation have evolved, we have seen corporate labs and research organizations extend their remits to take responsibility and drive innovation across corporations. Intel Labs Europe transformed Intel's approach to innovation in Europe using the Open Innovation 2.0 paradigm and developed a new approach for holistically valuing research results using the 8R value model. In another example, MasterCard labs enables, catalyzes, and delivers new innovation capabilities and innovations for MasterCard and its customers. The Innovation Value Institute now orchestrates a Directed Open Collaborative Ecosystem for Digital Health demonstrating very promising results.

Appendix A: Case Studies in Innovation

Two case studies are in Appendix A. One explores public sector innovation at the City of Westminster and the other traces the path of Intel's work in automating IT support whenever possible. These case studies are written in the style of a business school case and are based on interviews with the innovators to understand the challenges they faced and their strategies for success.

Appendix B: Innovation Assessment Tools

Appendix B contains a modified version of Intel's innovation self-assessment instrument and an example of how to incorporate innovation capability maturity into individual performance appraisals.

Appendix C: Open Innovation 2.0

Appendix C contains three case studies that illustrate Open Innovation 2.0 (OI2). The first outlines the Intel Labs Europe journey to excellence using Open Innovation 2.0 designed to help develop new and emerging Intel and other technologies. The second shares the Irish Health Service Executive Digital Collaborative ecosystems and the last case study outlines the Innovation Value Institute research clusters to develop digital transformation platforms, products and pathways as Open Collaborative Ecosystems.

Summary

This chapter introduces IT and digital innovation, defines our innovation terminology, and sets a direction for the remainder of the book. We believe that innovation can and should be managed in a systematic and systemic way. We believe that the combination of IT/digital and innovation is a powerful one that is capable of transforming a company in a multitude of different ways. And. we believe that IT or digital innovation is no longer optional, it is an imperative to survive and an opportunity to thrive. Wayne Gretzky famously said, "Move to where this puck is going, rather than where the puck is" so we will discuss the evolution of innovation from an organization capability to an ecosystem capability and necessity in our concluding chapter.

Chapter 2
Business Value Management

Research turns money into knowledge; innovation turns knowledge into money. – Author Unknown

Innovation and value are intricately linked and in this chapter we discuss how to link innovation efforts to value and how to help quantify that value. Innovation happens at the intersection of technology opportunity, business need, and customer experience. Separated by terminology and organizational lines, IT or labs organizations and finance managers often appear to be at odds with each other. Investments in IT and digital innovation cost money and historically the IT cost center had no charter or mandate to think in terms of profit or a return on investment (ROI).

In the past the IT strategy was primarily to be as operationally efficient as possible, thus minimizing cost while providing for enterprise computing needs. And, IT spoke the language of availability, backup-and-restore, multitier architectures, parallel code optimization, and so on. Business and finance managers viewed IT as a cost of goods sold, that second entry on the income statement that subtracts away from revenue and shrinks bottom-line profit. Rather than seeking an optimum IT spend, finance often looked for a minimum level of funding.

This state of affairs began to shift as IT systems were ever more deeply integrated with critical enterprise business processes. Innovative IT systems can and do deliver increases in market share and improvements in profitability. IT and business value go hand-in-hand.

The Importance of a Common Language

The importance of a common language cannot be overstated. In order to achieve a common understanding, IT and innovation professionals need to learn more about finance, and business managers need to learn more about IT's capabilities. Company executives constitute a third community with different concerns, as shown in Figure 2.1.

– IT professionals have been trained to understand information technologies, such as multi-tier architectures and symmetric multiprocessors. In fact, understanding IT terms and technologies is absolutely critical to engineering agile IT infrastructure and delivering reliable IT capability.

https://doi.org/10.1515/9781501507335-002

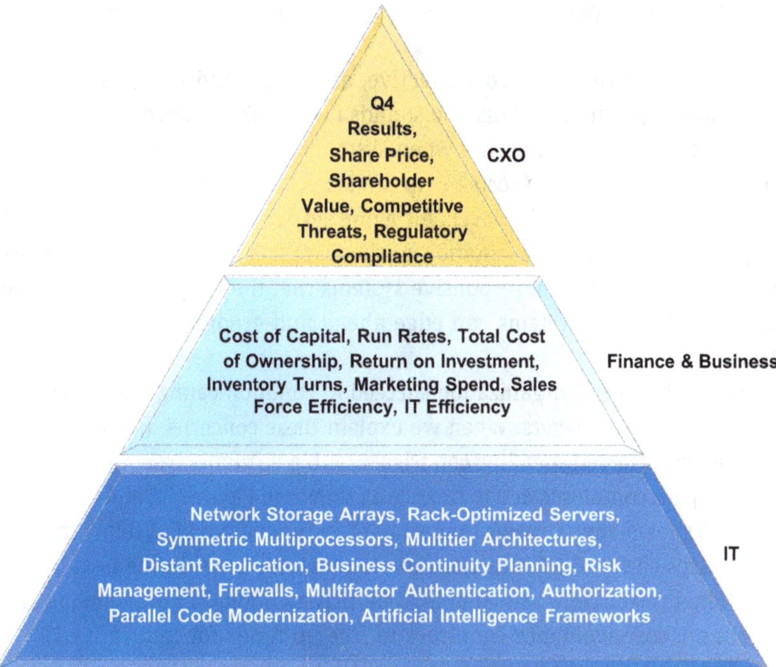

Figure 2.1: Terminology in the Enterprise: A Layered Architecture.
Source: Intel IT.

- Business and finance professionals talk about returns on investments, total cost of ownership, and opportunity costs. Thoughtful financial analyses are crucial to monitoring the organization's planning and execution processes.
- Executives are strategists who should not focus on the minutiae of operations, but rather look outward at the competitive landscape. CXOs need highly condensed information from business, finance, and IT.

The Cost of Miscommunication

The downstream consequences of deferred investments present an unfortunately common example of the risks of miscommunication. IT analysts have long been aware of the lifecycle for IT system replacement and maintenance costs. Early on, systems are more reliable and their performance is at or near state-of-the-art. Over time (measured in months, not years) systems begin to lag behind newer technologies that offer lower price/performance ratios. Moreover, maintenance costs begin to grow, software needs to be upgraded, and support for new types of storage or networking must be added.

To refresh too early is not cost effective, as finance and IT agree. To defer investment and maintain the status quo sounds ideal to the finance officer, but IT can see the vicious cycle that occurs when systems are maintained beyond their useful life. Rising maintenance costs tie up funds that could have been invested in innovative new systems. Service levels for aging systems may falter as well, leading to opportunity costs. The reputation of the IT organization can be tarnished by users who do not have the responsive systems that they expect IT to provide. Competitors with better systems can edge ahead and erode the enterprise customer base.

It is critical that the IT organization succeed in communicating this scenario to finance and business managers. When we explain these concerns, we contrast the vicious circle that deferred spending can trigger with a virtuous circle, underpinned by a spending plan communicated to finance as shown in Figures 2.2 and 2.3.

Figure 2.2 shows how a modest investment in innovative IT systems that improve IT services can lead to reductions in maintenance costs. In the next budget cycle, additional resources are available to launch additional improvements and, as time goes on, cost avoidance continues to free up funds for innovative IT systems. Figure 2.3 applies time value of money (TVM) concepts to the same IT spending model. As time passes, the incremental value, in net present value (NPV) dollars, grows sharply due to the discounting of net future value (NFV).

Generally speaking, when IT strategists approach business and finance managers, they need to speak in terms commonly used by their audience.

In this case, the key terms are *dollars* and *compounding investments* leading to *business value*. The wrong terms would be *system availability* and *response time* improvements leading to a more *state-of-the-art IT solution.*

Business Value Dials

Business value dials are metrics that measure improvements and successes for the enterprise. Figure 2.4 provides examples of dials shown symbolizing their purpose as gauges. These metrics are common- language terms for financial and business planners. Inventory turns, for example, or the time it takes for a complete rotation of products in inventory, is a solid standard across most industries.

The term *value dial* was coined at Intel and a library of dials has been developed over the years. The authoritative presentation of the Intel business value dial library is found in Sward (2006). David Sward provides a typology of value

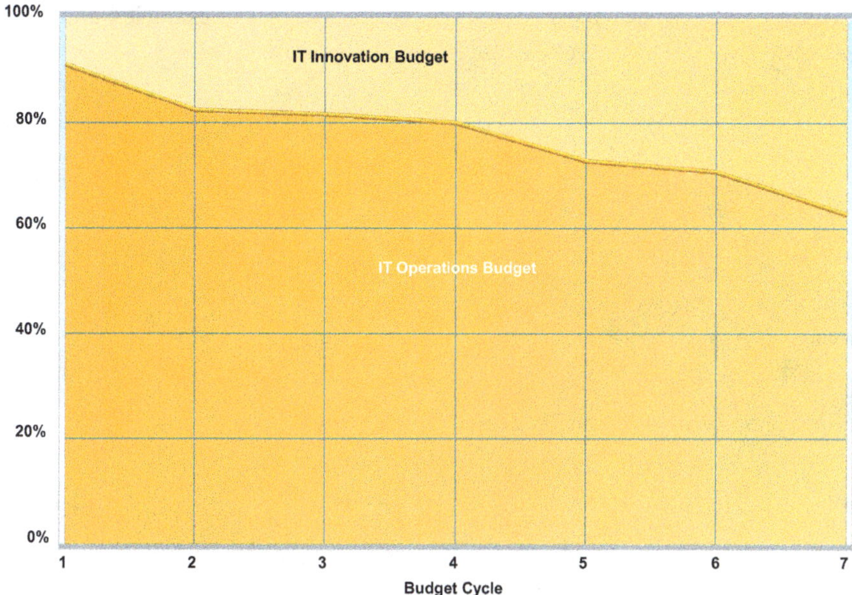

Figure 2.2: Growing the IT Innovation/Digital Innovation Budget.
Source: Intel IT.

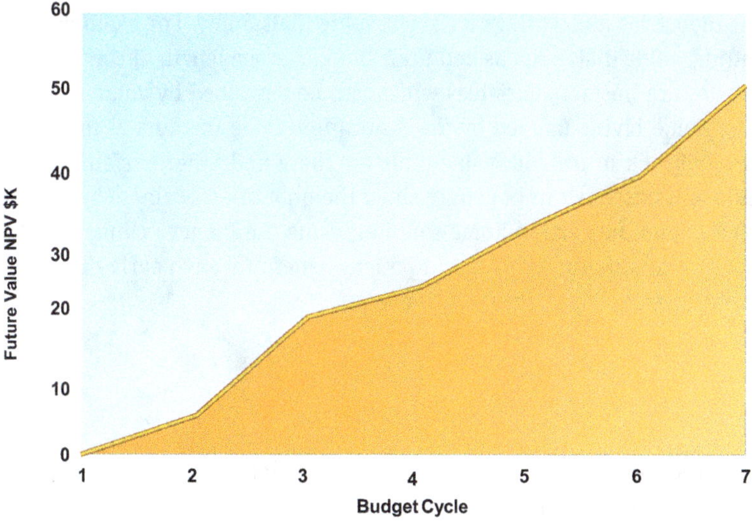

Figure 2.3: Cumulative Value in Net Present Value (NPV) Dollars.
Source: Intel IT.

dials (e.g., expense avoidance dials, revenue dials), tables of examples, and sample calculations. He also provides advice for getting started.

Figure 2.4: Intel's Business Value Dials.
Source: Intel IT.

In different industries and settings different value dials apply. For example in a hospital setting, value dials such as bed utilization, average length of stay and readmission rates are business variables which can be described by value dials. In a hospital at Home Living Lab led by the Innovation Value Institute at the Royal Hospital Donnybrook in Ireland, value dials for these and other variables have been defined and baselined to hopefully show the quantified business benefit of using a novel Digital hospital-at-home solution, using the Blueeye clinic product from RedZinc, in addition to clinical and patient benefit through early discharge of stroke patients and monitoring from home.

Time Value of Money in a Nutshell

Financial analysts factor in the time value of money (TVM) when projecting initial investments, operating expenses, and returns over time. Innovation and IT professionals should be comfortable with the basic concepts.

1. Which is more valuable, $100 today or $100 in five years' time? Setting aside risk, $100 present value is more valuable in five years' time because, had the

money been invested at a five percent annual compounded rate of return, the future value (FV) would be $128. That's why we as individuals do not keep our savings in our mattresses. The four salient variables for TVM calculations are present value (PV), FV, term, and rate of return. Knowing any three, we can calculate the fourth.

2. IT promises Finance it will produce $100 in FV in five years' time with a rate of return is 5%. What is the PV of that future return? This process is called *discounting*. $78 today is equivalent to $100 in five years' time. The acid test, in this tiny example, is the question, "Should IT invest $90 today to generate $100 in five years' time?" And the answer is "No." If IT can return $100 in five years for $50 today, then the answer is "Maybe."
3. "Maybe" is the answer because an IT investment decision is not made in isolation. There could be a better investment, an investment that is strategically necessary, or a less risky investment. Business conditions could elevate the need for one option and reduce the need for another. IT professionals need to be adept in understanding both the insights that financial analyses provide and their limitations.

It this discussion, cash flow has been set aside. At each period in an investment, both cost and value accrue. Business models that deliver value more quickly must be weighed against long-term gains when cash-flow concepts are integrated into the TVM calculations. Net present value (NPV) and NFV are calculations that take cash flow into account.

Last, financial analysts often solve for rate of return with estimates of NPV, NFV, and term. This calculation provides a metric for both ranking investment opportunities and setting a threshold, often called a hurdle rate, for investments that make good sense from a financial analysis perspective.

All of these techniques are helpful, but they represent a single dimension. Managing by spreadsheet is a risky approach and demonstrates low data analytics maturity as an organization. Integrating financial analyses with other business value indicators (e.g., reputational risk, market share growth) is a good approach in our experience.

A few of David Sward's top-level heuristics are as follows:

- Formulate, standardize, and hold firmly to the measurement definitions of value dials so that you can make year-after-year and project- versus-project comparisons using the same metric.
- Remember the importance of a baseline measure before diffusing new IT systems. A single value dial measurement after making a change provides little or no information for decision makers.

- Favor value dials that can be transformed into dollar values. Investment decisions are best informed by costs in dollars, benefits in dollars, and an event calendar to factor in the TVM.

Business Value and IT Efficiency

Some business managers have come to believe that gaining greater business value is at odds with gaining greater IT efficiency, and this is especially true for fielding innovative IT solutions. For those who believe that IT costs are a necessary evil, and such individuals do exist, the best way to direct IT resources is toward efficiencies that lower operating costs while doing no harm to the organization's overall competitiveness. Our view, to the contrary, is that business value and IT efficiency need not be at odds. In fact, there are plenty of opportunities to both improve business value contributions and increase IT efficiency. Figure 2.4 illustrates our thinking.

The framework shown in Figure 2.5 was introduced to Intel IT by the former CIO Doug Busch. The framework is supported by indices that estimate the impact of an investment on IT efficiency and business value. We also estimate financial attractiveness—the level of investment needed to field each potential IT project. A portfolio of investment opportunities can be plotted within this framework, and the best investments are those landing in the cells in the upper right corner. Investments on the diagonal may make sense as well. Here are some examples of better and best investments.

- Upgrading servers or consolidating server and storage systems may not contribute to business value, but is quite likely to improve IT efficiency. Infrastructure upgrades generally fall into the top center cell. The upgrading decision was made more complex when cloud computing entered the picture as an option, with different aspects of cost and security for different types of data. The compelling economics of cloud computing have driven fast adoption and additional IT efficiencies.
- Investments that streamline inventory and supply chain management may not improve IT efficiency, but they contribute to greater business value by expediting the movement of goods for the enterprise.
- The most desirable investments are those that improve both indica- tors. Examples include investments in wireless connectivity. IT efficiencies are gained since IT staff need not maintain wireline services, which ordinarily requires direct visits to the user's work- space. Business value is gained due to increased productivity for IT's customers. See Sward (2006) for a detailed discussion of the impact of mobile computing on employee productivity.

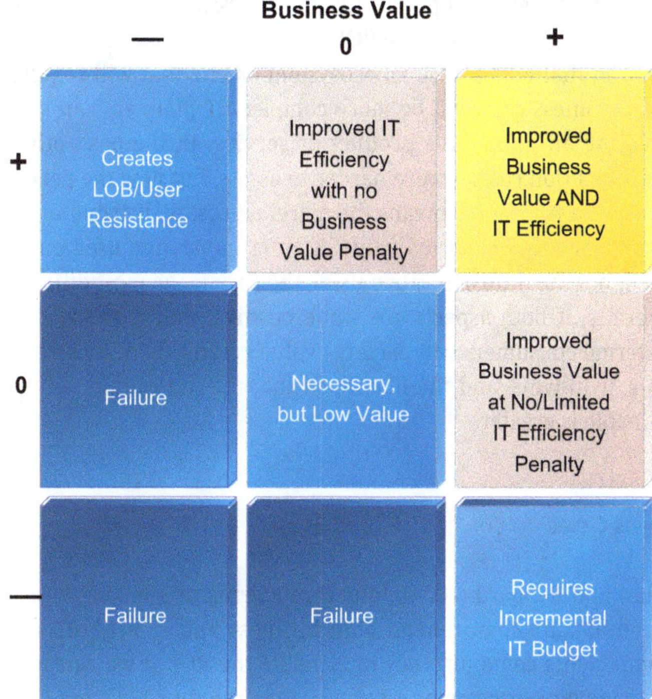

Business Value
—
0
+
+
Creates LOB/User Resistance
Improved IT Efficiency with no Business Value Penalty
Improved Business Value AND IT Efficiency
0
Failure
Necessary, but Low Value
Improved Business Value at No/Limited IT Efficiency Penalty
—
Failure
Failure
Requires Incremental IT Budget

Figure 2.5: Business Value Versus IT Efficiency.
Source: Intel IT.

Building Innovation Business Cases

Innovation business cases often need to be considered at both a micro and macro level. If an IT innovation occurs within the boundaries of a firm, then a microbusiness case will work. However, if the IT innovation diffuses across the firm's boundaries and into a business ecosystem or into a broader part of society, then a macro business case is needed.

For an IT or digital innovation (or any other type of innovation) to be sustainable, the economics of the business case must be viable for both the producer and consumer. Consumers purchase products and services when value is greater than price. Producers make products and deliver services when price is greater than cost.

Business cases for innovative IT systems deployed within the firm are simpler to prepare. The IT organization can identify and estimate costs and the population of consumers is both well-known and captive. Business value dials and other measures of value can be brought into play. Thus, the necessary ingredients are available to estimate both investment and the ROI.

For an IT innovation that cuts across an ecosystem or one that will require societal adoption, the business case will be more complex. IT planners can estimate the cost of creating an innovative product or service. In the past, other costs – particularly distribution costs – were harder to assess, but now the pervasiveness of the Internet and App stores means the marginal cost of distribution of solution is approaching zero. The expected value of an IT innovation used internally can be estimated, but the diffusion rate outside the firm is the most difficult estimate of all. Generally, if both aspects are value positive, that is to say that both internal and external consumers will perceive value greater than price, then the IT innovation is a "win-win," and the likelihood that the innovation will be successful and sustainable is greater.

IT Innovation Business Cases

As defined by Tiernan and Peppard (2004), four components of a business case need to be considered to fully comprehend both business and IT benefits and costs. These four components come together to estimate the ROI. If we consider the output of an IT innovation process as a service, then the four business case components are as follows:

- BB—Business benefits represent the value that will accrue to the business. This could include IT benefits such as improved head-count efficiency due to a server consolidation, for example.

  BB are also measured by value dials such as improved profitability or productivity.
- SRC—Service running costs are the ongoing costs associated with providing the IT service. It is important to note that the SRC will likely exceed the original investment required to create the service. Gartner and other IT research organizations report that for each dollar spent on the original investment, up to five dollars might be spent over the lifetime to maintain and support the software.
- SCI—The service creation investment includes all the infrastructure, software acquisition, development and integration costs needed to bring the IT service into being. This is sometimes mistakenly viewed as the total cost of the project when computing ROI, which is unfortunate.
- BCI—The business change investment is the cost of preparing IT's customers to use the new service offering. Elements of cost include the development

and delivery of training courses, the time that employees are away from their jobs to learn about the service, and the lower efficiency experienced until users are familiar with the service.

According to Peppard and Tiernan, these three categories of cost are mutually exclusive and exhaustive, and all are necessary to compute the ROI. Typically, ROIs are reported for a specified length of time, which varies in different companies. Standardization within a company is useful when comparing ROI estimates for several competing projects. At Intel, we typically compute ROI for a three-year period.

The cost of the IT investment is the sum of SCI and BCI. The net ROI is the value delivered (BB) minus the ongoing cost of running the service (SCR). The ratio of net benefit to total investment is ordinarily multiplied by 100 to express ROI as a percentage. The equation is as follows:

$$\%\,ROI = \frac{BB - SRC}{SCI + BCI} \cdot 100$$

ROI estimates are used in several different ways.

- Taken alone, an ROI calculation could be a negative number, and that simply means that, as planned, the investment should not be made. In the case of IT solutions, IT innovators may need to return to the drawing board. Or, perhaps over time, technology costs will be reduced.
- When comparing investment opportunities, ROI provides a way to rank projects. Note that ROI is unlikely to be the solitary ranking for a portfolio of innovative IT applications. The company's strategic plan, for example, may elevate an investment with a lower return.
- The ROI estimate can also be compared to the company's hurdle rate. The hurdle rate is the threshold ROI that is acceptable to the company. If the return is sufficiently high, then the project is fundable.
- We see many business cases where the business change investment is not included, nor are considerations about resistance to adoption of an innovation for a variety of reasons such as culture and the ability of an organization to metabolize further change.

Articulation of the business case in this manner ensures both business and IT managers have a shared, comprehensive understanding of the business benefits and costs associated with the innovation. Refer to Curley (2004) and Sward (2006) for use of other multidimensional measures of business value which are important to consider in choosing a particular investment. In particular, internal rate of return, the payback period, and profitability index are useful.

xAAS

With the explosion of "x as a service" models that include infrastructure, software, containers, hardware and many others, until X becomes "everything" are leading to opportunities to free IT teams from lower value add activities by focusing on higher value delivered through business strategy and innovation science. This makes it more and more important for businesses to ensure they understand the total cost of operations (TCO) and ROI of their new innovation investments. In these days of cloud computing where scaling to the cloud can be low cost to begin with and increase in cost as an enterprise grows, this model needs careful consideration and Peppard and Tiernan's work is even more relevant.

Portfolio Management

Often the overall IT budget and the IT innovation budget are constrained. The objective of portfolio management is to create the highest level of return within funding constraints available. These funding constraints will be determined by both the IT and business budgets available. As a general rule, having a project co-funded by both IT and business significantly increases the probability of success of a particular IT innovation as both organizations have invested in the gain and risk/return possibilities. Having a senior business sponsor associated with a particular innovation will substantially increase the possibility of success, as such a person can calmly quiet the naysayers or corporate antibodies that consistently try to squelch interest in innovation.

Rapid iteration of the business case is essential as rapid solution proto- typing, and proof of concept tests are performed. The quality and reliability of financial information in the business case will be increasingly more reliable and precise if this process is followed.

Post-Implementation Review

A key factor in the success of a particular innovation is to perform post - implementation reviews (PIRs) on each innovation to determine whether the value promised was actually delivered. Doing this will substantially increase the probability that benefits will be delivered. If business conditions change, the innovation team may have to be creative and change course midstream to deliver the benefits, but having a specific target is much better than having an open-ended innovation proposition that starts with "Let's see what happens . . ." To maintain balance, management needs to recognize that not all innovations will be successful. In innovation failures, it is important to fail fast and learn fast so we can quickly determine which roads we should not follow toward a particular solution.

Finally, as innovation becomes more predictable, a next step in maturity is to build the benefits promised in a business case into the following year's business and financial plans. This step can significantly increase the pressure to meet performance expectations and lead to more predictable, controllable, and sustainable innovation.

Summary

This chapter highlighted the importance of clear communication between the IT or digital innovation organization and finance. We looked at ways to carve out a budget for innovation and provided a nutshell explanation for the TVM. We explained ROI, a term used with different meanings across the IT industry.

We introduced our concept of business dials, which are the metrics we use to measure the return on IT investments. We took a closer look at the trade-off between IT efficiency and business value, concluding that there is a win-win potential in reviewing a portfolio of choices. We ended with a discussion of portfolio management and PIRs. For a more detailed review of business value concepts, see Curley (2004).

Chapter 3
IT and Digital Innovation

An innovation, to grow organically from within, has to be based on an intact tradition.
—Yo Yo Ma

IT innovation or digital innovation as a management discipline lies at the intersection of two disciplines: information technology (IT) and innovation, as shown in Figure 3.1. Both of these disciplines still have ample room to mature. IT is a volatile management domain due to the high rate of technology change. Changing technology, however, fuels the innovation process as new IT capabilities emerge, and IT can act as an innovation resource, a catalyst for enabling innovation, or as an enabling platform to manage the process of innovation.

Jim Andrew, Senior VP of Innovation at Boston Consulting Group, rightly calls information the *jet fuel* of innovation. IT provides the capability to digitize and easily distribute potential innovations, which keeps the marginal cost of replicating and diffusing the innovation very low. IT, or digital innovation, offers not only the challenge of creating, modifying, or repurposing new and improved ideas, but also the opportunity for accelerated diffusion.

Shifting Intel personnel to wireless laptop computers is a good example. While this is now the norm in business, a decade or two ago most companies provided desktop computers to employees. To explore the potential and business case for broad adoption of laptops by employees at Intel, we studied workgroup behavior, ran experiments to make sure that the laptop environment matched users' needs, and developed a business case. We identified the business dials that measured business value contributions. Finally, with support from finance and line-of-business managers, we rolled out new laptops quickly and systematically. A case study (Intel 2003) provides a detailed account of our decision to shift to wireless laptop computing.

The trend is consistent to repeatedly move employees to further scalable, collaborative and virtual solutions. When internal digital innovation fills an unmet need it is ripe to become an external product enabling enterprises everywhere. The Intel IT Innovation and Research organization created a collaboration tool for use in their conference rooms that began with being able to wirelessly connect to conference room projectors from a laptop and then was incrementally improved to allow everyone to connect to any display and collaborate. People working remotely could receive a code and connect and participate. This collaboration tool was so effective it was productized and sold as a product to Intel customers as the Intel Unite™ product. It uses a simple "share" and PIN access process allowing

https://doi.org/10.1515/9781501507335-003

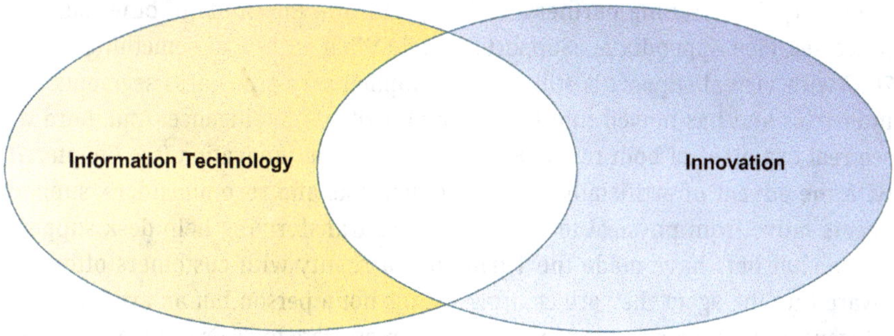

Figure 3.1: The Intersection of IT and Innovation.
Source: Intel Corporation.

people to securely connect to live content from anywhere. The natural incremental progression of this in industry has led to other solutions for collaboration such as Zoom™ and Microsoft Teams™ which grew exponentially when no one was in the office during the COVID pandemic.

The Special Case of IT and Digital Innovation

IT is an unconventional resource, and it has a special relationship to innovation. Unlike most other resources consumed by enterprises, the cost of IT systems continues to drop dramatically while its performance, capacity, and flexibility continue to improve. As a result, IT provides a strong foundation for launching new and innovative solutions to enhance all types of business processes. With each passing year, returns on IT investments can increase, thus widening profit margins, not pressuring them.

IT can be a catalyst to the innovation process because managing infor- mation is itself a key part of the innovation process. For example, needs, requirements, and good ideas from IT's customers must be captured, stored, and sorted. In addition, IT infrastructure provides an accelerated method for diffusing or deploying new solutions. Overnight and around the globe, IT solutions can find their way to desktops and servers at the speed of light. When IT's customers log in with their morning tea and coffee, new features and updated information are installed and ready to go.

The marginal cost of replicating an IT innovation approximates to zero. Consider an investment in a new platform for providing support to IT customers. The yield is an improved help desk. However, the support platform can be reused to automate personnel activities for HR's customers, to assist the billing function for the enterprise's trading partners, and to perform a multitude of other support processes. (See Appendix A, eSupport at Intel.) What we saw as something new in 2007 with virtual support is still being re-applied across business segments and industries and has moved into the space of artificial intelligence. And, here we see real examples of both re-applied and incremental innovation (see Chapter 1), with the advent of artificially intelligent chat bots and recommenders, support agents move from physical to virtual and are transforming help desk support. These chat bots have made the Turing test a reality with customers often not aware that the agent they are chatting with is not a person but an artificially intelligent performance support system that can escalate to IT or customer support employees as needed.

IT innovation can completely transform the way an organization accomplishes its objectives. In the City of Westminster, for example, policing is simply a different function when wedded with the City's extensive network of cameras. Officers can be dispatched immediately when observers see suspicious activity. The City's mobile workers can bring IT connectivity with them when conducting inspections or managing parking. With the addition of natural language processing (NLP) and image recognition, the security of digital cities is being transformed. The cameras can now stream data in order to process images for high risk people and events and provide early warning and alerts to the officers and other security services. (See Appendix A, Wireless Westminster.)

The Six Parallel Vectors of IT Innovation

We describe the pathway from innovation to diffusion with a set of six parallel vectors that begin with a vision and end with a measured result. On the one hand, these vectors, shown in Figure 3.2, are ordered as phases in the creation and absorption of IT innovations. At the same time, and more important, the vectors operate in parallel. Later phases often cause rethinking of early ones. For example, the proof of concept proto- type is likely to change the vision of the new idea. Or, an unfavorable business case may call for additional prototyping.

Ergonomic Advising Software: Overview

At Intel, software monitors the use of the mouse by IT's customers to improve safety. Frequent mouse clicking is correlated with repetitive stress disorder. Our software can help computer users by making them aware of their mouse-clicking behavior. The application can also interrupt work to caution the customer and suggest a stretch break. Finally, data collected by the software can be mined to better understand mouse behavior for different departments and job functions.

The idea of mouse monitoring came from conversations in the corridor between an Intel safety representative and an Intel IT professional. The project exemplified the six vectors of innovation management in action, became an internal product, and then was replaced by an XaaS solution.

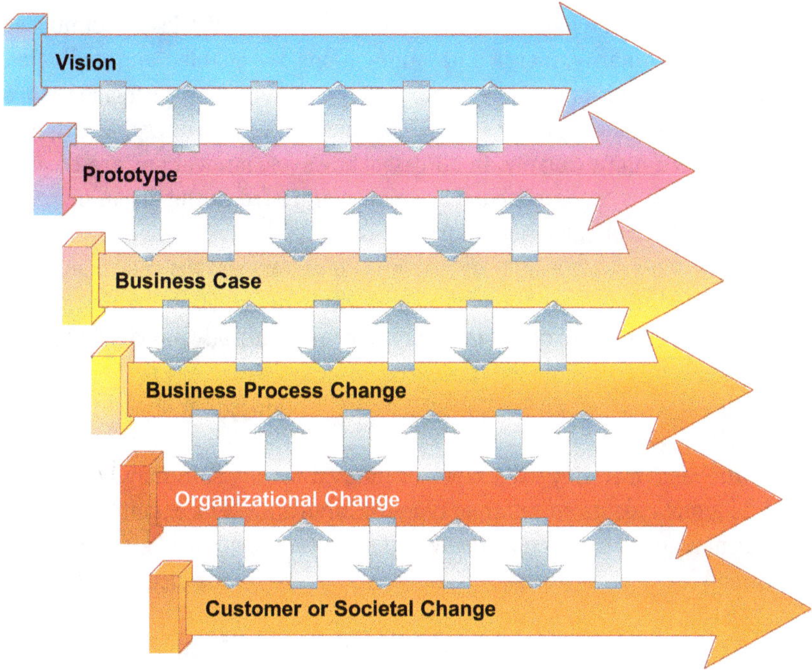

Figure 3.2: The Six Parallel Vectors of IT Innovation.
Source: Martin Curley.

Vision

Most innovations actually come from a stated need or opportunity. We have all heard the generally accepted axiom of innovation, "Necessity is the mother of invention." At the same time, some of the most powerful innovations are conceptualized and motivated by compelling visions.

Consider the case of the transformation of the City of Westminster shown in Appendix A. CEO Peter Rogers had a vision of how the City could be transformed through the use of wireless technology. In Rogers's vision, city employees could spend more time on the streets providing safety and services to the City's residents, businesses, and visitors. While being more productive, these employees also could potentially be provided with better quality of life, enabling working from home, etc. A BHAG (i.e., a big hairy audacious goal) can often create the momentum, enthusiasm, and energy needed to mobilize resources and people to work together to develop and realize an innovation. BHAG goals can be key drivers for value dials, for example, to "reduce the total cost of ownership by 25%."

However, not all innovations are as earth shattering as Wireless Westminster was in its time. Ordinarily, incremental innovations are enabled and motivated through incremental visions of how a particular task might be performed more quickly, how a particular product might perform better, or how that product could be produced more cheaply. In all cases, however, innovations are created in two phases. First is the intellectual creation manifested in the vision or need; next comes the physical implementation.

When the timing is right and the vision is clear, innovations can spring into life, diffuse rapidly, and quickly realize significant benefits. Thus, the first vector is aimed at creating a vision of solving a problem or taking advantage of a particular opportunity. Or, in the words of Robert Kennedy, "There are those that look at things the way they are, and ask why? I dream of things that never were, and ask why not?"

Using the lens of Keeley's ten types of innovation, a vision may be focused either on just one type or on multiple types of innovation. For example, a vision could focus narrowly on an innovative way to improve customers' experience, or a vision could aim to transform customers' experience, while also changing the business model.

For example, the Walt Disney Company introduced a Photopass system enabling after-the-fact purchase of photos taken at Disney theme parks. Professional photographers roam the park snapping pictures, which are immediately available or available later on a website. This innovation changed the user experience for visitors and also changed the business model. A Disney visitor could continue to purchase products from Disney days after the visit was over. Photopass created improved customer service and enhanced revenue streams for Disney. Continuous experimentation and prototyping was a hallmark of making this particular IT innovation work. Early prototypes were not immediately successful.

Thus, the first vector is aimed at creating a vision of a better way to perform a business process with an IT capability. The vision should be user-centered and describe how a business process could be better accomplished. Tracking down problematic processes and observing the people who perform the work are common ethnographic methods for drawing out process requirements and understanding where potential technology solutions might be applied. (See Chapter 5 for a discussion of ethnographic research.)

To move an innovation from the vision to the prototype stage, it is important to clearly communicate the vision to gain buy-in from management and to ensure that the vision is shared by the team that is expected to make it successful.

Ergonomic Advising Software: Vision

Repetitive motion injuries related to use of the mouse were appearing in the Intel safety organization's database and researchers were reporting a linkage to the frequency of mouse clicks and the duration of uninterrupted work.

Meanwhile, a shareware program called MouseCount was published by KittyFeet Software and was being used by a small number of IT customers in Intel. MouseCount monitored users' mouse click behavior and wrote raw data to files each day, month, and year. The inventor envisioned MouseCount as a platform for a contest for the *most* clicks.

These two unrelated events triggered the idea of building an ergonomic monitoring system to an Intel safety officer at Ireland Fab Operations, Tom Mooney. What if software could monitor the behavior of computer users and measure the risk due to overwork with the mouse? What if safety engineers could study usage in different communities to see which job categories were at greater risk? And, finally, what if the software could warn users and suggest that they take a break from mousing?

At this point in the process, the safety engineer had recognized a problem, an opportunity, and a reapplication of an existing innovation to a new usage. Namely, repetitive motion can cause injury, we can identify those at risk and warn people, and the idea of counting mouse clicks can be put to use as an early warning system. In the end, the ergonomic advising software turned out to be 20 percent invention and 80 percent reapplication.

From Vision to Prototype

Visions are best communicated by example. A prototype is a small-scale solution that certifies that the IT solution is viable. Prototypes also demonstrate the vision to stakeholders and provide a test bed for making improvements based on new ideas and potential concerns. Prototypes are also useful for estimating how much a business process can be improved and thus what the business value contribution is likely to be.

A prototype in the hands of a user is invaluable for deciding if the innovation will be able to meet its intended function and use.

Ergonomic Advising Software: Prototype

MouseCount provided a simple platform for initial experiments prior to prototyping. Tom approached Brendan Cannon of the IT Innovation Centre with some of the early MouseCount usage data, passed on some suggestions on how the product could be improved, and the two speculated on the potential for an expanded application. Intel IT collected data for twenty-seven weeks from twenty-six volunteers. The raw data not only highlighted the high rate of mouse clicking, but also helped to identify additional functionality that was needed. Daily counts, for example, was too coarse a grain size. To provide preemptive advice to the user, hourly measures are needed.

Manual analysis of the data, while acceptable during this experimental stage and, in fact, attractive to the engineering mind, would need to be automated to make the system practical and efficient for a broader base of users. Similarly, a production system would need a central repository for the data to support studies of variances within and among departments, job categories, and applications. And, based on conversations with IT customers, the issue of privacy emerged as important.

To be accepted, the prototyping team reasoned, employees must feel comfortable sharing these data. And, Intel has explicit policies about protecting employee privacy. This thinking led the Intel team to include the capability for employees to choose anonymity when reporting data to the central database.

Prototypes vary in sophistication. Simple prototypes can be a computer simulation or can developed during a workshop. They must communicate a vision and gain buy-in for further exploration of an innovation's potential. More complex prototypes require buy-in from management to allocate the resources. As highlighted by the ergonomic monitoring prototype, it is crucial to build a prototype with which to test the scope and the requirements of a finished product. Many IT technologists believe that the hard part of innovation is building the technology solution. It is difficult to wrestle with complexity and sometimes there is significant technical risk. However, in our experience with IT innovations, solving technical problems is very often the easy part. Soft factors such as business process and organizational change often emerge as the most difficult. Joint accountability between the business and IT is essential for the successful development and adoption of an IT-based innovation.

The use of locode and nocode environments can dramatically increase the speed of development of solutions. For example Zendra Health in Ireland have created a locode environment for building medical apps very quickly. The value proposition of Zendra Health is that they could replace the average >$300k and fifteen months it took to develop a medical grade app by providing a certified platform which allowed rapid locode development of new clinical grade apps. In 2020 Nurse Aislinn Gannon was provided with training on the Zendra Locode environment and in twenty-four hours was able to develop a patient-centered app for chronic type 2 diabetes. The application was presented to the Health Service Executive board as part of a broader digital transformation strategy presentation and it was a key datapoint in demonstrating the possibility of accelerating the digital transformation of the Irish Health Service.

When an IT innovation is realized, the prototype is ready to be converted first into a minimum viable product (MVP) before being eventually evolved into a product and is often offered as a service. We think in terms of the principles articulated in Geoffrey Moore's *Crossing the Chasm* 2002). Early adopters are happy to exercise a prototype, which may have intricacies and incompleteness. To aim for the early majority, however, means building a complete product that fits into the user's experience as comfortably as possible.

Thus, when a new IT service can reuse existing user interfaces or the look-and-feel of familiar services, the barrier to successful adoption will be significantly lowered. Moreover, when a new IT service can use an existing architecture and reuse code modules, the cost of both development and maintenance can be substantially reduced. This is aligned with the concept of a platform which we will discuss in Chapter 10.

The disciplines and skills of prototyping are not the same as those needed to engineer production systems. Also, while a prototype and subsequent MVP is an important step forward, it is but the second step on the path to delivering business value. The third step is building the business case.

Business Case

We believe that the importance of building a business case is illustrated by the wide swings in IT investment over the past two decades. Before the dotcom crash, many IT innovations were funded due to irrational optimism fueled by the disruptive adoption of the Internet and the compelling need to remain competitive in a changing world. In other words, no business case was required.

This was followed by a period of irrational pessimism where many IT business cases were rejected out of hand due to the bad experience in the dotcom crash or the unavailability of capital for further IT investments. We also see this in the world of artificial intelligence where initial enthusiasm was followed by a "winter." Over-investment in Internet-enabled innovations combined with investments made to mitigate Year 2000 risk brought many businesses to the point of having neither time nor capital to invest.

We are happy to report that a modicum of balance has been regained. Good IT investments with strong business cases are often reviewed with objectivity and many are approved. One legacy of the wild swings of irrational optimism and pessimism is that few innovations are funded without a strong business case. And this is as it should be: the presence of a credible and compelling business case substantially increases the probability of a successful innovation and the associated conversion of value potential into value creation.

When considering whether to experiment or adopt a new or emerging technology, we suggest it is useful to check in which part of the Gartner hype cycle the technology is located. More risk adverse organizations may want to wait until the best use or a candidate dominant design has emerged from the normal Cambrian explosion of experimentation which usually accompanies the arrival of any new potential disruptive technology.

Often the old adage of "Let chaos reign, and then reign in chaos" is observed as a new disruptive technology such as blockchain emerges.

Business Cases, Prototypes, and Vision

Typically, for an innovation to be viable and sustainable, a return on investment (ROI) needs to be created for the producer's costs, operating costs, and the consumer's benefits. In the early stages of an innovation project, some form of valuation is necessary to justify and sustain the investment. At the vision stage, it is difficult to estimate value with any precision, and methodologies such as using a business value index (Curley 2004) can be useful. A pro forma business case is also useful.

As the innovation journeys through the product lifecycle pipeline, more information becomes available. We review and refine our business cases regularly. We also use rapid solution prototyping in conjunction with real-time business case iteration to produce business cases with improved confidence and precision in a few weeks' time. Decision makers tracking innovative IT projects can look at the work in progress and re- estimate costs and business value contributions.

Note that the prototype and business case should confirm or refine the vision. It is not uncommon for adjustments to be made, and this is a good place in the pipeline process for a stage gate.

Moreover, often the decision to invest in an innovative IT solution is a differential one. Among a collection of choices, and taking into account the available budget, we must choose the best candidates.

Go, No Go

Decision makers, informed by business cases, launch or stall innovative IT projects. When launched, the IT development organization hardens the prototype, expands it to be complete, tests it repeatedly, and integrates it with other IT systems. If we are successful, then an innovative IT project and a conventional IT project will both be well managed. We want to identify and mitigate technical risks in the prototyping phase when sunk costs remain small. When the decision is *go*, we aim to deliver on time, on budget, and on specification.

> **Stage Gates**
> Stage gating divides the product innovation process into stages – typically five or six. Between the stages are virtual gates (often virtual meetings or digital decision tools) that act as checkpoints at which the gate can be opened or closed for a project to move to the next stage.

Business Process Change

Ergonomic Advising Software: Business Case
When Intel can invest a few thousand dollars to improve employee safety, they will do it every time and in an instant. Intel IT innovators explained their vision to different groups and folded statements of support from a broad constituency into their business plan.

Prototyping had expanded their vision. The ergonomic monitoring system could provide data useful to the software development community. Some software applications require more mouse clicks than others. Software developers could use this data to reconsider the design of their user interfaces.

Moreover, when evaluated as potential intellectual property, the ergonomic monitoring system qualified and Intel IT initiated the patent process. Intel IT deferred the decision of whether to build and sell such a product or to license others to do so.

When innovative digital solutions roll out, they inevitably cause changes in business processes. Process owners will need to endorse these changes and training is often required for staff members who will re-engage work in a different way.

For some innovations, the switchover from old methods to new ones can be quite complex. Old and new systems may need to coexist for a period of time until process owners gain confidence in the new solution. Such was the situation with the option of moving to the cloud as opposed to internal server requirements. Adoption of business change will often require a change manager who actively attends to the change process. This is another case where the technology solution may have been difficult to achieve, but the acceptance of changes in business processes may be even harder for IT's customers. The more perceived benefits associated with a particular innovation, the more likely the business process change is to be adopted.

Organizational Change

Many IT innovations require organizational changes in order to realize value. If an organization is unwilling to change, or is already exhausted from trying to assimilate too many other innovations, then failure is likely. Most organizations have a certain tolerance for change, and the wise IT strategist keeps this rate in mind.

Ergonomic Advising Software: Business Process Change
The ergonomic software was offered on a voluntary basis to Intel IT's customers and it diffused throughout the Intel Ireland community quite quickly. One of the first findings when mining the centralized database was seasonality. Not surprisingly, when budgets were about to be set, finan-

cial analysts were clicking at a ferocious rate. Safety officers learned when and where to sound alerts.

IT customers reported that they were more aware of their mouse behavior and that they were proactively looking for alternatives. This in turn led to innovations in mousepad options, which in turn add to complexity. A computer user can modify choices to make two-click operations into one-click operations or other innovations ported over to the PC, brought into play by necessity in cell phone technology.

IT and business people alike will resist the adoption of innovation if it puts their job at risk or if it substantially changes their work-life balance or working conditions. Creating win-win scenarios can be very helpful in ensuring that organizational change comes about through commitment rather than compliance.

Innovative IT solutions can also instigate change to the IT organization. For example, when Intel IT's *People, Intellectual Capital, and Solutions Group* realized we were one of the largest consumers of IT solutions, we realized we were uniquely suited to document what we had learned and to share this knowledge with fellow IT travelers.

We brought in writers and editors to work with IT subject-matter experts to produce white papers on best-known methods. The project grew from a single idea until it reached a critical mass that led to the formation of a new dedicated group called IT@Intel which today continues to share knowledge across companies engineer-to-engineer, supporting innovation adoption.

Customer or Societal Change

Because we define innovation as the adoption of something new which creates value, this final vector of customer adoption is critically important. As IT becomes more and more pervasive, IT innovations touch many aspects of society. For any innovation to be adopted, it has to meet at least three primary criteria:

- Utility—The solution solves a real problem.
- Ease of use—The solution is appealing to the customer.
- Business benefit—The company delivers shareholder value.

Ergonomic Advising Software: Organizational Change

In the case of office ergonomics, IT and Safety formed a team to explore Tom Mooney's bright idea. While organizational change often refers to large-scale adjustments, partnerships like this one reflect organizational teamwork that is critical to the success of most IT innovations. IT and Marketing, IT and Engineering, IT and Finance, and a host of other partnerships are necessary.

The ergonomic monitoring system radically changed the tasks performed by Intel's office ergonomics teams. Rather than observing work with ethnographic techniques, these professionals could now study a journal of events captured in a database. And, the monitoring system provided a platform capable of capturing additional events as needed. The ergonomic advising software became a general-purpose instrument panel focused on individual behavior when using a personal computer.

A producer must be willing to invest in the innovation, customers or users must be willing to pay for the innovation, and business value benefit must accrue. These are the hardline facts about IT innovation in business.

The Public Sector

We speak in business value terms because that is the context of our direct experience. We recognize that there are other contexts, particularly public sector organizations. For those who seek to provide the best possible services to their customers on a nonprofit basis, most of these same principles apply.

The concepts of cost and ROI remain firmly in place. The goal of cost avoidance remains the same. Why spend more when efficiencies allow a nonprofit to spend less? Market share applies as well—a successful nonprofit can afford to reach out more widely. Customer satisfaction remains in place.

The slippery slope for the public sector is the absence of a profit metric. In business, we expect dollars returned for our investments. In the case of the public sector, the profit metric is replaced by quality of service, reduction of risk, and measures that show quality-of-life improvements for customers served. The nonprofit public sector organization can be run like a business, and we recommend this approach. See the case study on Wireless Westminster in Appendix A.

In healthcare for example, improvements in variables such as average reduced length of stay or reduced readmission rates can be directly monetized.

Customer Sensitivities

Digital innovations can be threatening to IT's customers. Customers and users must come to believe that the benefits of using the innovation are greater than the downside risks associated with the collection of personal data. An everyday example that is increasingly common is the retail loyalty card. Shoppers use loyalty cards to qualify for discounts on goods and services, even though most know their personal shopping patterns are being collected and analyzed. With the advent of artificial intelligence to include highly accurate image and voice recognition this no longer becomes an "opt-in" concern and moves to other concerns with the challenges of managing privacy across the many legal compliance requirements around the world. Data anonymization grew from privacy requirements allowing AI advances while protecting "shoppers", "patients" and others.

Ergonomic Advising Software: Customer or Societal Change

The most immediate benefits of ergonomic advising software are identifying and measuring a risk to computer users. When it comes to office ergonomics, the adage *forewarned is fore-armed* takes hold. Intel IT customers were made aware that excessive mouse clicking is a manageable risk. They can measure their behavior against benchmarks, and safety programs can provide mitigation strategies to reduce risk. They can target their efforts.

The ergonomic advising software is well positioned to inform the software design society as well. While Douglas Engelbart's mouse was a radical innovation, understanding its weaknesses is critical to improving the quality of software and hardware designs. Graphical user interfaces are often viewed as an art form. The ergonomic advising software provides empirical data that nudges the design effort from art to science. Measured results galvanize engineers to improve products.

Gmail is an innovative IT service that, on the face of it, has a pure advertising business model (i.e., a free lunch for users) and has been adopted. However, in countries such as Germany, initially adoption rates were much lower due to a higher level of concern about privacy implications of IT. While Gmail may successfully satisfy the five other vectors of innovation management, the degree of alignment with all six vectors was a limit to its adoption at first.

Most recently Facebook's innovation, the Messenger application, then created a storm of reaction as they pushed the limits of personal data gathering.

As the diffusion process continues, we do expect to see changes in customer or societal behavior. For example, at Intel we saw that the installation of sensors in conference rooms to detect motion and turn lights off after periods of no movement led to generating of Dilbert™ cartoons. Other innovations hopefully have brought more productive changes.

- The advent of instant messaging (IM) caused people in meetings to start asking clarifying questions of other attendees without interrupting the meeting. However, for others, it creates a situation where non important and urgent messages can take precedence over more important and non-urgent tasks (Covey 2020).

  Repeated interruption from IM messages and also the consumption of CPU cycles on an already overtaxed laptop mean that people often turn off IM where possible.
- The adoption of the smartphone message system was an interesting IT innovation to watch in action. It transformed the communication flow to and from executives creating a just-in-time or real-time workflow for business decision making.

  On the downside, some users of smartphones found it was addictive and repeatedly checked for new e-mail messages. This practice has become a concern for many smartphone users today. This causes a deflection of concentration in meetings resulting in a continuous partial attention phenomenon. It also caused a different social norm to emerge, as people are seen communicating via their devices while in the same room or even sitting on the same couch.

- Wireless home networks enable employees to do work at home while watching TV or even in bed. Pervasive use of IT where and when people want to use it.
- The advent of web video collaboration has had to address research which indicates that people are uncomfortable seeing themselves on camera and don't like their private spaces shared to the world. This has led to the introduction of innovative digital backdrop libraries to shield employees' home environments, and the camera on/off option still allows people to work unshaven or in pajamas. Be aware that some applications default to the camera being on when entering a meeting, which can get interesting if someone is running late and too quickly skips the option to turn it off.

The biggest reward for innovators is often the opportunity to observe the changes their vision in action has made in the lives of their customers, or even in society as a whole. For example, the creators of our ergonomic advising software know that they are contributing to making their colleagues' lives better by helping prevent injury.

Innovation and Societal Change in India

An example from Intel's India Innovation Centre is the use of web cameras for telemedicine. Rural India has scarce access to medical experts. Because medical examination and diagnosis often require days of travel, web cameras are now being set up to allow opticians to make preliminary examinations and determine whether it is necessary to make a trip for treatment. The next iteration of this will be the use of artificial intelligence for image analysis to assist the opticians to make better decisions.

Again, in India, the migration of certain government services to the Internet is allowing farmers to remain home and work their land instead of having to spend several days traveling into cities to obtain business licenses, birth and marriage certificates, and other licenses and permits. Rural PC kiosks that are making this possible are becoming part of the social fabric of the villages and gathering places for the residents.

Summary

Managing the six vectors concurrently can lead to more predictable innovation. Conversely, managing IT innovation without concurrent re-examination of all vectors is a recipe for failure. A missing vector, such as the absence of a business case, is a clear invitation for failure.

One of the biggest challenges to successful innovations and innovation leadership is resistance to change. Three of the six vectors are related to change. Along with excellent communications, understanding change management is critical to long-term success of an innovation by helping to avoid organizational immune reactions and rejection. Involving users and customers in the agile process of co-designing and iterating solutions is critical in ensuring new digital innovations meet customer needs and have the highest adoption levels. We will discuss the concept of living labs as a mechanism for introducing more radical digital innovations in Chapter 10 on Open Innovation 2.0.

Chapter 4
Systemic Innovation

> *Systematic innovation consists in the purposeful and organized search for changes, and in the systematic analysis of the opportunities such changes might offer for economic or social innovation.*
> — Peter F. Drucker

Systemic innovation is the pervasive and ongoing search for new ideas that improve business processes and deliver business value. Innova- tion is systemic when it becomes a way of life. In this chapter we examine the whole of systemic innovation and identify different levels of maturity and sophistication. Later chapters will look into facets of systemic innovation in greater detail. Our objective here is to provide a reference model.

This is a chapter that applies both to digital innovation and to innovation in general. In our digital world, IT organizations that excel in managing their own innovation processes are well positioned to provide value to the organization and then share that expertise with the enterprise as a whole. Demonstrated success within the IT organization is also a powerful way to gain corporate-wide respect.

Especially in the case of innovation infrastructure—the tools and methods learned, developed, and tailored to a company's industry and markets—the IT organization's experience in solution development and delivery can be highly leveraged and the investment in digital innovation can find even greater returns.

Managing Systemic Innovation

In the early days at Intel, quality, safety, and innovation shared a reputation for being unmanageable. People spoke of quality as an art that could neither be measured nor managed, and that the size of a manufacturing run should be increased to cover the inevitable number of defects. Similarly, improvements in safety were haphazard. Today we know this is ludicrous. These two functions, in turn, have been brought under methodical control and achieved world class levels. We believe that managers of systemic innovation can learn from past experiences with quality and safety management.

You Will!
In the 1980s, Intel faced competitors who began to use quality as a differentiator. According to then-CEO Craig Barrett, "When other companies began to compete on quality, then the equation changed and people's attitudes had to change."

https://doi.org/10.1515/9781501507335-004

Barrett went on to say, "We approached quality like any standard engineering problem at Intel. We found that if you defined the problem, collected data, intelligently used statistics, and made data- based decisions, you could improve the quality of any process or product."

To emphasize his commitment to quality, Barrett added the phrase, "You Will" in the margin of his presentation graphics. As Barrett put it, "[This was my] message that things had to change." And the message resounded throughout Intel.

"The rest is history," Barrett summarized some years later. "We trained the whole company on how to use statistics to make valid decisions, we implemented process controls throughout the manufacturing process, we found that we could consistently exceed our own expectations on yields and quality, and we continue to do so today."

Most companies consider innovation part of their culture, but to maintain their competitive edge, they need to foster long-term systemic innovation. Today's companies need to move beyond historically recognized—though still very important—innovation agendas such as obtaining patents and developing new technology. They need to embrace new innovation targets such as business models, process innovation and delivery innovations. The value returned for companies like Amazon, which focused on delivery innovation, are unquestionable. A systemic innovation program enables a company to manage innovation as a culture in the same way that quality and safety have come to be managed.

Saying that quality cannot be measured and managed sounds ludicrous today. When Craig Barrett implemented quality management at Intel, he provided the links between existing tools and the support required to use them, such as training and process controls. In a similar fashion, companies that have embraced an environmental health and safety culture can tell you the financial value of having a safety culture, and those that adopted a safety culture late can also tell you the cost of being behind that curve. There is risk in being behind the curve for implementing a culture of innovation. The inflection point for other companies and countries using innovation as a strategic competitive weapon has long arrived.

Systematic Innovation and Systemic Innovation

When we describe innovation as systemic, we mean that the innovation capability is pervasive throughout the company and innovation is a way of life. Like quality and safety, innovation is always a part of what we do. It is woven into the company's genetic code and replicated as a rite of passage for new employees. It is celebrated and rewarded. Systemic innovation is more of an end-state and less of a roadmap.

We also mean that managing excellence in innovation can be a rational and methodical process. Innovation does not simply become systemic; effort, skills, and investments are required. Without careful management, innovation efforts can be ineffective. As Drucker (1985) argued, with management, innovation efforts become purposeful and measured.

We focus on both systemic and systematic innovation to provide a balanced view. Each term contributes to a comprehensive discussion.

Systemic innovation is not an art that demands unmanaged creativity, nor is it used exclusively by the research and development department. Systemic innovation is a discipline in which everyone can be engaged and involved. Then it adds measurable value to the bottom line.

Systemic Innovation

We view systemic innovation as a four-stage process that operates much like a control loop. As Figure 4.1 shows, the process is ongoing and cyclical. Innovation can be managed like a business. Strategic and tactical management decisions determine the innovation budget. The budget fuels the innovation capabilities that deliver new solutions. Then, finally, as innovations are diffused, they reach realization and generate business value. Like a business, managers monitor the relationship between investment and payoff as the control loop is closed. This is very much in line with the dynamic capabilities thinking of David Teece (1997). Dynamic capabilities are about the continuous and purposeful adaption of an organizations resources in response to changing conditions and strategies. In the innovation strategy dynamic capabilities model, strategy, budget and capability can all be modified to maximize output value and there is continuous closing of the loop to optimize for outputs.

This is a general-purpose model that applies equally well when systemically innovating a company's business models, engineering processes, and its products and services. At the same time, we shall continue to use Digital innovation as our base case. In a nutshell, when the four stages in the systemic innovation control loop are mature, each stage operates as follows:

- In the *Manage Innovation Like a Business* stage, managers set innovation strategy and allocate the budget in accordance with that strategy. They review the results of prior investments to optimize the innovation portfolio spend. On a regular basis, these stakeholders review the innovation project pipeline and adjust resources in line with progress reports on each project. They often review and realign their shifting requirements as the company responds to shifting markets.
- Based on guidance from the managers of innovation investment, IT and business managers *Manage the Innovation Budget* in a dynamic fashion. Innovative projects may be accelerated or retarded for a variety of reasons. Managers can also stretch the budget by working with open innovation consortia or supplement it by licensing innovations to other organizations.
- The heart of the innovation process lies in *Manage the Innovation Capability*. This is a broad category and includes innovation infrastructure, both for the

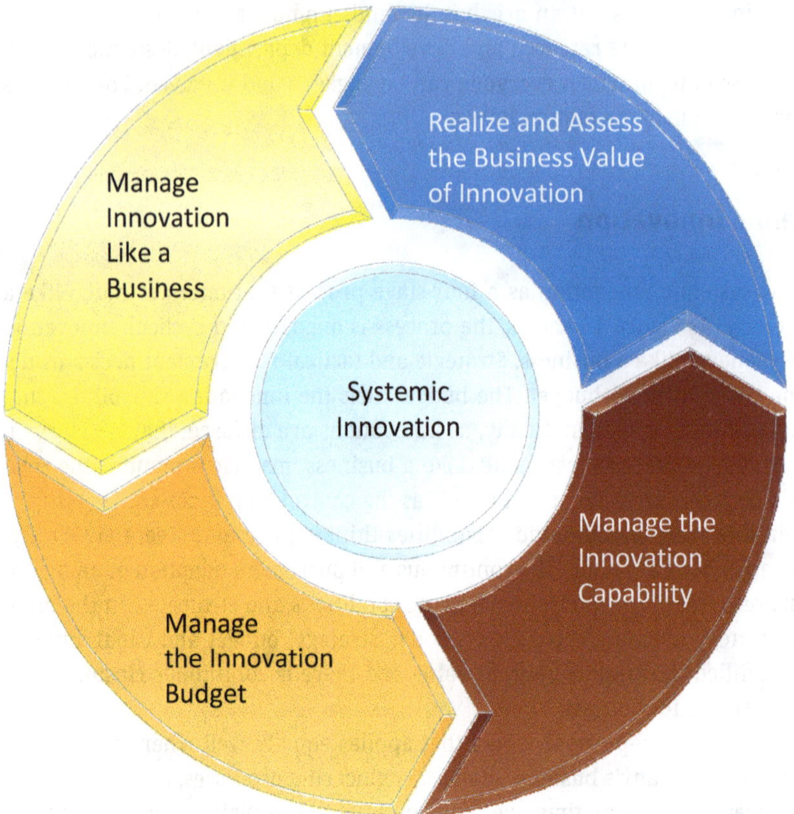

Figure 4.1: Control loop stages.

IT organization and for the enterprise at large. Innovation capability includes maintaining professional skillsets. Digital systems that capture and manage suggestions and requirements from internal users and customers are also a part of the innovation capability. When ideas, suggestions and requirements are not acknowledged, tracked and managed, participation in idea generation drops dramatically and the system usually fails. People can perceive their ideas are going into a "black hole" and stop participating, so feedback is essential to sustain the system.

The tools and techniques for diffusing digital innovations are critical as well. Accelerated diffusion and adoption of solutions result in accelerated value capture. With a distributed, global infrastructure, new digital solutions can be deployed very quickly to accelerate value creation.

- The final stage in the control loop is *Realize and Assess the Business Value of Innovations*. In a mature organization, this means that the pipeline of innovations deliver real systems in a timely fashion and that those systems produce measured business benefits to the enterprise. Especially for IT and other support organizations, customer satisfaction is an important benefit. Other benefits include revenue creation, accelerating work, improving quality, and supporting collaboration.

Of particular interest is IT-led business innovation. Business value accrues when entrepreneurial leaders from the IT organization deliver or help to create new business products, services, or models that generate income.

The control loop is closed, as shown in Figure 4.1, when tools and metrics are in place to capture the information needed to *manage innovation* in the *digital world*, like a business.

Capability Maturity Framework for Systemic Innovation

In our experience, systemic innovation capabilities are not mature when innovation programs are launched. The innovation *capability maturity framework* (CMF) shown in Table 4.1 describes the evolutionary manner in which competencies grow. The CMF breaks out critical processes from larger bundles called macro-processes. Our control loop stages in Figure 4.1 become the macro-processes for the Innovation CMF.

Ad Hoc

In many organizations, efficiency and cost-effectiveness dominate the planning process. Innovative opportunities will arise from time to time, but they are not budgeted on a regular basis and there is no infrastructure available to support them. When customers voice their needs loudly enough, the manager forms a team to address the issue or hires a consultant who is a specialist in the area of concern.

When a system is fielded and customer complaints diminish, the team is disbanded until the next customer crisis. In a nutshell, in the *initial maturity level* shown in the bottom row of the CMF shown in Table 4.1, the organization is averse to innovation and the risk that it brings to everyday operations. This level of maturity is often called *chaos* in the management literature.

Table 4.1: Capability Maturity Framework for Systemic Innovation, Source: M. Curley inspired by CMU SEI CMMI.

Maturity Levely	Macro-processes			
	Manage Innovation Like a Business	**Manage the Innovation Budget**	**Manage the Innovation Capability**	**Realize and Assess Business Value**
Optimizing	Continuous realignment	Amplified budget	Innovation excellence	Predictable, probable, and profitable
Advanced	Explicit strategy	Significant co-Funding	Infrastructure integrated	Proactive Change Management
Intermediate	Management commitment	Formal budget allocation	Infrastructure established	Active change management
Basic	Tacit tolerance	Informal Budget Allocation	Occasional skunk works	Informal Assessment
Initial			← *Ad Hoc* →	

Digital Innovation CMF Basic Level of Maturity

The primitive signs that innovation is maturing begin with management awareness and tacit tolerance, as shown in the *basic maturity level* in Table 4.1. Early innovative projects are ordinarily driven by a hero—a professional who takes on a challenge, fights to squeeze a few funds out of the budget, and brings a novel capability to life. There is no innovation budget, but managers are willing, from time to time, to free up funds and time, often under pressure from users or business managers. Occasionally, teams are formed and the "skunk works" produces a result. Sometimes pet projects are funded when an idea finds a manager to champion it, but funding is based on emotion, not data. Most often, value assessment is informal, often lacking a baseline against which to measure improvement.

At the basic level there is frequently a mélange of tools and systems that are supporting the existing levels of innovation in the company. For example, there might be training for problem solving, people might practice brainstorming, and the engineering community might be designing experiments and developing prototypes as part of the product development lifecycle. However, the existing tools are not components of an integrated innovation system.

It is difficult to find employee communications on the topic of innovation and an innovation strategy is lacking. Furthermore, there is often resistance from designated or incumbent innovators, such as members of the research and development team, to establishing an innovation system for all employees or managers. At the basic level, innovation is associated with creativity and the majority of investment in innovation is for product development.

Digital Innovation CMF Intermediate Level of Maturity

The cornerstone of improving innovation capabilities is management commitment, which describes the *intermediate level of maturity* for the innovation CMF. Leaders in the company with authority and vision must decide that innovative excellence is a core competency that the company must have. For companies in the middle of a pack of competitors, an emphasis on innovation can be a breakaway strategy. For companies aiming to enter a market filled with incumbent players, innovation provides differentiation. Industry leaders view innovation as a necessary competence in order to maintain market share and to create new markets.

With management support comes oversight and visibility. Ideally, the fledgling innovation function can work with counsel from a committee of both business and technical managers. This group provides a sounding board for new ideas and also can bring problems that need to be solved, and be advertised to find their innovators, to expedite the company's business processes and growth.

Companies need to move beyond a historically recognized—though still very important—innovation focus at the basic level, such as patents and new technology, to embrace less obvious innovation such as business model, process innovation, and delivery innovations. This might also include having individuals share best practices on how to manage a project, for example, or discussions among employees about better collaboration methods.

At the intermediate level, a systemic innovation program enables a company to manage innovation as a culture in the same way that quality and safety are managed. Innovation metrics begin to appear and the organization starts to apply engineering discipline and marketing techniques to actively diffuse innovation throughout the organization. It is often at this level when companies realize that competitors are successfully using innovation as a strategic advantage. That realization creates a sense of urgency in management to commit to investment in innovation.

Innovation Budget

With management support, a formal budget allocation is established, the stage is set for methodical activities across the CMF. Over budget cycles, the innovation budget can grow if the new solutions improve overall efficiency. Efficiency gains are especially large when innovative solutions replace high-maintenance legacy systems. Cost avoidance and cost reduction often provide the greatest contribution from digital innovation and other systems at the intermediate level of maturity.

Innovation Capability in the App and Development Arena

Since the advent of the iPhone the realm of technical innovation has broadened to include just about every form of business. Before, technical innovation was largely seen as the domain of technology or academic-centered organizations. Major changes have been seen in sales, marketing, media and the supply chain with the advent of innovators like Salesforce.Inc, social media platforms and recommendation engines. As a result, every organization has a need for innovation in technology that can take advantage of new opportunities. To capitalize on these opportunities effectively over time requires a level of commitment beyond the basic level.

A typical first activity at the intermediate level is building infrastructure. Education and training come first. Members of the organization need to learn about the opportunities and risks that are characteristic of innovative application development. For many organizations dominated by financial and enterprise resource planning (ERP) systems maintenance, new software tool and language competencies will need to develop. In other organizations, the capability may need to be understood universally in the marketing, sales, warehousing, distribution and other departments, creating a need for technology expertise and for broad-based capability training to harness the tools that may lead to innovative products or practices.

With the advent of artificial intelligence entering almost every business segment, there is a critical shortage of data scientists. Quality experts make an ideal target for re-training in data science practices, and need some training support moving them into this area, since they are already using many traditional data and statistical tools. This skills shortage has given rise to further AI innovation by allowing abstraction of the AI model development and training and AutoML software to emerge. These abstraction and automation tools allow more rapid digital prototyping and testing of AI models.

Rapid solution prototyping, agile and user-centered design concepts and methods are particularly important for innovation-oriented digital practitioners. AI tools such as Microsoft Edge Co-pilot and ChatGPT can be useful tools for visualization in the prototyping stage.

Managers assigned to create innovative digital capabilities need not build and collapse their organizations, as the ad hoc skunk works managers did.

Rather, experience can accrue as a growing stream of innovative products emerge. Continuity in the creation process leads to greater efficiencies as good ideas actualized in one part of the company can be copied exactly or adapted to needs elsewhere in the company. Winning projects can be rewarded, whereas the reward for the skunk works team was often disbandment.

The newly formed innovation team must learn about the critical role of active diffusion when deploying innovative capabilities. When a valuable system is not used, it gives back no value. At this intermediate level of maturity, we would expect the organization to spend more time announcing new capabilities and explaining why customers should put them to use. Initially, this is often an informal process. An advocate or champion might socialize the innovation by instant messaging colleagues, initiating video chats or simply going from instant message to online chat and other digital meeting forums to demonstrate the capability or usage or posting videos on YouTube, Instagram or Snapchat or even TikTok. It is easy in this digital age to create groups in your social media of choice and share ("take a look at this.")

Creating an innovation pipeline begins at the intermediate level. The formal budget sets a cap on the number of innovation projects that can be launched. A queue is needed and the organization needs to track these projects through prototyping, development, and deployment. As explained in greater depth in Chapter 7, there are advantages in blending innovative projects with traditional ones if the organization has an existing pipeline management methodology.

For its own purposes and for the enterprise at large, the IT organization is well suited to and has the skills to develop idea capture and development systems. Off-the-shelf options the likes of Mural are readily available and some of them have rich campaign capabilities that allow group and crowd creation. Archiving ideas from across the enterprise and from trading partners and customers outside the enterprise is a valuable activity. These systems are often web-based to support widespread access. Without archiving systems like this, ideas are generated in brainstorming sessions and then lost, and a cycle repeats itself with these unused intellectual assets being repeatedly wasted.

Finally, at this level the organization begins offering innovation training and workshops for its own staff and for others in the company. We call these offerings innovation services.

Business Value Realized and Assessed

Active, methodical assessment processes are formalized at the intermediate level of maturity. The organization cultivates a collection of metrics such as the business value dials described in Chapter 2, and collecting data, both before and after an innovation is introduced, becomes the norm.

The process of change management comes into focus as experience in rolling out innovative, often digital, solutions accumulates.

As demonstrated with our six vectors of innovation described in Chapter 3, the organization now knows that the realization of innovative solutions affects business processes, organizations, and ultimately the customers and culture of the company. Different metrics are needed to tap into all three of the outcome categories.

Digital Innovation CMF Advanced Level of Maturity

The advanced level of *innovation capability* is marked by a shift from merely creating business value to maximizing business value. Innovation managers pay increased attention to longer-term planning and to those innovation opportunities with the best likelihood of payback. Business leaders look to the innovation team for an explicit statement of strategy that provides structure, purpose, and priority to the innovation process. As the number of innovative products grows, the innovation team creates portfolios of similar projects and the pipeline management process becomes finely grained.

Investment managers formalize measures of business value as a part of the planning process, and a business case is required for each innovation opportunity. In our experience, when innovation is valued, there are always too many good ideas. It is the task of the innovation managers to choose the best ideas and to muster resources in accordance with cost, benefit, and risk. Also, in our experience, when innovative digital opportunities are evaluated in this way, priorities are not hard to set and contention among those arguing merely for the cleverness of a new idea is quelled. The systemic innovation process rests on a rational business foundation.

Innovation Budget

At the advanced level of maturity, innovation managers begin to find ways to defend a growing budget. Demonstrated business value over several budget cycles provides the foundation, of course. At this level, innovation managers are keenly aware that they are competing for each investment dollar. Should the enterprise spend more on manufacturing technologies, product marketing efforts, or a digital innovation? The decision is differential, and the innovators must differentiate themselves in order to succeed.

Co-funding is another way to leverage the innovation budget. A compelling customer care prototype in support might trigger investment from the sales department. An environmental program that saves significant costs through recycling could attract funding from external collaborators. An innovative forecasting application developed for the finance department may be attractive to the strategic marketing group, especially since a second deployment would be less costly. In many corners of the world, funds for innovation and training are available from government agencies, labor unions, and other stake- holders. The Horizon Europe program is one example; Saudi Arabia's Vision 2030 NEOM Project and the Chinese government five-year plans are others. The Irish Development Authority is especially adept at leading innovation for business investment, and it is no surprise to find their former employees in development authorities around the world. The U.S. Department of Commerce issues funding to invest in regional technology and innovation hubs as part of President Biden's Investing in America strategy (TechHubs.gov.). Finding funds for innovation often comes down to knowing where to look.

Stakeholder commitment to innovation grows as the digital systems for cultivating enterprise-wide innovation emerge. Investments for these systems can directly transform an enterprise to be far more innovative. The reputation of the enterprise is enhanced when customers and trading partners can see visible support for innovation. Enterprises that are adept at innovation create products and services that open new markets and reach out to new customers. When IT delivers robust support to the enterprise, potential gains in business value are enormous. This was especially noticeable during the COVID-19 pandemic when IT organizations and entrepreneurs stepped into the gap with digital innovation to keep companies connected, innovating and alive.

Innovation Capability

An integrated infrastructure is the trademark of an *advanced level of innovation capability*. Workshops, assessment techniques, and skillsets form a pipeline, not for projects, but for IT and business professionals. Courseware and workshops bring newly hired employees systematically into the culture of innovation.

The development of innovation labs to focus on new technologies, transforming and managing data and developing products from apps to industry efforts in the quantum arena push technology forward at an ever increasing pace. At this level of maturity, the organization has a well-developed understanding of the different audiences that it serves. Customers are directly involved in innovative system and application development.

Guided by management and budget allocation, innovation managers align their work with enterprise goals and objectives. Major innovations such as executing improved supply chain management always have an equally major business sponsor. The melding of business and technical expertise in support of innovation is key to success at this level of maturity.

Creating innovative capabilities is user-centered at the advanced maturity level. The kernel of user-centered design and *design thinking* is equality between developer and user. In prior levels of maturity, users were involved, but until recently in the extreme, the IT organization imposed its solution on its customers. This effect has enabled customer-centric start-ups, fresh with new innovations, to take market share away from competitors with less mature innovation capability.

At the advanced level, innovators are concerned with collections of *user interactions* that make up the entire *user experience*. An AI help desk agent can learn from user interaction to provide better experiences and personnel can use IT systems to expedite their work, as shown in the case study on innovative eSupport at Intel, in Appendix A. However, it is important for innovators to understand the entire context in which this work is embedded.

In addition to running campaigns to push innovations toward internal customers, in the advanced maturity level, diffusion managers use technology itself. In some cases, innovations can be bundled with new platforms when hardware refreshment occurs. Many innovations are invisible and simply assist users behind the scenes. Others can be offered as a part of the operating environment image and do not need to be downloaded from a website. They are part of the app that can morph as new and better innovations occur. Technology-based push is one of the reasons why digital innovation can diffuse very rapidly. Moving an innovation to the cloud, user workstations or personal devices in an internetworked world happens in seconds. The rapid advances in the fintech world have enabled changes to your bank's websites that make them barely recognizable compared to a few years ago. Ad's pop up on your smartphone because of a transactions you made seconds ago. These are all innovations that get copied and replicated, but can be key in driving a startup, new business or enable operations to function from anywhere at anytime for existing companies.

Business Value Realized and Assessed

Proactive change management marks the advanced level of maturity for realizing and assessing innovative digital solutions. There are a number of change management models that can be used. The Kotter eight step change model (Kotter 2012) blends very well with the innovation adoption cycle adding three important steps: create short-term wins; don't let up; make it stick.

Streamlined distribution channels accelerate innovations into widespread usage and the assessment process gains sophistication as well. Organizations at this level address the challenges of converting soft benefits into dollar terms.

One category of traditionally soft benefits is improvements in productivity. Controlled experiments can measure time spent on typical tasks for existing and proposed solutions. These experiments generate estimates of time saved, and employee time can be transformed into monetary units (Sward 2007).

Innovation CMF Optimizing Level of Maturity

Notice that this level of maturity is called *optimizing* and not optimized. Here and in other writing (Curley 2004), we contend that most organizations do not become mature; rather, they reach a high level of performance and then improvement becomes incremental and continuous. In some cases the increments will be smaller; large improvements can occur between lower levels of maturity, to be sure. However, marginal returns can be higher due to reuse of innovations and the amortization of infrastructure costs over many innovation projects. The other scenario is disrupting innovations that can even eliminate incumbents by focusing on delivery innovation that appeals to users through giving them time back, making their lives easier or making access convenient (Christensen 1997). The Blockbuster incumbents could never have incrementally innovated past leapfrogging digital technology such at Netflix. Digital innovation allows leapfrogging especially with the explosion of data science. Data science has allowed innovators to more precisely pinpoint where they can add value.

Changes in the enterprise goals and objectives combined with improvements in information technologies such as data mining, demand a continuous monitoring of the alignment of innovations with business needs. It used to be that the concept car built three years ago may be ready for daily use at a reasonable price point, for example. However, as the rise of digital innovation has accelerated time to value and time to market, companies can no longer afford three years to develop concept cars. Digital twinning is a key tool for car designers to simulate and test without building physical models. Competitive pressure may elevate the priority of innovations aimed at reducing time to market as mentioned in the banking industry. Current digital innovations are using artificial intelligence to assist banks in making lending risk assessments such as Upstart Holdings Inc. At the same time blockchain technology is becoming foundational to disrupt banking, deliver cybersecurity and protect digital assets such as digital currencies. Walmart began offering local pickup or same day delivery from local stores to fight Amazon's overnight delivery. The stakes are high and the systems required meant huge and rapid development. Thus, even the best-managed innovation organization will experience constant change, disruptive digital innovation and, as a result, adjustments will be necessary in order to maximize returns.

Innovation Budget

An amplified budget is one where the organization begins to generate a revenue stream from outside the enterprise. This is accomplished primarily by licensing the organization's intellectual property, spinning off a compelling product or service into a separate entity or leveraging the XaaS or micro service business models. Innovations can sometimes be productized and marketed more effectively by third parties or by utilizing partnership for an as a service (aaS) business model mentioned in Chapter 2.

Participating in open innovation consortia is another way to amplify the innovation budget. This approach is not primarily a cost-avoidance strategy aimed at lowering the investment in R&D by sharing costs with others. Rather, open innovation consortia often deliver higher quality results more quickly that a single company's efforts. The open source software movement is a good example of open innovation. The Lawrence Livermore National Labs Magpie project is a good example of how people come together to solve real problems. With artificial intelligence (AI) entering every business segment, IT managers are being asked to provide the infrastructure to support it. An existing high performance computing (HPC) software environment is very different from that of AI. The Magpie project provides open source tools to converge these two infrastructures into one, reduce the cost of adopting AI and show greater utilization of the traditional HPC environment. Intel contributed to the Magpie project in order to make sure their customers could run AI and data analytics in a converged infrastructure using optimized software for the Intel© Xeon™ processors for better performance and infrastructure utilization.

In some industries, consortia might be non-competing companies serving the same vertical market, for example, hospital IT groups from different communities or public utilities that are assigned a monopoly over a geographical area. In other cases, open innovation consortia may include competitors. The focus is not on competitive advantage, per se, but on making the industry as a whole more efficient, perhaps by standardization paired with innovation. Such is the case with consortia like the Industrial Internet Consortium, seeking internet of things (IOT) standards and solutions.

Innovation budgets must remain flexible. As Curley (2004) pointed out, investments in IT are like options—their future value varies over time. Like the holder of a stock option, the innovation manager need not remain committed to a project that shows increasing signs of risk. When enterprise strategy shifts, as it often does, innovation investment managers may want to accelerate projects that are more closely related to new corporate objectives. For a company with an increased interest in reducing time-to-market, accelerating a supply-chain management innovation would better align digital innovation with corporate goals.

Innovation Capability

At the *optimizing level of maturity*, the tension between operational excellence and innovation is minimized and the groups respect each other's contribution to the overall success of the enterprise. It is essential to have efficient, available, and replicated core systems, such as ERP or a CRM in place.

Those systems should mitigate every conceivable risk. At the same time, the measured risks inherent in developing innovative solutions can be managed. Without innovation, the organization will quickly become a laggard and be vulnerable to competitive pressures or new developments which could impact the viability of the organization.

Innovation centers provide a vital role in reinventing organizations in this digital world and sharing new capabilities both within and beyond the company. An innovation center, which we describe in detail in Chapter 9, provides a setting for continuing education in innovative methods. The center can be a showcase for concept cars, prototypes, and fielded systems as well as a working environment for innovation in action. For companies participating in an open innovation community, the innovation center is a meeting place to share ideas with fellow travelers. Moreover, the innovation infrastructure team can also complement physical centers with web-based virtual centers, including augmented reality or virtual reality.

The innovation creation team becomes sustaining when the creation of better IT systems is woven into the culture of the entire enterprise. At the corporate level, innovation excellence can bolster the company's reputation. Throughout the enterprise, programs exist that reward all who sit around the innovation table—executive managers, IT innovation investment managers, infrastructure managers, and diffusion managers are all on the innovation team.

In a nutshell, the innovation capability of the organization is mature when information is recognized as the jet fuel for innovation across the enterprise.

Business Value Realized and Assessed

Predictability, probability, and profitability are the signals that innovations are delivering business value. Due to user-centered design, innovations are predictably appropriate for the organization's customers. At the same time, there is a high probability that innovative projects entering the pipeline will survive and reach their intended markets and deliver predicted value. In many industries the data revolution has meant that companies must innovate just to remain competitive. This is especially true in marketing, where customers are literally being taken from those who are not up-to-date on the technology. This is due to excellent vetting procedures and careful pipeline management. Lastly, in an optimizing innovation organization, the enterprise is demonstrably more profitable due to the new ideas and improvements delivered by IT. Instrumentation is in place to actively monitor business value results.

Highly successful organizations have conquered the diffusion challenge. Marketing expertise is available in the organization and new capabilities are launched with a campaign commensurate with their scope and importance. For innovations created for a limited audience, such as an improved customer tracking system for the sales department, the campaign may require investment in new technologies like artificial intelligence (AI) for genuine customer preference tracking and prediction. For an innovation aimed at every computer user in a global company, a strong commitment to, and budget for, diffusion will be needed. The importance of *active diffusion* is now firmly cemented in place.

Through portals, workshops, webinars and roadshows, the pipeline of innovations is visible throughout the organization. Customers can see what to expect and when. As partners with IT and other organizations, these customers can express satisfaction or frustration with capabilities and expect that innovators will celebrate the satisfaction and address the frustration as an opportunity.

Idea capture and management systems provide enterprise-wide support for ideas of all kinds. For example, at Intel the first innovation ideation application supported the company's technology strategic long-range planning. The first systems increased the submissions of abstracts by a factor of three, and these sketches of new ideas were of higher quality. All abstracts could be viewed by everyone in the company.

Figure 4.2 provides a snapshot of a web-enabled innovation ideation application in action. Each of the stars in the sky launches a different idea management function.

The macro-process called *realize and assess the business value of innovations* is an autonomous process and a living reality within and beyond the IT organization.

Innovation Excellence and Operations Excellence

While daily operations of backbone systems will certainly dominate project activities in the organization, innovation is a recognized project category. Several innovation projects are likely to be at different phases of their lifecycle. Using innovation infrastructure capabilities, project teams can reach customers to invite them to test versions of ideas under development. There is a growing awareness by the creation team that some aspects of innovative development are the same as conven-

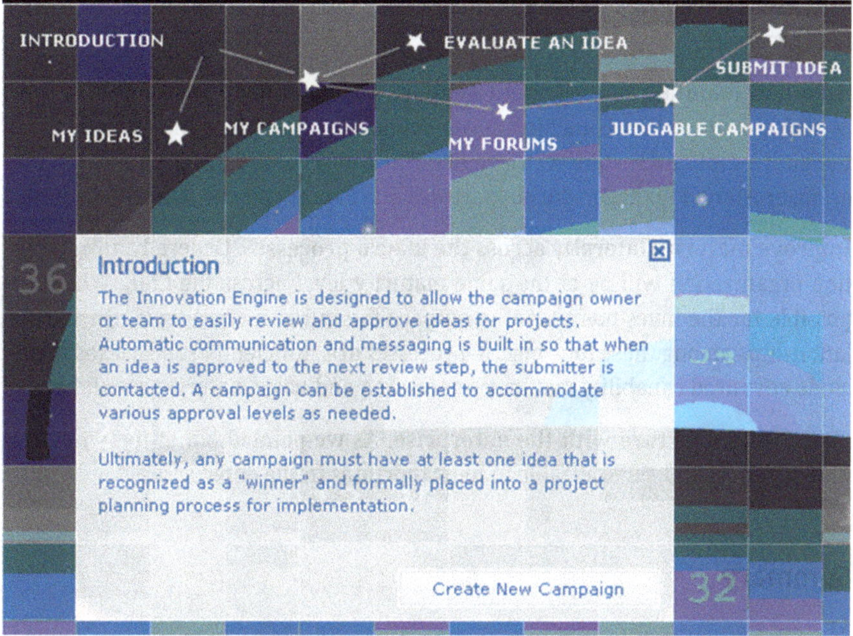

Figure 4.2: An Innovation Ideation Application.
Source: Intel IT.

tional development and others are novel. Creating novel solutions is not an invitation to ignore software quality and careful documentation, for example.

Systemic Innovation Imperatives

For organizations seeking to improve their innovative capabilities, the innovation Capability Management Framework provides both diagnostic and prescriptive advice, some of which we wish to underscore and highlight. Here are the major take-home messages stated as imperatives for the organization:

Make innovation a systemic process. Our experience has shown us that with thought and careful management we can manage risk, chart progress, and keep innovation in alignment with corporate strategy. Innovation need not be an *ad hoc*, chaotic, and random business process.

Deliver measured business value. While all systems should deliver business value, it is the innovative uses of technology that have the potential to move markets, gain competitive advantage, and dramatically improve the efficiency of business processes.

Gain and maintain management support. We identified management support as *sine qua non* when launching an innovation program. It is the cornerstone of the entire CMF. And while we have described an ever-maturing innovation program, erosion of management support will quickly reverse the maturity process.

Improve maturity laterally across the macro-processes. Generally, the innovation organization will be at the same maturity level across the CMF. While it is possible for the investment team to outpace the infrastructure team, the interrelationships among these four macro- processes are sufficiently robust so as to preclude advanced capability maturity in one area and basic maturity in another.

Share infrastructure with the enterprise. As we pointed out at the onset, this CMF is robust and generalizable to most functions in the enterprise.

Summary

We believe that there are four key innovation capabilities that work together in a control loop, and we offer a capability maturity framework to identify growth in each of the four key areas. Over time and with diligence, an organization can improve its innovation capabilities. The Digital Innovation CMF provides a roadmap for systematically improving digital innovation capability and output. With increasing maturity, the process of innovation becomes systemic throughout the whole company, and innovation becomes a core competency and a way of life.

Chapter 5 Innovation Capability

> *Capability is the ability to perform actions. In human terms capability is the sum of expertise and capacity.* — Wikipedia

Innovation capability, taken broadly, comprises the methods, tools, and skills necessary to support and streamline systemic innovation. Training and education are part of innovation capability, for example, because they provide the necessary skillsets for innovators. The scope of our thinking about innovation capability is as broad as our definition of systemic innovation. Workshops and courses that address ideation are within the scope of innovation capability along with more traditional innovation capabilities such as prototyping tools and user experience design skills.

While some of the capabilities in this chapter are specific to developing and diffusing digital innovations, others are quite general and could be put to use throughout the company. Web-based idea capture and management with intellectual property protection capabilities, for example, are needed throughout the enterprise.

We believe that Keeley's ten types of innovation introduced in chapter one and his research findings underpin the importance of disseminating innovation infrastructure throughout a company. There are opportunities to generate significant business value when innovating in the areas of finance, process, offerings, and delivery. While some innovations in the delivery of the company's products or services may require innovative IT capabilities, others may not. Systemic innovation methods can be helpful when rethinking the company's channel marketing or branding strategy, for example.

Innovation Project Stages

Most innovation process capabilities align with a stage of an innovation project. Figure 5.1 shows the stages that we use to organize our thinking.

- Stage 1 is the ideation process—thinking of new ways to improve capabilities. Methods and tools for gathering information about user needs and current business processes, conceptualizing possible solutions to problems, and planning the innovation project fit in this stage. Preparing for this stage is very important and should involve observation, understanding needs and opportunity analysis.

https://doi.org/10.1515/9781501507335-005

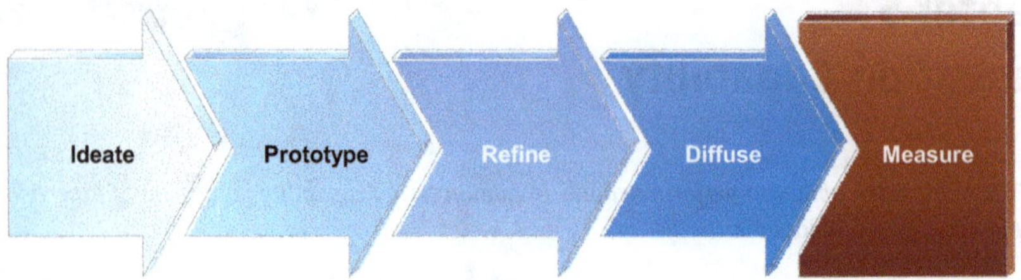

Figure 5.1: Development Stages for an Innovative Capability.
Source: Intel IT.

- Stage 2 is prototyping—building inexpensive test solutions so that the feasibility of the project can be tested. Rapid prototyping tools and usability experiments are tools relevant to this stage. Prototypes can be physical or digital. Video and simulation can play important roles at this stage. Digital twinning, AI and generative design are increasingly useful tools at this stage.
- Stage 3 is refinement—extending a prototype to a full production system that is tested, integrated with other systems, and ready to deploy. The interim step to build a minimum viable product (MVP) is a critical milestone in the refinement or iteration process. The refinement stage also includes packaging software, delivering apps, documenting their usage, and building support and training systems.
- Stage 4 is diffusion—for us, diffusing is the active acceleration of the adoption process. When IT innovation is managed like a business, its products are actively marketed to its customers, their stakeholders and the employees of the company and then adopted because of the value they bring.
- Stage 5 is measurement—business value dials will be needed to translate the impact of an innovation into monetary terms. Without monetary units, the actual return on investment cannot be calculated. The use of business value dials is explained in Chapter 2 and Chapter 9.

Ideate

Ideation is ordinarily the first step teams use in the innovation process. There is pre-work needed for this step. There is an old adage that 80% of innovation comes from a stated need. Based on knowledge of a user's need obtained through observation or data collection, innovators begin by thinking about what a potential solution would look like. The outcome for the ideation stage is a solution description that is rich enough to support a prototyping effort.

Brainstorming

The ideation tool most familiar to people is the *brainstorming* process. Brainstorming is the free flow and capture of ideas in the absence of ongoing evaluation. That is, participants avoid making judgments about the ideas until the flow of ideas ends and then the ideas are evaluated. There is usually little to no structure in the brainstorming process. There are other tools and methods that rely on how the brain works or use a process to generate ideas, and brainstorming is sometimes embedded in a longer methodology. These methods are outlined below.

Brainstorming at Intel

The Intel Materials Purchasing and Management group used an online brainstorming tool that yielded results very quickly. Brainstorming participants, working locally and remotely, participate and all ideas are captured automatically. Ideas are online and so there are no more flip charts or sticky notes to be transcribed, nor electronic whiteboard printouts to be distributed. The tool also supports prioritization of ideas and build an archive for future use. Unused ideas are no longer lost; they can be re-visited and used in the future.

Participants report the benefits to be speed, quality, and engagement. The application process can generate forty ideas in ten minutes and conduct a poll that enables participants to prioritize those ideas in ten more minutes. Discussion is focused and the ideas are of high quality. The team is efficient and energized by a brief but intense period of engagement. The widespread availability of products like Mural or Miro make virtual brainstorming easy and efficient as all inputs are recorded and available for persistent viewing. Using AI tools to generate ideas expands on this and can yield more diverse ideas.

Lateral Thinking

Lateral thinking is a method developed by Edward de Bono who held faculty positions at Cambridge, Oxford, Harvard and London and a renowned authority in the field of creative thinking (1986). Lateral thinking helps teams examine problems from six different perspectives. It is a step- by-step process that uses techniques such as fractionation, the reversal method, and random stimulation to generate alternatives. Innovators are encouraged to identify and consider critical factors, challenge assumptions, suspend judgement, and funnel dominant ideas to final selection. The resulting ideas generated are often startling in their diversity.

To teach his method, de Bono created *six thinking hats aligned to the way the brain processes.* By metaphorically changing hats, innovators systematically shift their perspective on the problem at hand and everyone is on the same page. Most importantly, the "hats" help teams avoid traditional adversarial thinking and ensure that the information to make decisions about an innovation is as complete as possible.

- Blue Hat: Manager of the overall thinking process. The blue hat thinker presents the problem or opportunity and identifies where the team needs to focus and what thinking techniques ought to be employed.
- Red Hat: When donning their red hats, the team focuses on communicating feelings and intuitions. The red hat brings emotions to the forefront and helps teams to reach consensus.
- White Hat: The white hat is an invitation to share what members of the team currently know. With all available information disclosed, the white hat thinkers identify missing information and seek it.
- Black Hat: When wearing black hats, the team takes a critical look at the solution under development. The goal is to identify risks, possible difficulties, barriers, weaknesses, or problems.
- Green Hat: The green-hat team generates ideas, captures alternatives, improves upon ideas. Putting on a green hat after wearing a black hat, you focus creatively on identified risks or problems.
- Yellow Hat: With the yellow hat of optimism, the team identifies benefits, explains feasibility, and highlights the aspects of the solution that are looking good.

A facilitator leads the innovation team in looking at a problem and examining the objectives that need to be achieved. The team then tries on each *hat* in turn to extract the total picture, manage risks, identify benefits and alternatives, and reach a consensus about next steps.

We recommend organizations embed ideation techniques such as lateral thinking and the Six Hats debriefing exercise into a Systemic Innovation for Teams (SIfT) Workshop, to allow teams to address relevant challenges or needs in the organization. The workshop should include other steps in the innovation process, such as prototype development.

TRIZ

TRIZ is the Russian acronym for the theory of inventive problem solving. It is a methodology for solving engineering problems. Developed by Genrich Altshuller[1] and his colleagues. The method is a collection of principles to apply one after another to generate possible solutions. Altshuller, was a Russian patent inspector. He based TRIZ (pronounced *trees*) on abstractions of the many clever ideas that crossed his desk (Livitov 2019).

The essence of TRIZ is the contradiction. For example, a company called OnTech came upon an interesting product packaging concept: beverages that could be stored on the shelf and could be heated at the press of a button without the aid of a stove or an oven.

The TRIZ approach suggests sharpening the contradiction and abstracting the essential feature. What's needed is a self-heating cup. The key element is heat. In the abstract, how can heat be created? Electricity, fire, and exothermic chemical reactions are three ways to produce heat. The third approach looks promising because it is portable and exothermic reactions can be triggered by mixing chemicals. OnTech designed a three-chamber cup with chemicals in two chambers and a beverage in the third. Pressing a button breaks a seal so that the chemicals mix and the beverage is heated.

TRIZ in Action

We recommend a number of organizations have a certified TRIZ trainer on their staff that provide TRIZ workshops for the company as a whole. Those courses are ordinarily given anywhere in the enterprise and primarily to engineers. Many of the TRIZ principles can be applied outside engineering. While we do not recommend TRIZ training for all professionals, TRIZ training is useful to most engineers including software engineers and user experience designers. TRIZ has a suite of tools and methods and is not something lightly adopted to build innovation capability.

The heart of TRIZ is re-applied innovation. Altshuller uses previous innovations in the form of patents to spark the cognitive process that allows re-application into a new area or to solve a new problem. People that are good at pattern recognition and have a basic understanding of problem framing and engineering principles can use the TRIZ process effectively. Altshuller (1994) provides an entertaining and tractable description of TRIZ. One particularly valuable method in the TRIZ training is the ability to predict the evolution of a technology and forecast where it can go.

---

1 Pavel Livotov, Vladimir Petrov, *TRIZ: Innovation and Inventive Problem Solving*. 2019.

While delivering an Innovation 201 Workshop to American Chamber of Commerce members in China, Esther noted that one of the attendees led a company that provided high-end lighting systems for cars. In an aside conversation with him she noted that using TRIZ car headlight evolution could predictably include infra-red technology in the future. Seeing the look of shock on his face she realized they were already doing research in this area but it was not public knowledge. She assured him that no one had "leaked" their research and that it was simply predictable using TRIZ. He became VERY interested in learning more about TRIZ. We now fast forward a few years and know that this technology is key for autonomous driving, night driving safety, supplements other sensors and could have been predicted sooner for implementation using TRIZ.

Ethnographic Research

Ethnographic methods are disciplined observation techniques. These methods were originally developed by anthropologists who analyzed behavior in other cultures by watching how typical human activities were undertaken. From these field notes, anthropologists extract regularities and contrast behavior in different cultures.

For digital innovation, ethnographic methods are used to understand how people behave when performing their daily work. While not limited to the classic time-and-motion studies conducted by efficiency experts, ethnographic observations often uncover difficult tasks that slow down a process or introduce error. These challenges become the basis for innovative digital solutions—IT systems that fit into and assist with daily work.

Ethnographic methods are open-ended and soft. This is in contrast to focused, hard measures such as surveys and questionnaires. Often the ethnographic observation generates the hard survey item. For example, ethnography may uncover that real-time network access at meetings is helpful. A corresponding survey could then ask IT customers how often they have needed network access during a meeting.

Ethnography in Action

In order to better understand the enterprise needs, the IT organization conducts ethnographic research as a necessary part of the IT innovation process. A typical ethnography report would be organized as follows:

- Methodology—the purpose of the research and how will it be conducted
- Data Sets—the behavior, task, or process that is the focus of the study, the characteristics to be observed, and the data to be recorded

- User Value Statements—detailed quotes and specific observations that indicate user value along with summary statements showing what users value in general
- Implications—observed trends and relationships between users and their work environment that indicate a digital innovation opportunity
- Recommendations—conclusions drawn by the ethnographer that underscore the most important opportunities. Since ethnography is not statistical, salience must come from the observer.

In our experience, the ethnographers have observed both internal and external customers and the focus externally is usually in the interest of understanding how they use the IT systems provided to work with us efficiently. For example, Intel has migrated to a 100% ebusiness model. Intel IT assisted that effort by studying how to create better systems to handle both sides of the ebusiness interface.

An IT study we saw focused on telephony choices such as wired, wireless and Wi-Fi phones. The ethnographers studied employee phone usage throughout the workday. A key finding was that phone usage is an overall capability for employees and should not be thought of from a device perspective. That is, it's not important how the phone works, but rather how it behaves.

The ethnographers were able to extract high-level requirements for any phone technology. These findings resulted in successful diffusion of new soft phone capabilities that met users' requirements. Ethnographers found that the array of options in use at Intel is inconsistent. Some phones mute, others do not, and muting commands vary. Signals such as busy were also inconsistent. Hands-free headphone capability and group- oriented speaker phone or virtual meeting space options were irregular.

Generally, ethnography is most useful in the early days of an innovation project. In this setting, we observe to understand and create requirements. We also observe with the use of prototypes to see whether our solution actually meets customer requirements.

Ethnography is also useful when developing business value dials. Especially for innovations that aim to improve employee productivity, we must identify and define how our new technology improves the quality or speed with which work can be accomplished.

LEAN Six Sigma

LEAN Six Sigma is a hybrid systemic practice to improve efficiency/eliminate waste and reduce defects and variability by effectively solving problems. Many of the tools and methods for LEAN Six Sigma overlap with innovation tools and methods. In the ideation stage, LEAN direct observation methods are valuable in understanding an environment, identifying problems, and preparing ideas to solve them. The same is true for other innovation process stages. Table 5.1 lists a menu of tools and their origins. There is a tendency for practitioners of various methods to become inflexible about the tools they use and want others to use. Our approach is to mix and match and choose the best tools for the job.

Table 5.1: Innovation Tools Mapped to the Process Stage.

Ideation	Prototype	Refine	Diffuse	Measure
Fish Bone Diagram	Body Storm	AIDA	Bullet Proofing	Labor-saving Calc's
Five Why's	Using Analogy	Stage Gates	DICE	Quality-saving Calc's
5 Problem Elements	A Day in the Life	Beta Testing	Copy Exactly	Time Motion Studies
Spaghetti Diagram	Basic Prototyping	House of Quality	Resistance to Change	LEAN Waste Tracker
Value Stream Map	Graphic Simulation	Process Decision Chart	Kotter	
Process Map	3D Print	PDPC (Process Decision Program Chart		
Waste Elimination				
Functional Analysis				
Contradictions				
IFR (Injury Frequency Rate)				
Seven Step Problem Solving				
Boundary Definition				
Affinity Diagram				
Scamper				
Concept Maps				
Mind Mapping				
Brain Sketching				

Table 5.1 (continued)

Ideation	Prototype	Refine	Diffuse	Measure
6 Thinking Hats				
Lateral Thinking				
Task Analysis				
Priz.guru				
Ideal State				
40 Inventive Principles				**
Smart Little People				
Brainstorming				
General Tool		TRIZ Tool		LEAN Tool

Source: Adapted from Dr. Frank Gleeson – Intel Ireland.

Prototype

Prototypes are usually scale models, that is, partially functional *first articles* that we use initially to test and improve upon an innovation before investing further and taking on operational risk. Prototypes share characteristics with children's toys, according to de Geus (1997). Prototypes are the systems we can afford to break in order to learn what is required for the mission-critical versions that really matter. Sometimes dimensionally accurate graphical simulations are appropriate prototypes. Prototypes are also one of the most effective tools for communicating the innovation vision and obtaining buy-in from both management and users. Some people call prototypes a proof of concept, a powerful way to describe the fact that a team has "proved it will work." Digital prototyping is growing in popularity as virtual reality and simulation capabilities are mature and even include artificial intelligence.

Concept Cars

Digital concept cars are based on the same notion as automotive industry concept cars—futuristic, novel, unique, and appealing vehicles used to try out new looks and capabilities, but not necessarily fully functioning.

They have just enough definition to get across to the end users you are trying to reach (Busch 2006).

The concept car program has resulted in such prototypes as global collaboration, home monitoring, virtual team tools, an instant meeting server tool, and work life effectiveness tools.

At Intel, there are R&D Councils that review requests for funding and an Innovation Assignment and Ventures program that frees people to work on the innovation. Some groups and sites additionally have innovation working groups with dedicated innovation budgets that support employees' ideas or Big Hairy Audacious Goals (BHAG) projects. The BHAG process is a very successful goal based innovation technique that often BEGINS with business value as the driver, e.g., "we need to reduce cost by 50%" or "we need to increase output by 50%." The innovation campaigns then support those goals.

Usage Models

A usage model is an explanation of who would use an innovation, how they would use the innovation, and what value the innovation would provide to the user and the company. When there are multiple users then each user type becomes a "persona." Usage models are a powerful way to communicate the vision of a new application or a reapplication.

Usage Models in Action

Usage models often rest on the results of ethnographic research. When an ethnographer describes an employee struggling to perform a task, an innovator might see a way to make the task simpler. This is one way that ethnographic research is reused. A single ethnographic study could lead to the development of several usage models.

Surveys are another source of information for building usage models. In the People's Republic of China, parents reported that they have a high level of stress when they have to return to work and their child is left with a child minder. They also felt stressed when their child begins kindergarten. Kindergarten teachers claimed that they were frequently interrupted by parents and grandparents that wanted to check on their child.

These findings led an innovator to suggest repurposing a simple remote monitoring system using web cameras and the internet. In fact, some kindergartens have installed cameras so that families can see their children from their personal computers and teachers report that the system has reduced parent interruptions.

At Intel we piloted a similar usage model. New parents could look in on their babies at home while they were at work. Off-the-shelf technologies were put to a new and innovative use. Our new parents innovated as well by inviting remote grandparents to look in on the baby as well. It was not hard to predict that the next stage for this usage would be commercially available video monitors to supplement the usual audio monitors. Which in fact became a reality.

User-Centered Design

User-centered design is a method of product development that is rooted in customer needs rather than in technology capabilities. Technology companies have a history of delivering new technology capabilities and not defining how these capabilities might be used—solutions looking for problems. While both the push of technology and the pull of the customer are important, the pull of the customer is more important.

Sometimes technology push works. For example the somewhat-sticky glue that 3M created enabled the sticky note that we all enjoy. More often, research and focus on the needs, wants, and limitations of the user are more effective. Business users who want to do their work efficiently and accurately will best inform the design process.

At Intel there are global product design centers that are dedicated to delivering solutions that meet the unique needs of a community through user-centered design. The early product designs that resulted from these centers included a PC that could be powered by a car battery during inclement weather, a mobile computing solution for children with a child-sized keyboard and a more rugged design, and an i-café PC configuration that enabled IT support teams to maintain the systems remotely.

When applied to the development of innovative IT capabilities, user-centered design begins with observation—what are people currently doing and how are they equipped to do their jobs? We interview managers to understand the context of their work. And, of course, we listen to the people closest to the work. We want to know the challenges they face, the problems that they encounter, and the steps in the process that are the most error-prone or time-consuming.

When we construct usage models and prototypes, we return to the user community for input. Input could be as simple as an opinion: “Does this interface make sense to you?” Input could be as precise as a study comparing elapsed time to complete a process with and without the innovative IT solution.

Sometimes the results swiftly change our direction. For example, in China, innovators wrote software to help children read and write *Hanzi* characters. The innovators used Hanzi text on the navigation menus, which worked well for adults who could read the characters. The children, however, were frustrated because they could not navigate. The product did go into production after modifications to add easier navigation.

Refine

It is traditional for IT and engineering organizations to develop their own solutions and move them into production locally or enterprise wide. This approach to building innovative digital solutions is viable, to be sure, but in some cases, refinement may be better resourced outside the IT organization. Self-developed solutions come with the burden of support that off-the-shelf solutions often don't have, which may result in resistance to funding their development or diffusion due to the cost of follow-on support.

Outsource

Outsourcing can work in two ways. Some organizations outsource conventional IT system development so that in-house staff can focus on innovation. Who better knows the company's processes, objectives, and infrastructure? Traditionally, IT organizations aim to fully understand competitive IT capabilities and only outsource non-strategic systems. Payroll is a common example.

Alternatively, the organization can turn to third parties for help in refining an innovative IT system. For projects involving new technologies, outsourcing can provide a route to scarce expertise or to skillsets not yet developed internally. In the current environment, where artificial intelligence (AI) is penetrating every industry and competition for data scientists and AI experts is fierce, outsourcing AI model development and data preparation is growing.

It is prudent to weigh the advantages of in-house versus outsourced development. In our experience we often end up constructing a hybrid form since eventually we will be deploying and supporting the new capabilities.

Open Source

Open source is one of the largest examples of open innovation that exists. Fueled by people's interest in a topic and their willingness to contribute, innovative software can be developed atop components that are of high quality and available at no charge. There are large communities dedicated to a wide variety of open-source solutions and Intel has actively supported many opensource developers via the Intel Developers Communities at www.intel.com/developers and on sharing sites like www.github.com. Artificial intelligence is one area being fueled by the opensource community. Intel, Google, IBM and other companies provides free training and resources for people wanting to learn about AI. In Ireland the problem of deploying an electronic health record (EHR) to people by the HSE IT organization has proved intractable and one division, HSE Social Inclusion, has turned to the OpenEMR open source EHR and deployed OpenEMR to over fifteen thousand patients in a large living lab which now looks promising for a national deployment to over five million people.

The power of open-source development is extending into all business segments and is made possible by collaboration tools noted in Thomas Friedman's *flat world.* (See Friedman's Flat World in Chapter 8.)

The slippery slope of open source is licensing. In most cases, the organization must agree to share improvements or extensions to open-source components. So-called *copy-left,* in contrast to copyright, provides a legal foundation to encourage sharing. *Copy-left* is in direct conflict with intellectual property protection, for example when participating in an open-source software development community all of the code innovation is shared publicly.

Software as a Service and Infrastructure as a Service

Software as a Service (SaaS) and Infrastructure as a Service (IaaS) are even more disruptive ways of refining and deploying innovative IT applications. This is a delivery model where users share access to software provided by an outside vendor. The IT organization would likely qualify the vendor, but would purchase neither software nor servers. The supplier takes responsibility for whatever servers and storage systems are needed and the consumer pays a usage fee.

One distinct advantage for SaaS and IaaS is access to IT expertise by small and midsize businesses. Salesforce.com and Microsoft offer sales force automation capabilities, for example, that would be difficult to support in smaller businesses.

XaaS

Growing out of the software as a service model we are now in a world of "anything" as a service (Xaas): software, platform, network, communications, data base, operating system and more. The advent of cloud computing and high bandwidth internet access is fueling this trend. A large number of products, tools and technologies can be delivered to users over a network, often the internet.

Infrastructure as a Service (IaaS) allows companies to pay for hardware and software as they use it instead an up front investment. This results in a reduction in physical overhead in both people and hard and soft assets. Many Cloud Service Providers (CSPs) operate under this model. The "as a service" model moves expenses from CapEx to OpEX.

Containers as a Service (CaaS) allows software to be distributed inside containers and avoid compatibility and other issues.

Platform as a Service (PaaS) provides preconfigured resources for application development and testing.

One might argue that paying a usage fee for a solution available to everyone was not innovative. We would reply that in the increasingly open world of digital innovation, applying the "as a service" (aaS) model to fill certain enterprise needs can be the most effective approach.

Open Innovation

In fact, more generally, organizations need to avoid the venerable *not invented here* syndrome and each of these different approaches to refinement highlight that need. Open Innovation occurs when two or more parties collaborate together to solve a problem or size an opportunity. In Chapter 11 we introduce Open Innovation 2.0 (OI2)

Diffuse

Web 2.0 Internet

Web 2.0 tools are being used to improve communications between individuals and groups. The way that we interact with each other has changed forever. Typical Web 2.0 capabilities are as follows:

- Blogs are web logs usually maintained by an individual and are similar to a diary or journal. Bloggers record and share their activities and thoughts with others that have access to their site. Companies invite employees to blog on their experiences e.g. Dell's "Direct from Developer" blogs.... "share technical details and how to configure Dell approved solution designs to make it easier for adoption. These designs have rich variety and the needs are defined under the capable leadership of Seamus Jones" their Director of Technical Marketing Engineering.
- Podcasts are audio or video recordings that can be shared among members of a community. They are another form of portable on- demand communications.

- Social media tools include chat rooms, forums, spaces that can be personalized with profiles and photos and then shared with others. Some spaces are hidden to members at large and are only visible to those invited to participate.

The impact of smartphones cannot be understated. The switch to app development based on the iPhone and later Android have ushered in a new era of innovation. On a user level, the impact is enormous and the breadth of possibilities is infinite. College friends, childhood friends, and former colleagues are staying in touch, re-connecting and socializing by forming communities using social media tools addressing unique audiences and of course Facebook, X (Twitter) and so on. Increasingly, games are being used as socialization tools as teams of people that have only met virtually get together for virtual team events or maybe to play cards or fight war games. These phones are pushing technology forward and remain a key to innovation success. Most powerfully, App Stores have massively reduced the advertising and particularly the distribution costs of new software solutions. Many small add on devices can now plug into the smartphones, using the Incremental innovation and "addition principle" to increase functionality e.g. point of sale systems, microscopes and medical devices.

The Tomorrow Project

Science fiction as a source for science fact is something that aligns with innovation. An Intel Europe project published a book of short stories by famous science fiction writers to ask them to predict the future of technology. This was re-applied in the USA, and then became a program for students with free online videos and stories that teachers could use in their classrooms to explore future uses of technology.

Mashups

A mashup is the intelligent combination of XML and HTML solutions that are combined together to create a useful experience for the user. The mashup enables do-it-yourself IT users to mix and match many of the web capabilities and tools into an environment that helps them transact their business. The term comes from the music world where disparate songs are *mashed* together to create a new song or sound.

An innovation portal that supports practitioners with many innovation products and services that can interact with each other, such as manage the pipeline, is an example of an IT innovation mashup that resulted from a service-oriented architecture approach. Web services are making many mashups possible and one company using the web service of another to generate business value is going to increase in frequency. IT organizations that focus on the service experience of innovation and intelligent re- combination of services into mashups will be winners. The mashup capability, and the ability to infer user preferences has given rise to Web 3.0.

Mashups also offer another way for organizations to think about innovation. The sharing and synthesis of ideas can lead to mashups of products themselves driving new collaborative innovations, speeding innovation by not having to build every piece yourself. This type of innovation allows partnering with others who may have best "as a service", open solutions or APIs that may enable a part of your product. This trend is increasing and going to market with best of class solutions you know will work may be a better option than build it yourself.

Web 3.0 Internet

Most enterprises have implemented Web 2.0 capabilities to improve how employees communicate with each other and we are now seeing the implementation of Web 3.0, the semantic web with AI and data-based tools that anticipate your needs and drive services to your connected devices, while enabling constant communication of information in any form at any time where data is collected, stored and used to identify virtually any trait that may be thought useful to those who may seek to benefit from it.

The growth of technologies like virtual reality, augmented reality and artificial intelligence is changing how we interact with the internet itself. Interactions are becoming predictable, preferential and immersive. Web 3.0 emerged as a movement away from applications that are dependent on a single supplier or a central location toward adaptive computing, with distributed databases that can interpret and act on natural language with machine reasoning and intelligent agents. Smart assistants and agents are making life easier for computer users in every business segment. This space is sure to be fueled by more innovation over time.

Crowdsourcing

Crowdsourcing is a term coined by *Wired* magazine to describe the process of taking a task ordinarily performed by an employee and offering it to a large group of people outside the organization. Promising applications are released to early-adopter users for what was once called alpha testing. No promises are made that a future product will behave like the prototype. This method promotes rapid feedback. It accelerates product iteration cycles without the full overhead of completing a beta test.

Wikipedia is a good example of a crowdsourced encyclopedia which then gave rise to crowdsourced book creation by multiple authors. Today crowdsourcing is a social media phenomenon supplying the entrepreneur, artists, or others seeking funding, an opportunity to gain funds by like-minded supporters.

The macro trend of mass collaboration which is an evolution of crowdsourcing is discussed in Chapter 11. Small scale venture capital crowd sourcing via platforms such as Kickstarter are an evolution of crowd sourcing.

Copy-Exactly

Copy-exactly was often perceived as a barrier to innovation at Intel because every factory had to agree to an innovation before it could be adopted. Needing buy-in to an innovation from every factory raised the threshold for selection of an innovation. However, positioning the concept differently—that it would greatly improve quality—helped copy-exactly to be perceived as an innovation advantage.

Because diffusion is often the most difficult part of innovation, the guarantee of diffusion embedded in copy-exactly is a real benefit in that once an innovation is approved, it is simultaneously diffused across the Intel factory network. For a long time, Intel employees were not permitted to talk externally about copy-exactly because of the high impact results it achieves to diffuse innovation. Today copy-exactly as a service is being provided by software platform vendors.

Other Diffusion Techniques

Workshops. Executive workshops are a very effective mechanism for both diffusing innovations and building creative solutions to hard problems. A well-designed workshop agenda can significantly help with the diffusion of ideas and innovations. Showcasing—whether standalone or through speakerships at conferences—is an excellent diffusion mechanism. Intel has actively supported technology adoption by delivering free workshops to engineers, IT professionals and the wider community on a wide variety of topics. The most recent Intel workshop, developed by one of this book's authors, is designed to help executives understand the uses of artificial intelligence, where it could add business value in their industry, and most importantly "how to get started."

Software Distribution. Automated software distribution tools can very quickly diffuse and remotely deploy applications to an entire enterprise of computers.

Intel® vPro™ processor technology can remotely wake up and power on PCs, install software updates, and then shut down the systems. This kind of technology enables reliable, efficient, and fast diffusion of new innovations. Github has become a software powerhouse for open-source innovation, collaboration and diffusion. The authors recommend always starting here when developing software innovations.

In-build. In-build is a method of distributing software and upgrades that are pushed to the client system and installed automatically as part of the operating environment. In-build eliminates or reduces annoying upgrade messages and repetitive re-boots that are disruptive. Thus, the in-build approach helps to overcome the *interruption tolerance barrier* for adoption.

Communities of Practice. Communities of practices are a good mechanism for addressing the socialization component of innovation diffusion. The process of moving from awareness of an innovation to finding it interesting, to actually using it, can be enabled by socialization, and both formal and informal communities of users are an effective means of diffusing innovations. Many professional organizations play an important role as innovation diffusers in their communities of practice. The value of membership, in such organizations as the Association for Computing Machinery (ACM), IEEE, or the likes of the Society for Petroleum Engineers, should not be underestimated for professionals wanting to stay current with their industry innovations.

Design Thinking

As thinking on and the practice of innovation has evolved, the role of design thinking has become much more central to the Innovation process. This offers a detailed overlapping option to the process already shared. Design thinking is now a widely adopted process to design solutions for complex problems using ethnographic approaches, system reasoning, intuition and iterative agile approaches. Historically, organizations, such as IDEO, Design Council and the DSchool at Stanford, have played important roles in developing and diffusing design thinking as a mainstream innovation technique. It is very suited to digital innovation based on the ability to very quickly build prototypes and test these in real-time with customers and solutions. Mastercard Advisors have an offering called Launchpad which cycles through a full design thinking process in a week, moving from a problem to a working prototype in that duration. Many financial institutions have benefitted from this process and sometimes the protypes produced have been subsequently evolved to full market offerings.

Increasingly, an extended design thinking process can be used on the full journey from idea to implementation and ultimately to value creation. We will discuss below how Martin's team at HSE Digital Transformation used a ten-step design thinking process to manage the full innovation journey. But first let's discuss the core elements of design thinking.

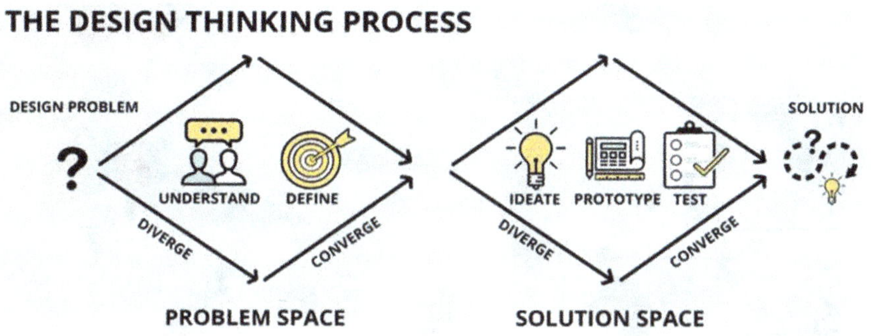

Figure 5.2: Design Thinking Double Diamond – source Design Council/Galvin.

The Double Diamond diagram originally introduced by the Design Council in 2004 is a great way to see an overview of a typical design thinking process. Every design thinking journey begins with a problem, but the authors prefer to widen this starting point lens also to an opportunity. Not every innovation comes from a problem, sometimes the use of imagination to create an innovation solution to an opportunity can deliver wonderful progress and benefits.

The double diamond consists of four phases: discover, define, develop and finally deliver as seen in Figure 5.2.

Once the problem or opportunity is defined the first step is to discover. Ethnography and walking in the shoes of the user or customer is an important step.

Divergence and convergence are important processes in design thinking and the output of the second phase ("define") is a specific agreement on the area to focus on. Generating options is an important part of the "develop" phase, while the "deliver" phase is all about delivering a solution from the finally selected best design. Using Agile methods for the development of the solution helps ensure an iterative, risk-minimized solution which best meets the needs of the customer is delivered. Martin, along with Intel colleagues Jim Kelly and Jonathan Walsh, ran a two-day design thinking process at Daimler headquarters in Stuttgart, the output of which was a new business venture for Daimler – Car2Go – which built on the strengths of Daimler and created a rental service revenue for the company building on their existing products.

Innovation as a Service:
Systemic Innovation for Teams (SIfT)

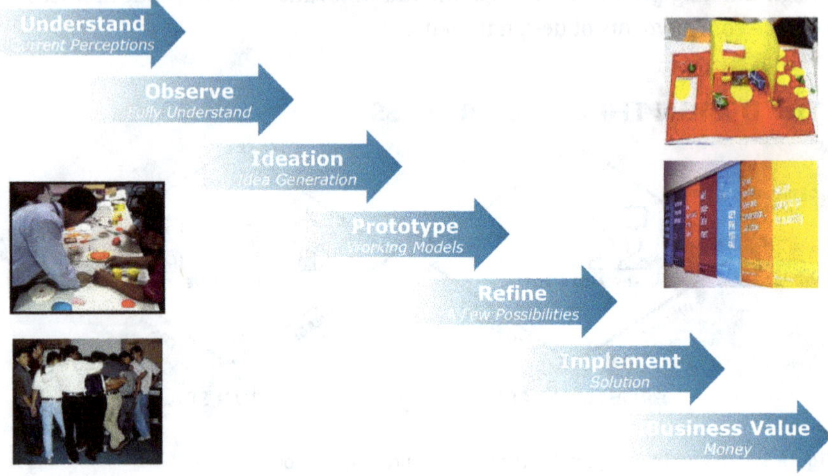

Figure 5.3: Intel SIFT (Systemic Innovation for Teams) Source Intel/Jim Kelly adapted from IDEO.

The Intel IT Innovation centers created a seven step design thinking process, adapted from the IDEO process (see Figure 5.3), called System Innovation for Teams (SIFT) led by Jim Kelly, now an Innovation Lead at Microsoft Garage. This became a repeatable process for a guided design thinking process which includes seven steps:

1. Understand
2. Observe
3. Ideation
4. Prototype
5. Refine
6. Implement
7. Business Value

The SIFT process becomes an invaluable part of the systemic innovation toolkit and proved a very efficient and effective mechanism for structured and productive innovation.

The process has been further refined and as a result of being implemented in China for BHAG cost reduction goals to reinforce "Why are we doing this?" The process became goal oriented up front, aligned to business value for example: "Reduce cost by 10%"; "Shrink the factory square footage by 10%"; "Reduce ramp time by 6 weeks." So it is now recommended that business value analysis be repeated in the beginning as the first step.

MiniCase Study: Using Design Thinking at HSE Digital Transformation

At HSE Digital Transformation and Innovation, we used design thinking extensively to manage the introduction of new innovations. Des O' Toole and Aileen Kileen jointly led our design thinking practice. It led to compelling co-created solutions such as the deployment of automated respiration rate management, across twenty-three hospitals, which eliminated errors in respiration rate measurement, but more importantly gave up to twelve hours' notice of a patient desaturating.

HSE Digital Transformation and Innovation introduced a 10-step extended design thinking-led process for the introduction of new innovations from an idea to an initial proof of concept in a living lab to full procurement and deployment and ultimately value creation. The ten steps are shown in Figure 5.4.

This process provides a very effective and repeatable process to go from idea to implementation (I2I) and ultimately to success. Beginning with communications and concept formation, the second step was to complete a one-page living lab template which documented the shared objectives, participants and critical success factors. The heavy lift was then done in the design thinking workshops where clinicians, patients, managers and technical staff would work through the design thinking process. Then followed funding and functionality confirmation phases, followed by design thinking feedback. Steps seven and eight managed the procurement process with step nine the critical development and delivery phase. Step ten was the benefits realization, success and celebration. Broadly using this process, multiple HSE digital transformation innovations with partners won Irish national healthcare awards including awards with companies providing telehealth (RedZinc), respiratory monitoring (PatientMPower), automated respiratory measurement (PMD Solutions), vital signs automation (Synchrophi), noncontact-temperature measurement (Trimedika) and others. Building a repeatable design thinking process and an associated design thinking capability is becoming an increasingly important feature of future innovation and organizational success.

Measurement

The final stage of the innovation process is measurement and this has been discussed in Chapter 2. For a more exhaustive discussion of measuring the value of digital solutions, we recommend Martin's book, *Managing IT for Business Value*,

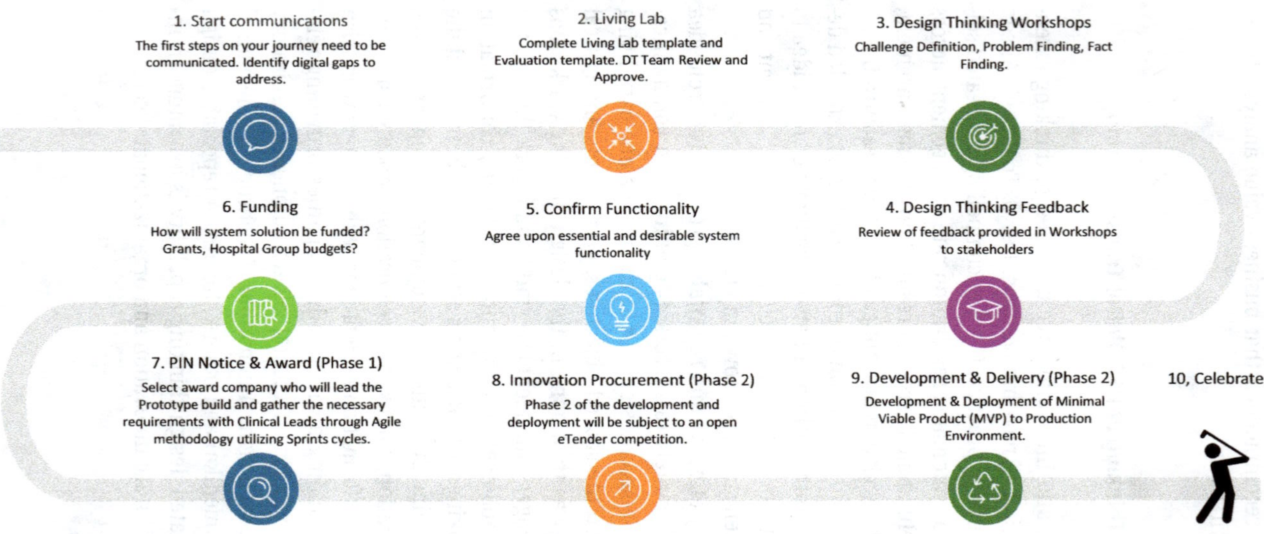

1. Start communications
The first steps on your journey need to be communicated. Identify digital gaps to address.
2. Living Lab
Complete Living Lab template and Evaluation template. DT Team Review and Approve.
3. Design Thinking Workshops
Challenge Definition, Problem Finding, Fact Finding.
4. Design Thinking Feedback
Review of feedback provided in Workshops to stakeholders
5. Confirm Functionality
Agree upon essential and desirable system functionality
6. Funding
How will system solution be funded? Grants, Hospital Group budgets?
7. PIN Notice & Award (Phase 1)
Select award company who will lead the Prototype build and gather the necessary requirements with Clinical Leads through Agile methodology utilizing Sprints cycles.
8. Innovation Procurement (Phase 2)
Phase 2 of the development and deployment will be subject to an open eTender competition.
9. Development & Delivery (Phase 2)
Development & Deployment of Minimal Viable Product (MVP) to Production Environment.
10, Celebrate

Figure 5.4: Ten Step Design Thinking Process – source HSE Digital Transformation and Innovation (Killeen/O' Toole).

and David Sward's *Measuring IT for Business Value*, both part of the Intel Press IT Best Practices Series. Carty and Lansfords' (2009) paper details the essential steps in setting up a comprehensive business value program, a very useful example of the Intel value dials and shares the results that Intel IT achieved using this approach. Intel co-founder and 1997 *Time* magazine's "Man of the Year" Andy Grove's mantra was "If you can't measure it, you can't manage it." This mantra is at the core of defining, designing and delivering for innovation value.

Summary

In this chapter, we have described some of the many methods and techniques available to guide innovators. Ideation can be stimulated with brainstorming sessions, for example, and by systematically examining emerging ideas with de Bono's lateral thinking techniques. Increasingly, tools like Mural and Miro can allow create brainstorming to happen virtually. Prototyping can take the form of a concept car, a simulation or a first-order approximation of a system heading toward immediate development. While refinement is traditionally the work of the development group, we emphasized alternative ways to acquire capabilities, such as outsourcing or obtaining "x" as a service. We reviewed our thinking about how to accelerate diffusion of systems. We recommend leveraging the company's existing distribution channels while actively partnering with marketing experts and advertising the availability of new and better solutions. We introduced design thinking as a crucial process in creating innovations which meet user and customers' needs. Moving forward we predict design thinking will become a core capability for organizations that wish to persist. Design thinking is especially suited to digital innovation because of the speed with which prototypes and full solutions can now be developed.

Chapter 6
Innovation Assessment

Stairs are climbed step by step. — Kurdish proverb

In this chapter we describe a self-assessment process that will systematically measure innovation maturity and help to chart a path to improved innovation competency. We begin by describing our self-assessment measurement instrument and explaining the steps involved in our assessment process. The assessment is designed for teams of people. We show how to use the results of the assessment to create an action plan for improvement.

The self-assessment instrument is in Appendix B. We encourage readers to peruse the instrument before reading this chapter. Our instrument was designed with common core business processes in mind. We expect that others will develop different instruments adapted to their specific core business processes. We offer our approach as a source of ideas. Our instrument establishes a team's level of innovation maturity. We then provide specific guidelines for moving up to the next level of the innovation capability maturity curve. Thus, the instrument is integrated with our overall view that stepwise growth is a healthy approach to improving innovation capabilities.

The Innovation Value Institute (IVI) in Maynooth, Ireland works in collaboration with a consortium of companies to develop a set of industry-wide assessment tools as part of the overarching IT Capability Maturity Framework (IT-CMF). The Boston Consulting Group (BCG) contributed strongly to the creation of the IVI innovation assessment that is also very valuable and assessments can be found at https://ivi.ie/assessments/ BCG's Matt Stack and Ralf Dreischmeier, as well as Chevron's Jack Anderson, made particularly strong contributions to the IVI Innovation assessment and associated capability maturity model. You can find out more information at www.ivi.ie.

In this chapter, we will offer suggestions about how to take advantage of this tool in both IT and non-IT organizations. We designed the instrument to apply to innovation in general —not just to IT innovation.

Innovation Self-Assessment Process

The innovation self-assessment tool was designed from the beginning to be a team-based process aimed at generating a score that describes the maturity level of the group's innovation capability. In a very large group — such as an entire IT

https://doi.org/10.1515/9781501507335-006

organization—a sampling of employees can be used to provide an estimate of strengths and weaknesses and a sense of the overall capability of the organization. An innovation self-assessment can also be conducted at the group or departmental level; for example, an assessment can be done within the desktop computing group or the software engineering group.

Assessment Teams

Our focus is on teams or groups, rather than individuals or departments, because research done shows that many companies use the team as its primary way of organizing work. A typical team has a manager and five to seven members. Data compiled by Eleanor Wynn, an Intel Principle Engineer, shows that a typical employee is on two to four teams, and a line manager oversees two to four teams.

The assessment teams include diverse participants from various jobs and experience levels who are trained to discuss behavioral anchors, one item at a time, and to conduct consensus-based scoring to arrive at a score based on a thorough and shared understanding of the strengths and weaknesses that exist within their own organizations. From this information, the teams are able to develop specific action plans for improvements.

The actual assessment tool is reproduced in Appendix B of this book. Before reading this chapter, we suggest going to the Appendix and examining the tool itself to become familiar with the characteristics it evaluates and to review the behavioral descriptions of strengths and weaknesses in innovation capability.

The Assessment Process

During the scoring phase, the team members share their knowledge of, and experience with, each set of behaviors to be scored. A guideline is provided to help them come to a consensus on scores. Once the scoring phase is complete, the team members revisit their notes, consider the high and low scoring areas, and proceed to define an action plan that will address their weaknesses.

Open discussion and group interaction during the scoring phase are important because at the end of the process, the team members will need to defend their scores by providing evidence of the strengths and weak- nesses identified to management to ensure management's validation and support for their action plan. Having a "group memory" of the process also reduces the risk of inconsistent scoring and promotes agreement on action plan priority tasks. Examples of action plans can be found later in this chapter.

The innovation self-assessment is an annual process, with results of the assessment leading to action items that are part of each employee's performance plan. Collectively, the action items are designed to move the team up the innovation maturity curve as successive assessments and action plans are completed.

Competencies and Behavioral Anchors

- Competencies are desirable characteristics and abilities, such as business innovation.
- Core competencies are the unique capabilities of an organization that enable it to create competitive advantage. A mature culture of innovation can be a core competency.
- Behavioral anchors are the actions, activities, and deliverables that demonstrate the achievement of a competency. They should be stated as specific, measurable, and attainable behaviors. Behavioral anchors for business innovation include observable actions such as: "consistently proposes ideas for improvement" and "challenges the status quo."

The Self-Assessment Framework

The innovation self-assessment tool measures six key organizational components that contribute to a culture of innovation accomplishment: management commitment, business responsibility, innovation competency, corporate values, innovation support, and innovation impact. These components and their relationships are shown in Figure 6.1. The following six numbered sections highlight the attributes or characteristics we feel are most important to consider in a self-assessment on innovation.

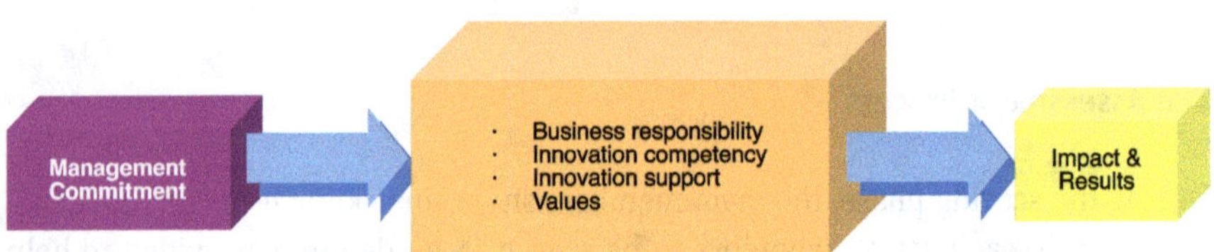

Figure 6.1: Components of a Self-Assessment Process.
Source: Intel IT.

Section 1. Management Commitment

The first step (Section 1) of the process is to acquire management commitment. There are seven steps in this process shown in Figure 6.2.

The first and fundamental step is obtaining a commitment from management to support an innovation system. In our experience, the most important section of

1.1 Management Involvement
1.2 Communication of Priorities
1.3 Upward Communications
1.4 Working Innovation Policy
1.5 Innovation as a Value
1.6 Resource Allocation
1.7 Key Innovation Assets Identified

Figure 6.2: Expectations of Management and Evaluating Commitment.
Source: Intel.

a self-assessment tool outlines the behavioral characteristics that indicate whether management is truly involved with and committed to innovation.

Innovation as a Value

The management commitment section evaluates management's actions regarding promoting innovation and whether management appears to consider innovation important. It asks, for example, whether management communications include topics of innovation and, if so, how managers communicate about innovation delivering communication upward and how they receive and respond to communications related to innovation from upper management.

Committed managers will have a working innovation strategy or agenda. The assessment tool asks for a concrete example of a documented or communicated innovation strategy. Without evidence of such a strategy, the score will be low for this category. On the other hand, being able to show that innovation is mentioned in progress reports or written about in company publications will warrant a higher score.

Resource Allocation

The way managers allocate their resources toward innovation demonstrates management commitment more than any other behavior. The resource allocation should be well documented, and any ratios that deter- mine the balance between innovation and other business objectives should be clearly stated. In any organization it can be difficult to obtain approval for the resources needed to develop a culture of innovation. As shown in Figure 6.3, an organization must make an initial investment in order to get the system off the ground.

Subsequently, as the system matures, fewer resources are needed to sustain it. This is true both for the overall system and for the assessment itself. Initial users of the assessment will have to invest quite a bit of time in understanding the expectations and the areas of the instrument itself.

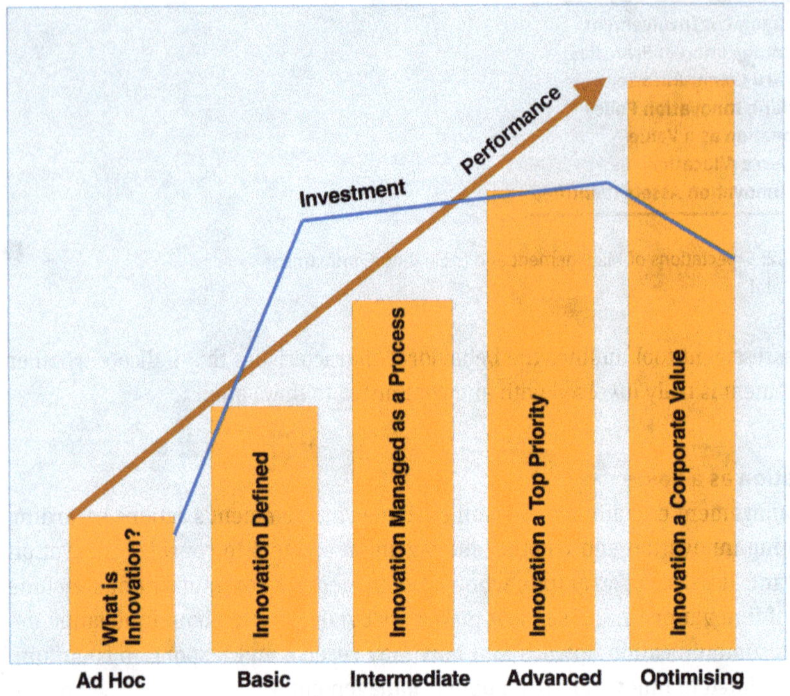

Figure 6.3: Innovation Investment Maturity Curve.
Source: Intel IT.

Key Innovation Assets Identified

Managers should also be aware of *innovation assets*—such as patent applications, intellectual property, physical assets, and people with key innovation skills—and understand how their innovation funding and resources are balanced with the resources required to keep the business running as usual.

Because validation of the innovation self-assessment includes defending the team's conclusions with evidence, a manager's ability to present an asset inventory to the validating senior manager can strongly support high scores.

Section 2. Business Responsibility

This section of the self-assessment measures how the pieces of an innovation program or system work together and highlights roles and responsibilities of employees in the innovation process. The steps are shown in Figure 6.4.

2.1 Organize Staff to Improve Innovation
2.2 Make Innovative Actions and Results Accountable
2.3 Adhere to Enterprise Standards for Innovation
2.4 Routinely Assess Innovative Initiatives
2.5 Involve Employees in Innovation Planning
2.6 Plan for Innovation Improvements
2.7 Discuss Innovation in Meetings and Communications

Figure 6.4: The Roles and Responsibilities in the Innovation Process.

Employee roles and responsibilities should be clearly defined, and methods of measurement for accountability should be well documented. Moreover, because the use of the innovation assessment itself fits into this category, there should be a system for routine innovation assessments that includes annual and quarterly reviews of the resulting action plans. Tools and systems must be in place that enable all employees to participate, and the availability of these tools should be widely publicized.

IT and other support organization employees are largely focused on keeping the business running, so it is important that their role in innovation be clearly understood and that the tools for their involvement are embedded into their routine work.

IT can also function as a catalyst for providing innovation as a service to the rest of the organization. As both users and developers of the innovation process and system, IT employees can act as subject matter experts who can facilitate and lead self-assessment sessions for other groups.

Finally, a document should exist that contains standard meeting notes and employee-management communications wherever innovation is part of the agenda.

Section 3. Innovation Competency

3.1 Innovation Training and Learning Programs
3.2 Innovation Training Improvement Process
3.3 Employee Development, and Improvement Systems

Figure 6.5: Measuring Innovation Competency.

Innovation should be listed as a competency in job training plans, and an innovation curriculum that is mapped to competencies and skill development should be made available to employees. The three topics to measure Innovation competency are shown in Figure 6.5.

We suggest using recognized training evaluation standards, such as Kirkpatrick's evaluation methods. Training quality and impact should be measured to ensure they achieve their desired objectives.

Kirkpatrick's Four Levels of Learning

Donald Kirkpatrick is known for creating a four-level model for evaluating learning.

In this model, evaluation begins with Level 1 (Reaction) and moves sequentially through levels 2 (Learning), 3 (Transfer), and 4 (Results). Each level is based on information from the previous level.

Level 1 evaluations simply measure how participants in a training program reacted to it—for example, whether the information presented was useful and whether they enjoyed the sessions—because participants' reactions have important consequences for learning.

Level 2 evaluations assess the amount of learning that occurred as a result of the training program, and often use tests conducted before training to establish a baseline and again after training to determine improvements in skills, knowledge, or attitude.

Level 3 evaluations are aimed at determining whether the acquired skills, knowledge, or attitude have been subsequently incorporated into the everyday behavior of the learner and usually done after some time has passed. Capturing from teams how they are using what they learned can lead to Level 4 value discovery.

Level 4 evaluations attempt to measure the success of the program in business value terms, such as increased production, improved quality, decreased costs, less waste, fewer accidents, increased sales, etc. While from a business perspective, such value may be the primary reason for a training program, measuring results in financial terms is difficult in itself and not easy to link directly with training. However, companies who expend the effort to develop metrics for measuring business value find it well worth the effort.

In addition, because communications play a vital role in developing, sustaining, and diffusing an innovation system, there should be a system for learning, developing, and improving communications.

Section 4. Enterprise Values

The section of the assessment that covers enterprise values measures how innovation maps to corporate values and their supporting infrastructure. When building a culture of innovation, innovation must be clearly spelled out as a corporate value. There should be methods for both capturing and applying customer feedback on new innovations and ways of measuring innovation in products and services, such as market share, adoption rate, or even some kind of "customer excitement" index.

If innovation is an enterprise value, it should also show up in Human Resource documents and be listed as a competency on performance appraisals. An example of including innovation competency in performance appraisals can be found in the section called Appraising Innovation Performance of Appendix B.

4.1 Communicate Enterprise Values
4.2 Seek Customer Input to Products and Services
4.3 Utilize Customer Input to Products and Services
4.4 Measure Customer Input to Products and Services
4.5 Include Innovation in Performance Appraisals
4.6 Track Innovation Systematically
4.7 Provide Awards for Innovation Excellence
4.8 Apply Innovation to the Margin of the Core Business
4.9 Manage Change and Risk Systematically
4.10 Conduct Post-Project Reviews
4.11 Track Ideas, Needs, and Challenges Systematically
4.12 Adopt a Failure Management Policy
4.13 Encourage Open Participation in Innovation
4.14 Recognize and Reward Innovation Systematically
4.15 Maintain and Share Goals for Innovation

Figure 6.6: Measuring Innovation as a Value.

Valuing innovation means not losing track of innovative ideas. As an innovation culture develops to an intermediate level of maturity, it sees the need to create an innovation pipeline so the IT organization can prioritize and track projects through prototyping, development, and deployment. There are fifteen areas to measure that indicate the maturity of how innovation is valued in the organization as seen in figure 6.6.

As the organization proceeds up the innovation maturity curve, it will encourage innovation by establishing a reward and recognition system for various forms of innovation—tangible and intangible, financial and nonfinancial. All employees should be encouraged to participate in fostering innovation, and awards for innovation excellence should range from low-level peer-to-peer recognition up to corporate-level and industry-level awards.

Finally, there should also be a reward system for benefiting from mistakes and learning lessons from conducting post-mortem reviews of projects that were not successful.

Mapping Innovation to Corporate Values

At Intel, an exercise to explicitly map innovation to our corporate values resulted in the following statements. Other organizations can perform the same exercise by printing a copy of their corporate values and discussing how each one of them relates to innovation. Questions to ask include "How does this value benefit from innovation?" and "How does it contribute to innovation?"

Customer orientation: We listen to our customers or stake- holders and respond to their needs in innovation, as research shows that most innovations can be tracked to customer input.

Discipline: An annual performance appraisal includes innovation as an item by which performance is measured. This supports risk taking and other Intel values and accelerates innovation through disciplined measurement systems.

Quality: We foster innovation in our work, products, and services. Much of our innovation involves incremental improvement to existing products and services to maintain high quality.

Risk taking: Innovation occurs when we challenge the status quo and embrace change. Innovation thrives on success and benefits from mistakes. Informed risk taking is rewarded. To assess risk taking and innovation, we hold meetings after projects are complete to learn from our successes and failures.

Great place to work: A challenging work environment provides our diverse employees with an opportunity to innovate; they are rewarded and recognized for their innovation.

Results orientation: We set challenging and competitive goals such as staying one generation ahead of the competition and reducing our total cost of ownership(TCO), and innovation helps us achieve those goals.

Section 5. Innovation Support

5.1 Processes for Innovation
5.2 Use of Innovation Experts
5.3 Use of IT Systems to Support Innovation
5.4 Business Planning and Innovation

Figure 6.7: Supporting Innovation.

The Innovation Support section of the assessment measures the role of innovation experts and enterprise infrastructure and tools—such as intranet websites, Internet websites, online support systems, virtual innovation centers, and online training and education—in supporting innovation. Supporting Innovation can be measured in 4 categories as shown in Figure 6.7. The authors recommend you pay particular attention to digital innovation support options in 5.3 and how digital innovation can be applied to all of the measurement options.

When we think of innovation experts, we think of Gladwell's descriptions of the different roles certain individuals can play to support the diffusion of new ideas. He describes some people as *connectors*—individuals with very large social circles who can deliver strong endorsements for new ideas to a large group of people. Guiding the connectors are *mavens*—people who are extremely knowledgeable about certain aspects of a market or a technology. (See Gladwell's Tipping Point in Chapter 8) In the author's experience we also rely on subject matter experts, on pathfinders who are willing to venture into uncharted territory, on champions who can effectively promote and support ideas, and on sponsors who can help us find funding for them.

Section 6. Impact of Innovation

6.1 Inventory of Innovations
6.2 Business Value of Innovations

Figure 6.8: Measuring the maturity of Innovation Impact.

The last section of the self-assessment measures the impact of innovation accomplishments and details innovation performance results (see Figure 6.8). It also provides a way for employees to measure how innovative the company's products and services are.

As we stated at the beginning of this section, management commitment is the foundation for combining business responsibility, innovation competency, corporate values, and innovation support to ultimately produce innovation impact.

Evidence that the self-assessment process has resulted in innovation capability maturity can clearly be seen in a well-designed and managed innovation pipeline and in the development and routine use of metrics that clearly show the business value of innovations that come out of it.

Scoring the Self- Assessment

We recommend beginning the scoring process by asking our teams to examine each scoring category as a basis for determining how their particular environment measures up with the examples of an optimized innovation environment listed in the right-hand column of the self-assessment tool shown in Appendix B. To accomplish this, the teams share their observations and experiences and write statements that describe the current state of their group's innovation capability.

For example, in Self-Assessment Section 1.1, Management Involvement, the standard for an optimized innovation environment would be one in which:

- An innovation strategy has been defined.
- The manager discusses and values innovation.
- Innovation assessment is conducted annually.
- Team innovation is recognized and rewarded.

The team members come up with a list of descriptions of their own group's progress with respect to these standards and then come to a consensus about the overall maturity of their system using the scoring chart shown in Table 6.1 as a reference for allocating points within each category.

Table 6.1: Assessment Scoring Summary.

Management commitment	Points possible
1.1 Management Involvement	50
1.2 Communication of Priorities	50
1.3 Upward Communications	20
1.4 Working Innovation Policy	30
1.5 Innovation as a Value	30
1.6 Resource Allocation	30
1.7 Key Innovation Assets Identified	30
Business responsibility	
2.1 Organize Staff to Improve Innovation	50
2.2 Make Innovative Actions and Results Accountable	50
2.3 Adhere to Enterprise Standards for Innovation	50
2.4 Routinely Assess Innovative Initiatives	30
2.5 Involve Employees in Innovation Planning	30
2.6 Plan for IT Innovation Improvements	30
2.7 Discuss Innovation in Meetings and Communications	20
Innovation competency	
3.1 Innovation Training and Learning Programs	40
3.2 Innovation Training Improvement Process	20
3.3 Employee Development, and Improvement Systems	10
Enterprise values	
4.1 Communicate Enterprise Values	20
4.2 Seek Customer Input to Products and Services	20
4.3 Utilize Customer Input to Products and Services	20
4.4 Measure Customer Input to Products and Services	20
4.5 Include Innovation in Performance Appraisals	20
4.6 Track Innovation Systematically	20
4.7 Provide awards for innovation excellence	10
4.8 Apply Innovation to the Margin of the Core Business	10
4.9 Manage Change and Risk Systematically	10
4.10 Conduct Post-Project Reviews	10
4.11 Track Ideas, Needs, and Challenges Systematically	20
4.12 Adopt a Failure Management Policy	20
4.13 Encourage Open Participation in Innovation	20
4.14 Recognize and Reward Innovation Systematically	20

Table 6.1 (continued)

Management commitment	Points possible
4.15 Maintain and Share Goals for Innovation	10
Innovation support	
5.1 Processes for Innovation	70
5.2 Use of Innovation Experts	30
5.3 Use of IT Systems to Support Innovation	20
5.4 Business Planning and Innovation	20
Impact of innovation	
6.1 Inventory of Innovations	120
6.2 Business Value of Innovations	120
Total points	**1200**

For example, a team's statements about management involvement in a group might include the following list:
- An innovation strategy has not been defined.
- Our manager often discusses and seems to value innovation.
- An innovation assessment is conducted annually.
- Team innovation is rarely recognized and rewarded.

Table 6.2: Rating an Innovation System's Maturity.

Maturity Score	Maturity Level
100%	World Class System: – Comprehensive documentation – Catalyst for other organizations – Vision plus organization and management commitment – Permanent innovation – Innovation culture
70–90%	– Excellent System: – Consistently good documentation – Frequent Innovation – Established innovative culture
40%–60%	Good system: – Generally good documentation – Good results in several areas – Committed management support – Frequent innovation

Table 6.2 (continued)

Maturity Score	Maturity Level
10–30%	Beginning of System: – Limited Documentation – Occasional Innovation
– 0%	No system: – No documentation available – Lack of innovation – No innovation vision or organization

Source: Intel IT.

Table 6.2 can be used as a guideline for scoring. For example, the team members might generally agree that they are in the beginning (10–30 percent) level and, after discussion, come to a consensus to give that category a score of 25 out of 50.

We offer the following guidelines for determining a maturity score.

Developing an Action Plan

Having completed the scoring of the self-assessment, the team proceeds to create an action plan that will be presented to their senior managers for approval. During this stage, the team looks at the lowest scores and areas of highest concern in relationship to the value dials that the orga- nization wants to manage.

They capture three types of information in each category to use in developing the action plan:

- Highlights—areas where evidence is strong about their innovation capabilities.
- Lowlights—places where the discussion revealed weaknesses, lack of evidence, or problems with the innovation system.
- Action items—actions that the team itself can initiate to catalyze improvement in their group. We have found that it is important to prioritize the actions and commit to what reasonably can be done in order to build confidence in future success.
- Recommendations—suggestions for actions management could take to facilitate innovation. For example, for a lowlight stated as "People are not recognized for innovation, and they don't know the expectations for innovation performance," a recommendation could be that HR and management should include innovation as an item in performance appraisals and include behavioral anchors to clarify expectations.

ACTION PLAN Rev 1.	
Evidence of a System (Highlights)	**Areas of Potential Improvements (Lowlights)**
– We maintain a website telling customers what's new and coming next from our organization. – Post project reviews are part of our methodology.	Low scores on management involvement: – Innovation is rarely mentioned in status meetings. – Innovation is not listed as a competency in job training. – People are not recognized for innovation, and they don't know the expectations for their performance as innovators. Low scores for utilizing customer input to products and services: – Customer satisfaction scores are dropping. – We don't feed complaints into the innovation process. – Many customers are unaware of our interest in input. – We focus our customers on services more than products. – We have no regular, predictable recognition process.
Actions to take	
– Include innovation as a regular agenda item for our weekly staff meetings. – Include innovation activities in progress reports. – Find an innovation champion for our group. – Contribute more frequently to the corporate newsletter. – Include mention of innovation in job training. – Revisit previous post-project reviews before launching new projects. – Give recognition to the developers of the "What's New" website and the operations manager at the next department-wide meeting. – Monitor the use of help systems to assess customer needs. Work with management to install a recognition system into existing systems.	
Recommendations	
– Include innovation goals in department plans. – Develop a clear mission statement that includes innovation. – HR and management should include innovation as performance appraisals and provide employees with the performance behavioral anchors that they can use to measure it. – Hold quarterly contests to seek out new ideas from customers. – Communicate that innovation is equal to other business priorities.	

Figure 6.9: Initial Action Plan.
Source: Intel IT.

ACTION PLAN Rev 2. One Year Later

Evidence of a System (Highlights)	Areas of Potential Improvements (Lowlights)
– Innovation is on the regular staff agenda and is discussed at most of our meetings. – Innovation articles have become part of corporate publications. – We have improved our "What's New" website. – Innovation is now listed as a competency in job training. – Our appraisal process explicitly identifies innovation as a competency and includes behavioral anchors for innovation. – We have an annual award for the best innovation. – Individuals can nominate others for recognition.	– There is no explicit innovation training curriculum, training sessions are merely motivational. – It is difficult to find time or funds for innovative projects. – We have no budget for innovation. – Low scores on processes for innovation – We collect ideas, but rarely take action to use them. – Our ideas are stored in email messages

Actions to take

- Provide feedback on training courses so instructors can improve them.
- Give recognition for all major highlights in this assessment.
- Present data to senior management on market share competitors' innovation programs and processes and communicate a sense of urgency.

Recommendations

- Provide a physical innovation environment.
- Have innovation experts work with training department to develop innovation training curriculum.
- Make a course on ethnography available.
- Create a website for capturing and tracking customer ideas.
- Establish online tools for sharing ideas and requirements throughout the organization.

Figure 6.10: Subsequent Action Plan.
Source: Intel IT.

Figures 6.9 and 6.10 show examples of two quarterly action plans developed by the same group, six months apart. The initial action plan illustrates how teams set basic goals and objectives for gaining innovation competence. The subsequent action plan shows that competency is improving and that new and higher expectations are set.

Moving to the Next Maturity Level

This section provides examples of how an organization can use action plans as a springboard to proactively advance to the next capability level within a category.

In order to cover a cross-section of the Self-Assessment Tool, we have selected one category in each of the Self-Assessment Tool's six sections— management commitment, business responsibility, innovation competency, enterprise values, innovation support, and impact—to use as an example of how to steadily move through the maturity stages from Level 1 (Initial) to Level 5 (Optimizing).

We have chosen the following sections:

- Section 1.1—Management Involvement
- Section 2.1—Organize Staff to Improve Innovation
- Section 3.1—Innovation Training and Learning Programs
- Section 4.7—Provide Awards for Innovation Excellence
- Section 5.3—Use of IT Systems to Support Innovation
- Section 6.2—Business Value of Innovations

Management Commitment

Management Involvement (Section 1.1)

Level 1: Initial

At the initial level, management is primarily concerned with efficiency and cost-effectiveness and tends to view innovation as a financial risk. There is no budget for creative opportunities and no infrastructure to support them. Senior management is not involved in innovation processes, and if innovation occurs at all, it happens by accident.

Steps to Take to Attain Level 2

- Present data to senior management on market-share competitors' innovation programs and processes.
- Present self-assessment and benchmark data to senior management.
- Introduce innovation programs to address known problems—for example, IT efficiency items that require improvement—and top Pareto items—that is, the 20 percent of activities that produce 80 percent of the benefits.

Level 2: Beginning

At this level, senior management is beginning to be aware of the value of innovation, but—while no longer averse to discussions of it—they are not yet enthusiastic. At this stage, an innovative project is usually driven by a hero.

While there is no budget for innovative projects, management can be persuaded into freeing up resources for a pet project. Funding at this level is based upon whether management likes the idea instead of on hard data. Most of the innovation that actually occurs is related to product development.

Senior management has come to realize that not innovating can be costly, and they are aware of competitive threats, but they are still likely to see spending on innovation as jeopardizing their R&D budgets.

Steps to Take to Attain Level 3

- Present innovation indicators and data per individual organization or department to senior management.
- Actively work with management to identify innovative solutions to issues.

Level 3: Intermediate

Senior management understands the competitive advantage of being seen as an innovative company, and some even see it as a competitive necessity. Moreover, as management sees efficiency gains and cost reductions resulting from IT innovations, the innovation budget is poised to grow. At this level, senior management is on the verge of deciding that innovative excellence is a core competency. While innovation has not yet been incorporated into business operations, management is providing oversight and visibility and is beginning to hold business units account- able for innovation performance.

Innovation is now beginning to become part of the company's culture and is now supported by a formal budget.

Metrics for determining the business value of innovations are being developed, as are standard methods for managing innovation. Most projects at this stage have an innovation component.

Steps to Take to Attain Level 4

- Present business value data to senior management.
- Obtain senior management's commitment to take a more active role in ensuring an innovative place to work.
- Define an innovation strategy.

Level 4: Advanced

At this level, emphasis has shifted from creating business value to maximizing it, and managers are now paying increased attention to longer term planning. Investment managers have formalized business value measures.

A clearly defined innovation strategy is in place with explicit goals and priorities. The innovation pipeline management process has become more refined and the queue of projects is managed with strong skillsets, purposeful diffusion, and supporting IT capabilities.

Innovation is becoming incorporated into business operations and is managed in the same way quality, safety, yield, etc., are managed.

As there are more innovation ideas in the pipeline than can be handled, the ideas must be prioritized, and a business case is required for new innovation opportunities.

Innovation experts are highly respected and viewed as partners, and the culture of innovation has enhanced the organization's reputation in the eyes of its customers and trading partners.

Steps to Take to Attain Level 5

- Present information around value- and results-based innovation programs.
- Facilitate senior management through this educational process.
- Work to define what the next level is for the organization.

Level 5: Optimizing

At this level of maturity, business value is routinely measured and realized.

Innovation is seamlessly integrated into business operations, and the innovation pipeline is visible throughout the organization by means of web portals, workshops, and road shows. A system for active diffusion of innovation is in place.

Business Responsibility

Organize Staff to Improve Innovation (Section 2.1)

Level 1: Initial

There is an innovation expert or designated individual within the company who champions innovation.

Steps to Take to Attain Level 2

- Begin to establish awareness for improving innovation.
- Develop company innovation expectations for higher-use work environments, such as R&D, product design centers, and problem solving teams.
- Make experts available for coaching and consulting.

Level 2: Beginning

Innovation is site-specific. However, an innovation team or committee has been formed, and innovation has champions.

Steps to Take to Attain Level 3

- Establish innovation expectations with the innovation team or committee members.
- Communicate and sell innovation expectations via the innovation committee members.
- Establish the "norming" innovation behaviors.

Level 3: Intermediate

Site innovation experts are role models for innovation, but management and supervisors are also starting to become role models for innovative behaviors. Employees participate in efforts to drive changes.

Steps to Take to Attain Level 4

- Management formally communicates their endorsement of role modeling innovation through staff meetings, etc.
- Innovation experts help to identify more industry innovation concepts and practices for the organization, for example, benchmarks, best-known methods, etc.

Level 4: Advanced

By this point, all of management is aware of innovation as a business process and routinely demonstrates commitment. Innovation experts help organizations to focus on training and behaviors.

Steps to Take to Attain Level 5

- Establish training, and work with the customer group to develop an approach to remove barriers to innovation.

- Develop indicators to track the group's performance.
- Encourage management to establish innovation as a core value.
- Expand the organization's behavioral focus on innovation to the industry environment.

Level 5: Optimized

All employees in the organization are committed to innovation and focus on behaviors that foster it.

Innovation Competency

Innovation Training and Learning Programs (Section 3.1)

Level 1: Initial

At this level, either no training exists or training in innovation is very informal. If there is informal training, it is merely the result of *ad hoc* support and interest.

Steps to Take to Attain Level 2

- Identify core innovation training requirements.
- Look for packaged innovation training programs to leverage innovation resources.

Level 2: Beginning

Basic innovation training is available and was probably developed to ensure consistency and terminology. Training sessions are typically led by innovation staff and committee members.

Steps to Take to Attain Level 3

- Have innovation experts begin to work with peers to establish a formal training program based upon competencies, policies, and known gaps.
- Have innovation experts solicit volunteers to teach the classes.

Level 3: Intermediate

The innovation curriculum has been expanded, and instructors are now from the innovation core group or interested volunteers. Web-based systems are available to support innovation training.

At this level, training assessment processes are formalized and data — including baseline data—is collected.

Steps to Take to Attain Level 4

- Have innovation experts engage the customers in the training process (e.g., creating, revising, etc.).
- Have innovation experts and the customers begin to establish certi- fication packages based upon job criteria.
- Have innovation experts partner with business management to provide resources for teaching innovation courses.

Level 4: Advanced

Online tools from Human Resources and job competency diagrams include innovation concepts. Business units are responsible for the tracking of training. Training classes are routinely being reviewed for quality.

Steps to Take to Attain and Maintain Level 5

- Establish behavior-based training.
- Have business groups take over tracking and integration of innovation training in their everyday business.
- Provide site-specific information from business units to training.
- Identify additional courses to meet future innovation needs.
- Ensure that training programs are aligned with policy and philosophy of the organization.
- Base revisions to training courses on feedback from all major stakeholders.

Level 5: Optimized

Business groups own training and ensure quality. The business organization ensures that resources are available to teach classes. Innovation training is integrated with all other operationally required training courses.

Enterprise Values

Provide Awards for Innovation Excellence (Section 4.7)

Level 1: Initial

Management has been provided information on basics and benefits of an innovation. Innovation awareness is promoted through posters and other symbols.

Innovation committees are not process-oriented, and reactions to innovation tend to be based on personal perception rather than on business value data or analysis.

Steps to Take to Attain Level 2

- Establish an innovation committee/team/interest group meeting process and develop an education package for the members.
- Have innovation experts work with innovation committees to establish a recognition system based on innovation suggestions.
- Establish visible identity of innovation committee members in the work place.

Level 2: Beginning

Basic systems are in place for establishing an innovation committee, an innovation suggestions pipeline, and chasm crossing. Awareness is increased by innovation poster contests and innovation campaigns.

Steps to Take to Attain Level 3

- Innovation experts work with management to implement a more advanced recognition system.
- Use self-assessments and action plans to improve innovation performance.
- The innovation committee works with HR and management to implement innovation as a line item in focal review.

Level 3: Intermediate

The organization has developed a system to recognize employees for innovations, suggestions, and ideas. Innovation rewards have been established for employee performance. The innovation staff is expected to solve problems, and the focus is on engineering solutions.

Steps to Take to Attain Level 4

- Have innovation experts work with management to further integrate a recognition system into the organization's culture.
- Incorporate innovation training into all other operationally required training courses.
- Establish expanded innovation expectations in the focal review process.

Level 4: Advanced

An innovation recognition system is incorporated into the organization's business recognition system, and innovation expectations are incorporated into the annual review process. Rewards are in place for active participation, rapid protyping learning quickly from failure, adoption rate, and value reporting.

Steps to Take to Attain and Maintain Level 5

- Increase visibility of recognition and awards for innovation through the normal business recognition systems, such as large staff meetings, website publication, and Corporate level achievement awards.

Level 5: Optimizing

The innovation recognition system is self-sustaining and inherent to success.

Innovation Support

Use of IT Systems to Support Innovation (Section 5.3)

Level 1: Initial

Innovation is handled by Corporate Legal and Human Resources for the purpose of protecting intellectual property. There is no established process for harvesting and capturing ideas. Locally developed tools exist, but with low adoption levels and manual processes.

Steps to Take to Attain Level 2

- Get innovation experts involved in driving innovation awareness.

Level 2: Beginning

Innovation experts support innovation campaigns by recruiting subject matter experts to perform vetting of all innovation campaign ideas and inputs. Interest is increasing for providing a physical innovation environment.

Steps to Take to Attain Level 3

- Have innovation experts encourage innovation committees to use industry tools, processes, value metrics, and standards to manage the pipeline.

Level 3: Intermediate

At this level, senior management realizes that commitment and participation are required for an innovation infrastructure and innovation systems.

The Innovation Committee reviews innovation ideas and is involved in the pipeline management process. Campaigns are conducted by site or group innovation staff. A system allows employee feedback on ideas.

Innovation indicators and pipeline evaluation reports begin to be created by business operations in partnership with innovation experts. Engineering or technical solutions are expected to complete the pipeline management process.

Steps to Take to Attain Level 4

- Have innovation experts work with management to develop innovation review meetings and steering committees.
- Assess the quality of tools and processes to evaluate the system.
- Use data to emphasize behavior as a leading indicator of innovation.

Level 4: Advanced

Business units drive innovation review meetings, and management representatives from all key areas are being reviewed. Innovation experts are engaged in the process. Employees can give input to improve ideas gathered during campaigns.

Business owners perform all pipeline management processing using a standard suite of tools.

The focus is now on employee innovation skills, training, and behaviors. Innovation ideas, problems, and challenges are starting to be seen as assets to be managed to their best end value.

Steps to Take to Attain and Maintain Level 5

- Have innovation experts ensure that management understands the need to include innovation in their management meetings.
- Have innovation experts work with management to move them from using lagging indicators to leading indicators.

Level 5: Optimizing

An innovation pipeline review is incorporated into the same level of operations as reviews of quality and business value.

Business owners routinely assess all pipeline gates to manage innovations to their best end value.

Innovation experts process and support all innovation campaign outputs, tools, and processes, but now only need to advise business owners on complex items.

Impact of Innovation

Business Value of Innovations (Section 6.2)

Level 1: Initial

Management is focused on stock prices and market share as indicators of business value. Innovation goals are established by senior management and are typically focused on the number of patents, number of invention disclosure forms, etc.

Steps to Take to Attain Level 2

- Obtain innovation cost data from finance.
- Define the need for a tracking system.
- Review innovation investment data to establish a baseline for costs and funding.
- Initiate a business value reporting philosophy.
- Establish a forum to report business value goals to management.
- Create a tracking system for innovation information and begin tracking indicators.

Level 2: Beginning

Metrics have expanded to include business value and innovation index items. Senior management or innovation committee members have established innovation goals that are included in business operation goals.

Steps to Take to Attain Level 3

- Track lagging indicators for management to use in business plans.
- Establish broader goals to improve innovation indicators.

Level 3: Intermediate

Metrics are focused on lagging indicators. Management is including innovation goals in business planning, and linking them with other corporation goals.

Management is beginning to associate goals for innovation business value and return on investment with their level of innovation investment.

Steps to Take to Attain Level 4

- Utilize self-sustaining tracking and reporting mechanisms for pipe- line management and engine reports.
- Have innovation experts work with the business organization to develop new metrics for measuring their performance.

Level 4: Advanced

The organization has world-class innovation rates and metrics and is looking for new metrics to drive innovation improvements. Unique innovation business goals have been established along with other business goals to drive improvements within their operations.

Steps to Take to Attain and Maintain Level 5

- Define and use leading indicators to help measure group performance, such as "number of innovation communications."
- Develop innovation surveys and other ongoing feedback systems to assess performance.
- Continue to look for new indicators to drive improvements in areas of identified need.

Level 5: Optimizing

At this level, business value is forecast, measured, and reported.

Senior management has come to rely on leading indicators, employee surveys, and formal assessment of management systems.

Business groups are responsible for establishing innovation goals, based on employee surveys, feedback, and leading indicators.

The Importance of Innovation Assessment

Innovation assessment is an important tool for establishing a baseline measurement of an organization's level of maturity in innovation. It enables a team, group, or organization to develop explicit plans to increase maturity over time. It also serves as a de facto training tool for both the employees who perform the assessment and the managers who review them.

When several teams have completed the assessment, senior management compares scores and profiles across the larger organization. In the beginning assessments are often handled with face-to-face training, interviews and group discussion for the scoring, report generation and action plan. Over time this process can be migrated to an online solution. Table 6.3 shows assessment results for four teams.

– While teams A and B have identical total scores, their profiles are quite different and revealing. Team B has superior innovation capabilities, but they have not been able to contribute to innovation in the company's products and services. While Team A needs additional training across the board, Team B needs some management attention to align their work with the offerings of the company.
– Team C is at an intermediate level of competence and should be encouraged to continue acquiring and polishing innovation skills and methods.
– Team D is in trouble, and the problem probably starts with a lack of management commitment. If management commitment is lacking, then all remaining assessment categories have low scores.

Table 6.3: Cross-Organizational Comparison of Completed Assessments.

	Team A	Team B	Team C	Team D
1. Management commitment	49%	92%	75%	16%
2. Business responsibility	40%	85%	64%	12%
3. Innovation competence	41%	97%	56%	7%
4. Intel values	40%	84%	70%	32%
5. Innovation support	45%	46%	91%	24%
6. Impact	42%	46%	60%	10%
7. Products and services	42%	5%	80%	0%
Total	43%	43%	75%	9%

Profiles like those shown in Table 6.3 provide feedback to supervisors, first-line managers, and team leaders. The very process of measuring and comparing scores often increases management commitment.

Summary

Assessment is sometimes viewed as a threatening process, but we believe it can be at the heart of a learning process. A thorough appraisal of a team's innovation capabilities provides a foundation for growth. Our five-level capability maturity framework identifies a developmental path. Management commitment and measured objectives in the team's action plans together ensure innovation skills will improve over time.

Chapter 7
Pipeline Management

Prediction is difficult, especially about the future. — Niels Bohr

As advances in information technologies fuel creativity, vision, and prototyping, companies will find that they have a backlog of innovation ideas that is larger than the innovation budget can support. In addition, innovative projects often present a greater management risk since they often depend on new technology ingredients. The organization's overall project pipeline will contain a mix of innovative digital projects along with well-proven systems necessary for the daily operations of the company.

One solution is to bypass the pipeline and manage innovative digital projects separately. While this is an understandable alternative, it does amplify several risks. For example, sidestepping disciplined software development methods raises the risk of creating production systems that are unstable. Also, proper integration of innovative systems with the IT infrastructure, and other IT systems is less likely if innovative digital solutions are developed outside of the mainstream process.

We believe that innovative digital projects should be managed along with other IT projects, but with a different management framework. For example, it may make sense to actively accelerate or retard the progress of an innovative digital project, whereas this is rarely acceptable for conventional IT projects.

The Digital Innovation Pipeline

The goal of pipeline management for innovative digital projects is to determine the value potential and relevance of the projects and expedite productization of those with the most value, both within and outside the enterprise. The traditional value path leads from research to operations within the company. Alternately, some innovations exit the company to be developed by others. Some innovations are purchased from others and released into the pipeline late in the process. The innovation pipeline management process is aimed at keeping a close watch on the innovation pipeline, cultivating the options it contains, and steering candidate innovation projects toward the most appropriate value path. We propose an innovation pipeline management methodology that identifies five stages and the value paths of the three basic product life cycles are shown in Figure 7.1.

https://doi.org/10.1515/9781501507335-007

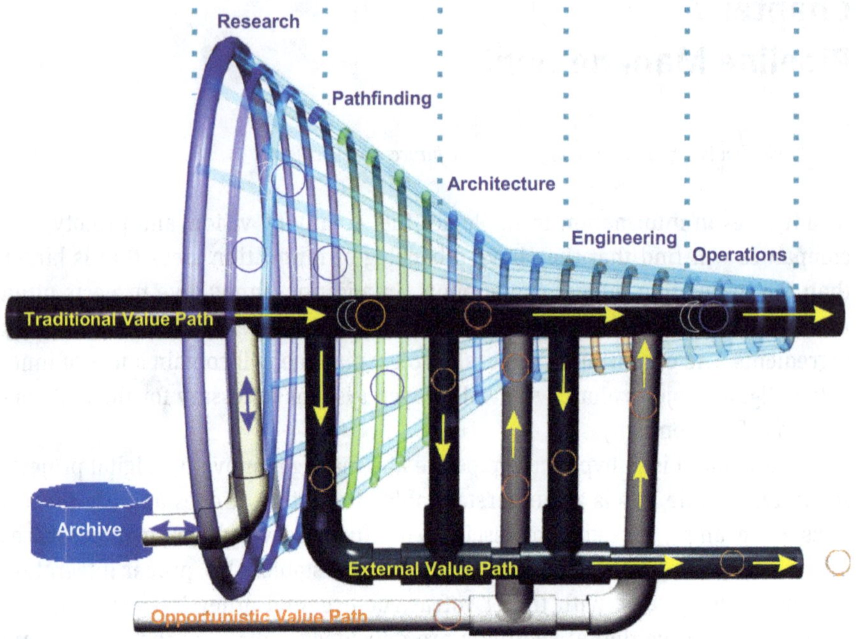

Figure 7.1: Pipeline Stages and Value Paths for Innovative Products and Services.
Source: Intel IT adapted from Henry Chesbrough.

Pipeline Stages

Note that there are multiple entry and exit points to the pipeline stages, which we shall describe below. Stages in the innovation pipeline are as follows:

- *Research*: At this stage, researchers are establishing a scientific foundation of information that is not yet aimed at solving real- world problems. Universities and government research laboratories are good partners at this stage. The development of the mouse at Stanford Research Institute and the invention of object-oriented programming at Xerox PARC are examples of research findings.
- *Pathfinding and Technology Development*: The pathfinding stage comprises early efforts to marry newly-discovered facts and relationships to build platforms and solutions. Some organizations have individuals or teams that perform this role, especially those with researchers.

  Early adopters often have the skills that lend themselves to being pathfinders as part of their natural propensity to seek out the new and novel. Those that are good at recognizing patterns and emerging trends also make good pathfinders.

Corporate research groups and start-up companies can play the role of pathfinding. The Xerox Alto, the first computer designed for use by an individual, is an example of a pathfinder's result.

- *Architecture*: At the architecture stage, the platforms and solutions provided by pathfinders are organized into functional systems. Architectures emerge as IT suppliers compete to establish standard interfaces among component technologies. The client-server architecture is an example of an architecture that emerged as networks merged personal computers and shared computing resources.
  - *Engineering*: Guided by an architecture, IT organizations assemble and test solutions that address the information processing needs of the enterprise. Common problems give rise to suppliers who exploit economies of scale to engineer and sell standard solutions. Enterprise resource planning and customer relationship management are two examples of pre-engineered solutions available to IT organizations. There is a growing trend for original equipment manufacturers (OEMs) like Dell and Lenovo to assemble, test and validate solutions in emerging areas of usage for their customers to adopt with confidence. (See https://infohub.delltechnologies.com/en-us/t/workload-solutionsOperations: Whether custom built or based on packaged software, digital solutions exit the engineering stage and are put into operations. At this stage, operations focus on making solutions efficient and available while diffusion managers aim to bring solutions into usage as quickly as possible so that business value will begin to accrue.

Organizations vary in their appetite for participating in the early stages of innovation. Generally, larger and more information-dependent enterprises participate earlier in the pipeline. Global financial services firms, for example, were early participants in hammering out secure networks that could be trusted to carry currency transactions (e.g., SWIFT). Similarly, supply-line management systems were engineered by consortia-building systems for the automotive and electronic industries.

Midsize and smaller companies most commonly innovate by purchasing packaged software and tailoring it to their needs. While decades ago, the build vs. buy decision often led to a coding effort in COBOL, in recent years the quality and variety of pre-engineered solutions have dominated the IT solution set. As described by Rogers (2003) and Moore (1991), these companies are generally a part of the early and late majority. Their use of innovative solutions is signaled when successful products cross Moore's chasm.

Pipeline Value Paths

As Figure 7.1 (shown previously) also illustrates, innovation projects have three distinct value paths, as follows:

- *Traditional value path:* On the conventional path, projects move results from research activities and transform them into production systems ready for deployment. As noted, this path is typical on the supply side, but increasingly rare on the demand side.
- *Opportunistic value path:* Especially for innovative digital projects that adapt and reapply technology previously developed for another usage; it is possible to bring a project into the pipeline relatively late. This is accomplished by licensing technology from third-party vendors. The opportunistic path is also used when organizations redeploy existing technology solutions and adapt them to other company needs.

External value path: Research organizations occasionally produce inventions that, while valuable, are not consistent with the strategy of the enterprise. These innovations have the potential to become products. Innovations on this value path move out of the pipeline and are licensed to third-parties for productization and diffusion.

Miramar

Miramar is an example of the commercialization path to value. Intel IT Innovation and Research developed an advanced 3-D collaboration prototype we called *Miramar*. After a business case analysis, the IT organization decided that it should not fund the full development. Instead, we licensed the prototype and its underlying technologies to an external company, QWAQ, who branded their product *QWAQ Forum*. In return for our technology, QWAQ provided Intel with a full license to use the *QWAQ Forum* product and paid royalties from QWAQ sales.

The value paths we recommend are similar in many ways to Chesbrough's open innovation model. The multiple paths reflect the fact that innovative digital projects are qualitatively different than ordinary IT. Upgrading storage capacity, fielding a new database in support of compliance requirements, and extending network infrastructure are the types of traditional activities that IT must deliver on time and on budget. Projects such as Intel's ergonomic advising software or Miramar, on the other hand, may follow different paths within and outside the company.

Most innovations return financial value in dollar terms, while some return value in less tangible benefits, such as increased employee safety, improved customer satisfaction, or enhancement of the firm's reputation. Using an options management tool like a business value index can help manage and assess the value potential of putative innovations.

Managing the Innovation Pipeline

There are decisions to be made when formulating a management strategy for an innovation pipeline. In this section, we shall outline the available choices, the key decisions that need to be made, and the route that we recommend Our roadmap, shown in Figure 7.2, takes a clean-sheet approach, that is, the roadmap creates a management approach from scratch. There are six basic steps.

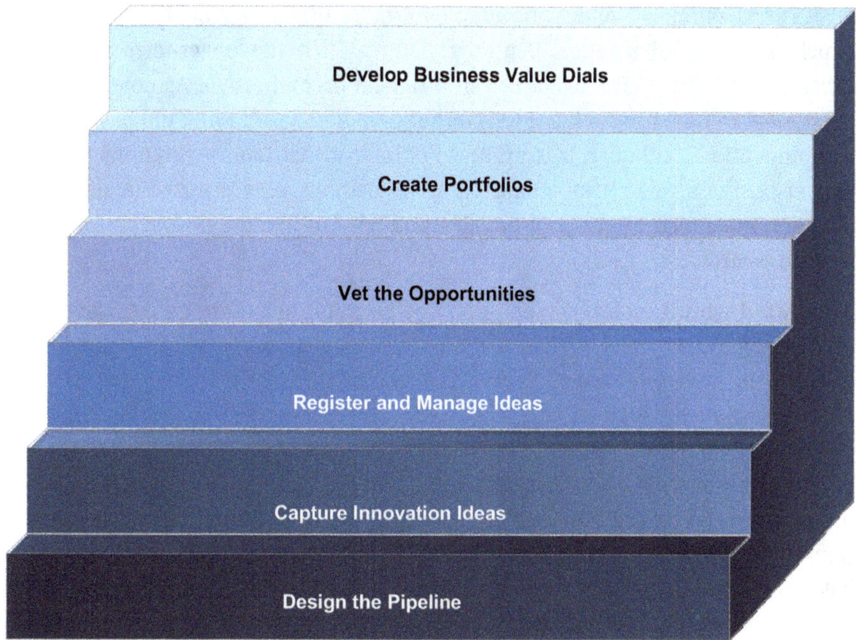

Figure 7.2: Formulating an Innovation Pipeline Management Strategy.
Source: Intel IT.

Step 1: Design the Pipeline

There are three key decisions to be made about the pipeline design: Will it follow an open innovation model or a closed, proprietary model? Will innovative projects, both digital and non digital, be mixed with conventional IT projects or will the types be managed separately? And will innovation be a centralized IT function or a function distributed throughout the organization? The decisions can be made independently, as shown in Figure 7.3.

Advantages and Disadvantages of Different Models

Distributed versus Centralized Innovation. The founders of Intel felt strongly that innovation should be distributed throughout the company's operations. In their prior experience, Robert Noyce and Gordon Moore realized that centralized innovation often generated ideas that never left the research laboratory. A tradition was established not to centralize innovation, which carries through until today. Intel innovation is pervasive and distributed, both within the IT organization and across the corporation as a whole.

Centralization of innovation may be a more effective model for companies which create digital products. Centralization may help the longer-term innovative process and increase the likelihood of a radical breakthrough. As noted, centralized research facilities such as SRI International and Xerox PARC did provide radical innovations, although it is useful to point out that both institutions failed to deliver business value from a long list of innovations. A centralized model for innovation must include the path to value and not fall into the trap of "researchers like to research".

Integrated versus Isolated Pipelines. One option is to integrate innovative projects with conventional ones because the two categories of IT will inevitably need to work together when deployed. In the last decade, the stovepipes of isolated IT applications have given way to systems and infrastructure that are interdependent.

We are not saying that centralized innovation with pipelines containing only innovative projects are impossible. We are saying that the path from an innovation being a research finding, leading to a workable idea by a pathfinder (i.e., basic research) and onward to an innovation ready for the development group needs to be well marked. The centralized scenario requires close communication, management of expectations, and understanding of the production environment that lies at the end of the pipeline.

Open versus Closed Pipelines. In the case of digital innovation, it is difficult to imagine an entirely closed innovation pipeline. The reason is that so many innovative tools are immediately available that accelerate the organization's work. Every make-versus-buy decision is a choice between the open and closed approach and certainly a modern IT organization would leverage existing products rather than recreate them. In our view, bringing outside innovation into the pipeline at the engineering step is always a good idea.

The more interesting question is whether and when to send ideas out of the pipeline for others to license. Intel IT and Intel Corporation have a strong commitment to externalization of ideas in nearly every case. The exceptions are for en-

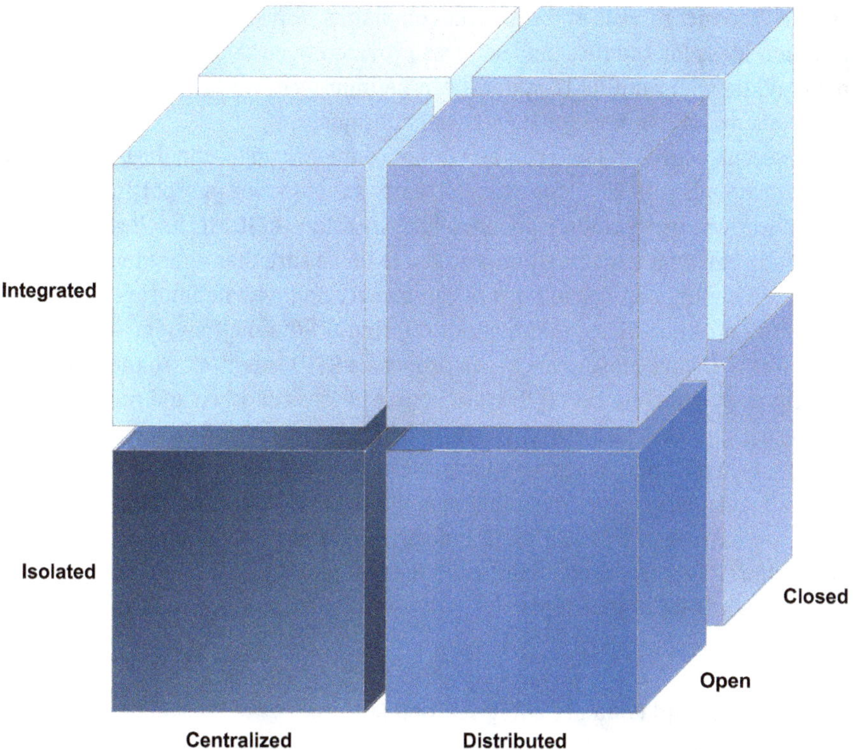

Figure 7.3: Pipeline Design Decisions.
Source: Intel IT.

abling technologies that are fundamental to Intel's core business, such as device physics and manufacturing process technology.

Step 2: Capture Innovation Ideas

Innovation ideas can be derived from several different functions in the company and with several different methods. One rich source is the support staff from IT and other organizations that have cross-company exposure to users and people with problems to solve. Incident tracking systems, from online call centers and escalations, identify recurring problems where innovations are needed. They reveal the nature of the problem as well as the people who are spending time away from work struggling with an issue. In some cases, support is needed, but in other cases an investment in improving an IT capability is in order. For innovation in general, product returns and customer complaints provide a similar source of innovation ideas for products and services provided to customers outside the company. While well-running IT systems can be improved, we have found that solving problems with innovation pays back handsomely.

A second source of ideas can be drawn from emerging technologies that offer new functionality. In 2005, for example, early adopters began reporting a variety of applications using radio frequency identification (RFID) technology. A standards body emerged as competitors worked to make sure that interoperability was assured. Vendors and consultants began showcasing new or improved capabilities based on RFID. IT suppliers began offering off-the-shelf systems for generic tracking needs and consultants began proposing RFID extensions to their clients.

The population of users is the final source of ideas. If asked and reinforced for answering, customers have a lot to say. In addition to problems that are tracked by support systems, these customers have suggestions for improvements or perhaps blue-sky ideas. New hires from other companies bring with them different experiences, perhaps even from different industries. Harvesting these ideas is a worthwhile effort. The current emerging trend for generative AI is a new source for both innovation and innovative ideas.

Step 3: Create and Populate a Registration System

A pipeline registration system stores ideas with descriptions in a repository that is a database of innovation raw materials. A simple innovation "engine" that provides a registry of innovation assets accepting input from global employees as well as business partners is relatively easy to deploy. A portal that allows innovators to enter a description of their idea, their names, and to state the type and maturity level of their proposed innovation everyone can participate in.

The result is a searchable pool of raw material for innovation projects. We have found that existing sources of innovation—online document libraries, R&D archives, technology development databases, internal conference papers and websites and product group monthly status reports—can often be mined to avoid having to start from scratch. While mining assets is time consuming and requires dedicated resources and tools, it is a good source of ideas. Mining also helps locate experts who can evaluate innovation ideas and thus is an efficient way to build the expert and prototype developers pool. With the advent of artificial intelligence and reasoning systems, this mining effort is drastically reduced and insights that were previously unseen are revealed.

An even more productive way to build an idea asset pool is by using campaigns to harvest ideas, needs, or challenges from individuals, teams, and communities. Most online innovation tools are designed to provide this functionality. Here are three examples from Intel:

- Intel IT campaigned for ideas that would improve IT efficiency. Templates provided by the Innovation Portal were made available to make posters quickly and consistently. We provided links to marketing and communication so that our campaigns appear in company newsletters.
- In anticipation of our first dual-core processor release, Intel polled employees and trading partners seeking usage models. With more powerful processing technology, in what new ways would our customers put our product to work? Employees provided over one hundred usage ideas.
- Intel has a technology strategic long range plan (T-SLRP). In anticipation of an annual update, the T-SLRP team campaigned with the question, "What next-generation technologies should Intel be investing in, and why?" This campaign generated over four thousand ideas, a four-fold increase over the prior year.

We found that our first campaigns were too open-ended and lacked focus. Having an open-ended asset capture system is rather like having a suggestion box. The ideas that spring from it can be so diverse that the effort required to evaluate, manage, and drive them to an end value is far greater than when a campaign is focused on a particular topic. With a topical campaign, we can identify our experts in advance and schedule them for vetting sessions.

Campaigns are contests and there is a winner—the best idea is identified and the person submitting that idea is rewarded. One reward is the opportunity to attend a conference, a privilege that most employees do not have. And we also offer technology gadgetry, which is especially popular among technology companies . . . What motivates people varies greatly from person to person, so having flexibility and allowing employees to choose their reward from a menu of options guarantees satisfaction and motivation for continued participation in the innovation process.

Step 4: Choose a Vetting Procedure

The vetting process for campaigns relies on a committee of experts who understand the technology issues for a campaign. This transfers the burden of vetting to people who are best equipped to judge the ideas. In the case of usage models for dual-core processors, the expert team was formed from several different business units and included an author of this book. We wanted the widest array of expertise possible. The committee divided ideas into three categories:

- Ideas that were infeasible, and thus set aside. And, as expected, we did receive some usage models that would be impossible to support.
- Ideas that were already in use, albeit in rarified environments. This category was surprisingly large and highly informative. Collectively, our employees were aware of a number of niche applications that could become mainstream with the dual-core processor's capabilities.
- The third category contained ideas deemed innovative—new, useful, and possible. Many ideas in this category were quite creative and, after some deliberation, we identified a winner. Using one core for multimedia and the other for processing was the winning usage model. The idea came from an Intel account representative who was not a member of the IT or R&D organizations.

On Ice

Much to the frustration of innovators, there is a history of innovations that are ahead of their time. While the innovator has a vision of something new, further exploration reveals that the barriers to creation or adoption are simply too high. Wise innovation managers archive these ideas so that they can be revisited at a later time.

Video chat is a classic example. Doug Engelbart invented and demonstrated the video chat concept in the 1960s, far in advance of affordable personal computers and available bandwidth. In our terms, Engelbart's system was a concept car.

Intel delivered the ProShare™ camera collaboration tools in the 1990s and once again the technology failed to diffuse. When the internet provided backbone bandwidth, the last mile adopted DSL and data over cable, and video cameras became less expensive, then video chatting became a reality and a core offering to business users.

Step 5: Manage the Innovation Project Portfolio

While innovative projects are tracked and stage-gated along with conventional IT projects, we do gather them into portfolios and we manage them more aggressively to mitigate risk. Innovations are new, and thus there is no history from which to draw lessons. The portfolio of innovative projects also allows for different development paths. For example, if engineers believe that an innovation cannot be fielded for a generation or two, then it may be held in archive or the innovation may be expressed as a concept car (see sidebar).

Other innovation projects may be vague and in need of refinement. In considering the deployment of wireless mobile technology at Intel, for example, we invested time in ethnographic studies to observe user behavior and in experimental studies to estimate productivity gains (Intel 2004).

Business cases are needed before a project launches into the engineering stage, and that is another facet of portfolio management. Our six- vector management model shown in Figure 3.2 in Chapter 3 highlights the possibility that an unfavorable business case may call for us to change our vision and develop a new prototype to test a different technology solution.

Finally, when to manage the portfolio of innovative projects, be willing to stop some projects, accelerate or decelerate others. While conventional systems follow a more predictable route and ordinarily deliver a necessary system, we find that innovative projects are more volatile.

- Accelerators include activities among our competitors that favor one project over another or larger-than-expected benefit estimates emerging from prototyping experiments.
- Decelerators include the need to reallocate resources to a high- priority project or the discovery that a new technology component is not as mature as expected.
- The most common reasons to stop a project are timing and a radical change in business value estimates, which are often related. At stage-gates, we reexamine the business value and cost estimates and reconsider ROI.

For example, if the conclusion is that a delay of a year will bring lower cost, higher performance, or greater maturity to a component technology then that change will tip the scale in favor of progressing. At that point it is best to archive the project in order to jump-start the effort in the near future.

Archiving the halted projects and reinspecting their status regularly ensures that a halted project is not a failed project to be discarded, ignored, and forgotten. There is much to be learned when prototypes fall short of expectations.

According to McNichol (2007), Google embraces a *fail-fast* approach. McNichol describes Google's method as *launch, listen, improve, launch again*. Innovative projects are experiments and should be conducted as efficiently as possible. Scientists and innovators can both learn a great deal from projects gone awry.

Adoption Fatigue and Tolerance for Interruption

Adoption fatigue is caused by too many changes in the environment and will lead to rejection of innovations. Many of us dread the release of a *new and improved* product because we know from past expe- rience that learning the differences takes time and can be quite frustrating.

Another barrier to adoption for some innovations is the level of tolerance people have for interruptions. For self-healing systems or tacit systems, the level of interruption can be higher than some users are willing to tolerate.

When one is working studiously and absorbed in a task, the solution that interrupts that process one too many times will be turned off or uninstalled. Examples of interrupting solutions include automated upgrades and patches, email compression utilities, and instant messaging—especially the latter.

By way of example we include the architecture of the Intel IT Innovation Pipeline as shown in Figure 7.4.

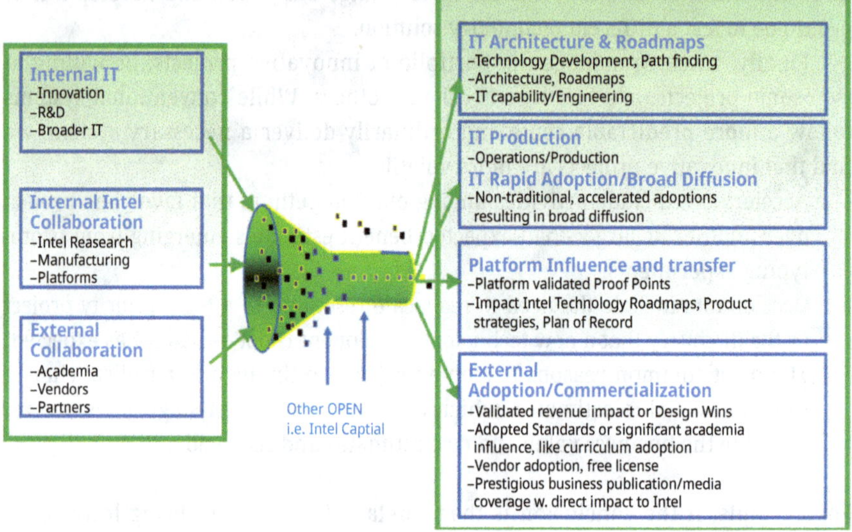

Figure 7.4: Intel IT Innovation Pipeline Architecture.
Source: Intel, Curley/Nisman.

The inputs to the pipeline recognized the inputs to the innovation process could come from three difference sources: internal to IT; internal to Intel from business units and the manufacturing organizations, for example; and then external (such as academia, vendors, customers and fellow travelers) to Intel. Having such a diverse input ensured creativity and diversity in the innovation pipeline flow. In the terms of output we had several defined value path across four types of impacts. Firstly, we looked for innovations which would impact IT architecture and roadmaps and then innovations which would make IT production systems and services more efficient, effective, reliable and secure. Secondly, we looked an innovations which would impact IT production/operations and innovations that would enable faster adoption. Thirdly, we would look at innovation which would influence Intel product roadmaps or provide proof points which would help with marketing of new Intel products. The development of VPro, a remote computing management technology which was hugely successful for Intel in the market, directly came from Intel IT employees who envisioned a better way of remotely managing and supporting computers. The fourth category of impact was in the external adoption and commercialization pathway. The Intel IT collaboration to help establish and drive the adoption of WIFI technology in the City of Westminster, discussed as a case study in the first appendix is an example of this. In the Intel IT Innovation centers, we often worked with Intel's customer's customers to envisage new usage models and drive adoption of new technologies. For example, Ivan Harrow from the Ireland IT Innovation center went on assignment to the UK's National Health System (NHS) Design Authority in Leeds and was instrumental in driving the adoption of Gigabit Ethernet across the UK Health service. Joe Hegarty and his Performance Learning Solutions team, including Peter Hamilton, developed an advanced eLearning solution called Skoool™ which stimulated the accelerated adoption of eLearning across Europe. Martin and Joe hosted multiple education departments from across Europe in the Ireland Innovation Centre and working with Trinity College, the National College of Ireland and others were able to demonstrate the benefits and business case of accelerated adoption of eLearning. The team won a prestigious Intel Achievement Award for their efforts and results in driving accelerated adoption of eLearning and consequent accelerated demand for Intel products and revenue. Celebrating success is important and the team travelled to the lovely Coronado Hotel in San Diego to receive the award from Intel CEO Paul Otellini.

Step 6: Establish and Use Value Realization Metrics

During the pipeline management process, a collateral effort is needed to develop and test business value dials. (See Business Value Dials in Chapter 2.) For innovative applications, new or modified value dials may be needed. And, baseline measures will be critical when assessing the impact of a new digital capability. Figure 7.5 shows a point-in-time snapshot of the Intel IT Innovation Centre's portfolio. It shows the actual value of different impact contributions and their relative contribution.

This example it shows that direct revenue impacts were 32% of the portfolio valuation with a $21.5 million contribution. Of equal importance was a contribution of $25 million in cost savings through innovations for Intel's manufacturing organization, TMG, through solutions such as predictive maintenance for high capital cost equipment such as Varian Implanters which improved availability by 2%. Such a small increase in equipment availability and utilization may not sound like much, but with each implanter costing about $20 million, small improvements created big savings. Productivity savings at $12 million and 18% of the portfolio was another important area of impact.

An old adage says you don't get what you expect, you get what you inspect. As a result, Intel has a wealth of metrics used continuously. Measures of interme-

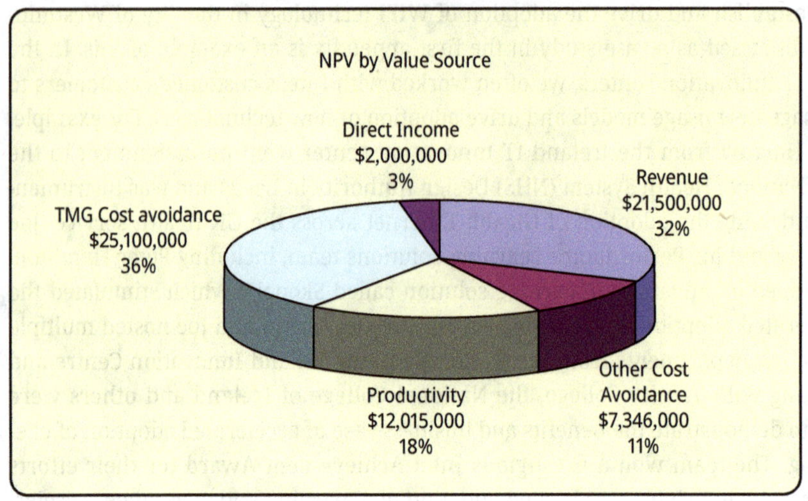

Figure 7.5: Portfolio Valuation Snapshot.
Source: Intel IT Innovation Centres.

diate quality permeate our fabrication processes. Our ebusiness systems monitor raw materials and finished products closely. And our planning processes demand measurable objectives. Consequently, this culture of measurement has transcended into our IT value metrics.

We cannot overstate the importance of establishing value metrics, especially for innovative projects. Finance and business managers remain skeptical of digital innovation activities and they often argue that innovations are solutions looking for problems. To succeed over time, the innovators and their organization must demonstrate a problem-solving approach with business value metrics expressed in monetary units.

Improving Yield for Digital Innovations

Closely monitor the innovation pipeline itself. Here are some of the metrics we recommend obtaining to show quarter-over-quarter trends in innovation activities:

- Success of innovation campaigns is measured by the number of campaigns, the number of ideas submitted during the campaign process, and the yield, that is, the number of ideas accepted for implementation.
- A key action, when an innovation occurs, is to ensure the innovators file an invention disclosure form. These forms are evaluated by legal and technical

experts. Track the number of forms submitted and, again looking toward yield, also track the number of innovations routed onward to be patent filings, preventive publications, or trade secrets.

By preventive publications, we refer to the practice of publishing ideas to establish prior art and eliminate the risk of a patent filing from another company. Look to online forums such as www.ip.com for more information.

- Count research and development proof points to see how many ideas are translated into working systems with a usage model and a simulation or a prototype. Proof points are demonstration systems that show which ideas are viable and better communicate a vision of an innovative capability.
- Track the proportion of awards (i.e., rewards and recognition actions) given by the company for innovations. We believe that awards are an important part of systemic innovation because they celebrate those who take the risk to suggest and develop new ideas. If an online award system is in place it is important to track the pattern of "givers". Leaders that seldom or never deliver recognition should be coached using the behavioural anchors shared in the appendix.

We also recommend actively monitoring awards outside the company. These events indicate overall industry leadership.

To monitor diffusion, keep an accounting of innovations that move from early adopters to the early majority, that is, innovations that cross Moore's chasm. These capabilities sometimes diffuse actively using a copy-exactly methodology, while in other cases they are adopted by individuals downloading the application from an early-access portal. A final measure of diffusion is the number of innovations that move into widespread usage virtually instantaneously. The adoption of wireless network technology is one example.

Tactics for Improving Yield

Our overall strategy for innovation pipeline management is expressed in our model's stages and value paths. Here are some more specific tactics we have found useful to ensure that innovative ideas receive appropriate attention and support and that innovation investments lead to breakthrough solutions, new products, or better business practices.

- Engage with technology architects and capability managers early in the development process to ensure readiness for adoption when the innovation has matured.

- Examine the company's product lines and operations to under- stand critical business and technology needs, influence roadmap direction, and the selection of innovation pipeline candidates.
- Maintain effective representation in relevant business decision- making forums and cultivate ongoing discussions with business managers.
- Capitalize on thorough planning, development, and deployment to influence outcomes and to capture the business value of innovation-initiated projects.
- Adopt a "learn fast, fail fast" strategy, that is, complete a cycle of rapid prototyping, discard what does not seem useful, and advance the results with the most potential. Disney and Google both espouse this approach.

Sample Results

By defining the end goal and grounding every innovation in a business need, innovation pipeline management can set forth a roadmap for keeping innovation and research investments clearly focused and delivering maximum value.

During one year, at Intel IT, thirteen projects emerged from the lifecycle pipeline and moved into production. Some examples include:

- A Business Value Capability Maturity Framework (BV CMF) workshop — a comprehensive and practical training class in IT value management for CIOs. The workshop can be delivered as part of the Innovation Center activities and is offered by the authors on request.
- SKuBA— an application that provides better sharing of real-time factory information from a fab back to designers. SKuBA helps to deliver better products and eliminates the need to perform several revisions of a new product when it is being introduced.
- An IT Innovation Zone (ITIZ) — is an early adopter innovation distribution channel and virtual community for cutting edge tools leveraging Web 2.0 and social software. Inputs to the pipeline can come from within an IT department, within the company, or from an external source.

Innovation Index

The metrics that we created to measure an innovation program evolved over time into a numerical innovation index. Of course, metrics vary by company and depend on the company's business model and strategic objectives. Our Innovation Index contains the following elements:

- Innovation Campaigns—the number of topics, requests entered using the online innovation engine.
- Ideas Submitted—the number of innovations submitted during the campaign process. This index item indicates the level of participation in the organization and helps identify innovators for specific topics.
- Ideas Accepted for Implementation—the number of innovations surviving expert review that are approved for further investment.
- Invention Disclosure Forms (IDFs)—the number of application forms completed by innovators for formal intellectual property (IP) protection. These forms are reviewed by the legal department and internal industry experts.
- Invention Disclosure Forms approved for patent filing, publication, or trade secrets—a yield function to monitor the IDF function.
- R&D Proof Points—the number of ideas that are translated into proof points having a usage model, simulation, or prototype that better communicates the vision and is used to explore the idea's viability.
- Innovation Reward and Recognition—the number of awards issued related to innovation and who is issuing them. Using an internal reward and recognition system with tools to track awards will reinforce innovation in the culture. We also encourage the applying for external innovation awards to demonstrate innovation leadership in industry.
- Crossing-the-Chasm Innovations—the number of innovations that are adopted and put to use by employees either informally, using the portal to download unofficially supported tools and processes, or formally, using the copy-exactly diffusion methodology.
- IT Hero Products—innovations that are adopted internally by the enterprise and end up becoming part of business-unit or enterprise builds or are published and shared externally to industry via online forums such as Github. We use the term *hero products* in place of *killer applications* which, while common in the industry, has negative connotations.)
- Innovation Assessment Score—the score from the innovation assessment that indicates the organization's innovation maturity.

Summary

In this chapter we addressed the issue of pipeline management for innovative digital projects. We offered different pathways to value and identified the stages in the pipeline. We shared with you our heuristics for maximizing yield and minimizing risk. Our take-home message is that innovative projects require keen management attention which, when applied, bring them into the product lifecycle and into adoption.

Chapter 8
Diffusion of Innovation

Getting a new idea adopted, even when it has obvious advantages, is difficult. — Everett Rogers

Diffusion is the active dissemination of proven good ideas and innovations. The term is borrowed from chemistry and physics, where it describes the random distribution of molecules in a medium over time. A drop of ink in a beaker of water diffuses over time until the entire beaker is evenly tinted. Innovation diffusion can occur randomly over time as new products and services, similar to molecules, move through social networks.

However, we believe that the diffusion of innovative ideas need not be random or accidental. In fact, it can be deliberately directed, managed, and accelerated within an organization. This can be accomplished especially in IT organizations, because the IT organization is in a position to promote and market its products to its customers to accelerate usage. In this chapter, we review the academic foundation of the concept of innovation diffusion in some detail, beginning with Rogers's (2003) foundation and ending with Freedman's thoughts about a flattened world. To these theoretical analyses, we add our insights and experience and provide a sequence of steps for systematically diffusing innovation throughout an enterprise. The more rapidly an innovation diffuses, the more quickly we can measure business benefits and report the return on our innovation investment.

Diffusion Fundamentals: How Innovations are Adopted

Used as a metaphor to explain how new ideas become widely adopted, *diffusion* has referred in the past to the dispersion of new ideas through social networks. Everett Rogers, originally an agriculture major at Iowa State University, achieved academic fame for his theory on innovation diffusion, published in his book *Diffusion of Innovation,* now in its fifth edition (Rogers, 2003).

Categories of Adopters

When Rogers collected data on adoption, he found that very few people took on an innovation when it was first available. Over time, uptake increased, peaked, and then the rate of uptake slowed and eventually just a few people jumped on

https://doi.org/10.1515/9781501507335-008

board and the market for the innovation was saturated. To make contrasts among these adopters, Rogers needed categories and so he turned to statistics and made an assumption common in science, which is that a normal distribution described his data.

In a normal distribution, 68% of the population lie within one standard deviation of the mean. As shown in Figure 8.1, Rogers named the 34% to the left of the mean as the *early majority* and 34% to the right of the mean as the *late majority*.

- Rogers named the next 13.5% of the population who adopted an innovation before the *early majority*, those between the first and second standard deviation in a normal distribution, to be *early adopters*.
- And for that 2.5% of the population to first adopt an innovation, those beyond the second standard deviation, Rogers adopted the name *innovators*.
- After the *late majority*, those 16% beyond the first standard deviation from the mean Rogers labelled *laggards*.

These statistically defined categories allowed Rogers and many other researchers to collect data on adoption and to contrast the characteristics of named subgroups in a consistent manner. Over many years of research, Rogers and colleagues studied diffusion of innovation using these categories.

These investigators found that willingness and ability to adopt new ideas is dependent on awareness, interest, and experience, and people could fall into different categories for adopting different ideas. A farmer, for example, might be quick to accept the idea of hybrid corn, but be a very late adopter of social media. We encourage innovators to read the fifth edition of *Diffusion of Innovations* (Rogers 2003), as it contains hundreds of thoughtful insights relevant to many industries and contexts.

The Chasm

In 1991, Geoffrey Moore used Rogers's normal distribution classification scheme to illustrate a particularly difficult transition in the diffusion of technology innovations. First, Moore combined innovators and early adopters into a single group named for the latter. Next, Moore speculated from his experience coaching technology start-up companies that products entering the marketplace had a particularly difficult time satisfying the needs of both early adopters and the early majority.

Moore observed that early adopters were technology enthusiasts and risk-takers seeking a radical shift in technology capability. These highly- skilled adopters were willing to work with incomplete products—raw material, if you will.

The early majority, in contrast, wants a whole product, a complete solution, and an easily understood implementation process.

Moore paid special attention to a gap in the graph that he identified as the *chasm,* as shown in Figure 8.1. The chasm was the point of greatest risk because young technology companies were pulled in two directions—to increase complexity and serve the early adopters or to increase simplicity and serve the early majority.

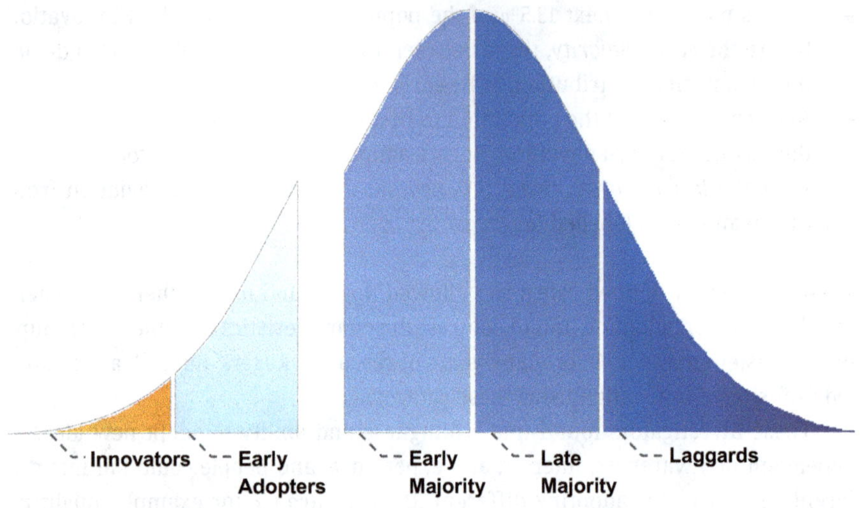

Figure 8.1: Adoption Concepts from Rogers and Moore.
Source: Adapted from Rogers and Moore.

Successful new technology suppliers take the latter tack. Highly successful technology suppliers have woven the chasm assumption into their product development lifecycle. In the world of R&D, researchers share results with early adopters, and developers build for the early majority. When technology companies allow engineers to dictate readiness of a product, there is great risk that the product is not really ready for the largest market, and failure or dissatisfaction can occur giving an opportunity to the later to market companies. Andy Grove, former CEO of Intel, went to an electronics store in the 1990s and observed people returning products. They had been expected to switch dip switches to set up their boards before they used them!! He returned and began the user experience requirements at Intel that align to Geoffrey Moore's early majority users.

Chasm Two

Moore is focusing his attention on the gap between early adopters and the early majority because he studied where good ideas can get stuck when they are departing from the development stage. In our experience, there is a second gap of which innovators should be cognizant. This is the gap between innovators and the early adopters, as shown in Figure 8.2.

Problems at this transition are aggravated by companies that compart- mentalize their research and development processes, we believe. And it will be the pathfinders who collect the discrete ideas from innovators and inventors and assemble them into a more organized collection of ideas that attract the attention of the early adopters.

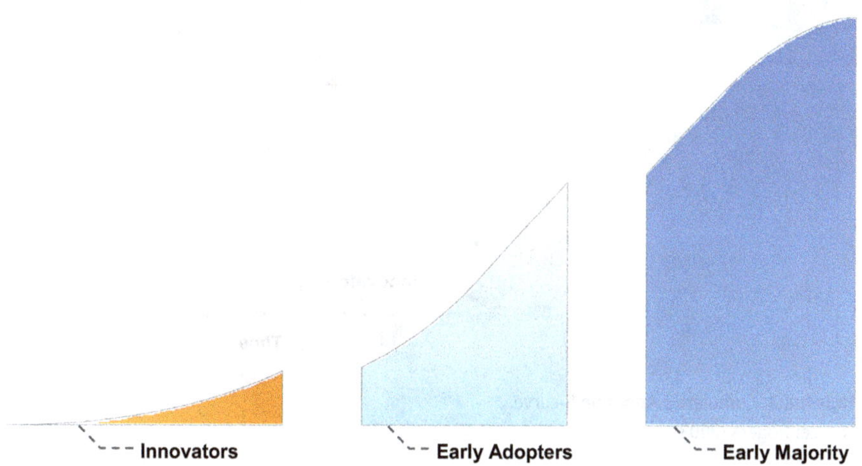

Figure 8.2: The Second Chasm.
Source: Intel IT, adapted from Moore and Rogers.

The S-curve Perspective

If we accept Rogers's normal distribution assumption and plot that distribution as accumulated adoption over time, an S-curve results, as shown in Figure 8.3. The S-curve perspective highlights how adoption accelerates when the early and late majority begin to adopt.

In an active and innovative organization, a family of S-curves will describe diffusion over time. Figure 8.4 illustrates the lessons learned from multiple S-curves.

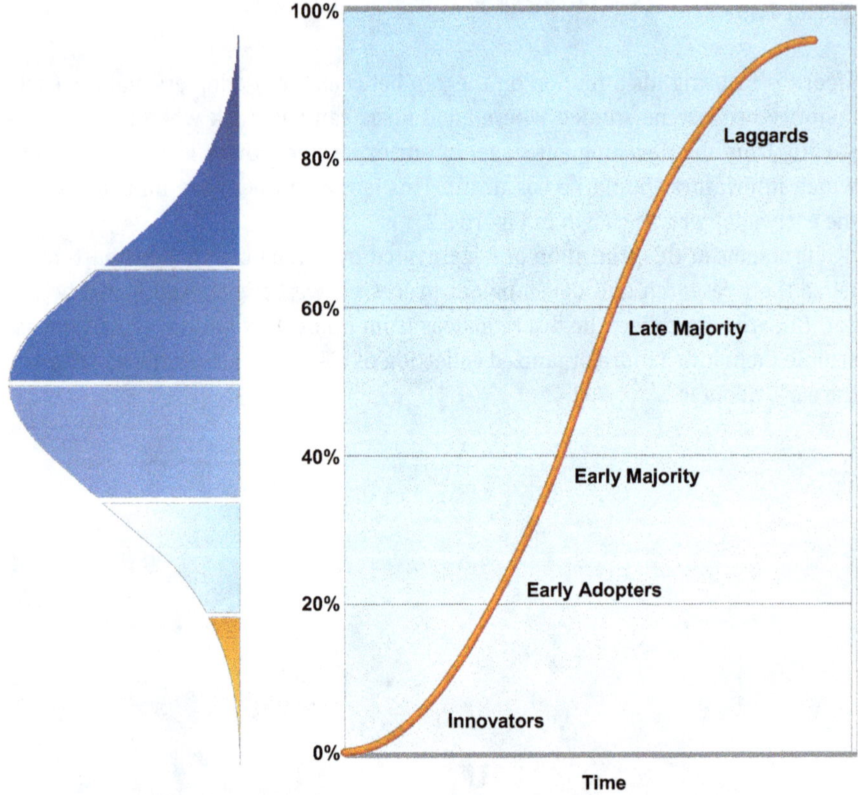

Figure 8.3: Cumulative Adoption S-curve.
Source: Rogers (2003).

We are assuming that 100% is the total population of the company. Here are the lessons:

As shown by curve A and curve B, not all innovations diffuse at the same rate. When plotting several diffusions, some will rise more quickly and flatten out sooner. This is especially true for digital innovations.

When an operating system upgrade goes out to every computer, the S-curve is nearly vertical, as shown by curve C. Elective downloads may diffuse for weeks or months.

– When 100% is the total population of the company, not all innovations reach all members—nor should they. An innovation for the marketing group may never have usage by engineering whereas desk/laptop innovations may impact nearly everyone in the company. Factoring in the total available market is important for innovation managers.

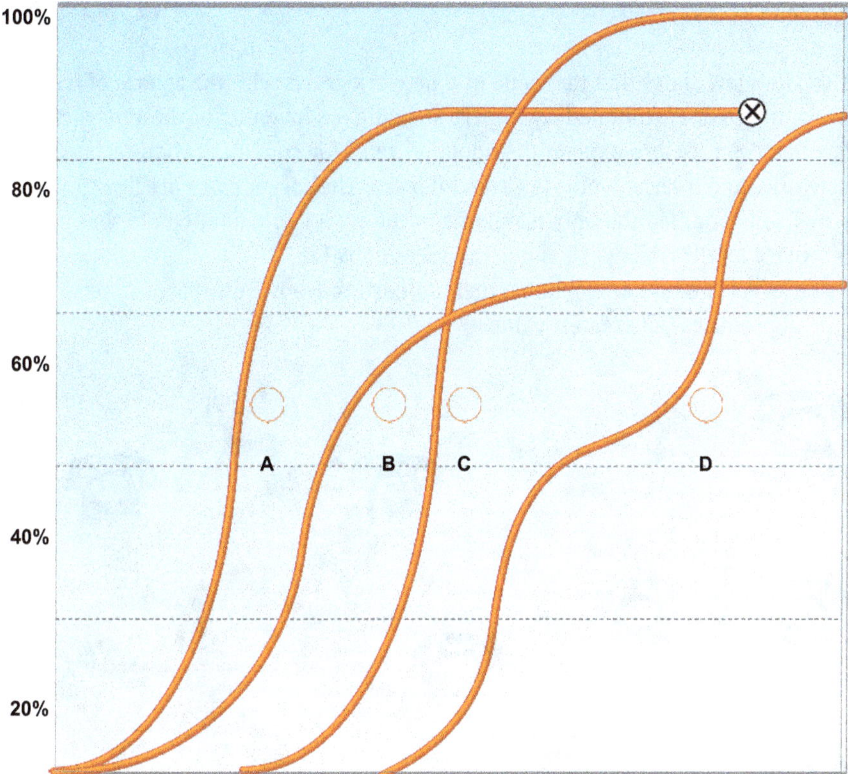

Figure 8.4: IT Diffusion S-curves.
Source: Intel IT.

As signified by the X at the end of cumulative curves in Figure 8.4, all IT capabilities are eventually decommissioned or brought to the end of their lives. The life span of an innovation is yet another variable for innovation investment managers to consider. It is highlighted by an S-curve analysis.

- Most large-scale diffusions are staged with the cumulative curve revealing releases in different departments, communities, or geographical areas, as shown by curve D. Scientists and statisticians agree: beware of the normal curve and the S-curve because they are idealized functions.

Metcalfe's Law

Metcalfe's law states that the value of a network grows with the square of the parties connected. Formulated by Robert Metcalfe, co-inventor of the Ethernet, this law has been used to explain the adoption rates for communication technologies, networks, and internetworks (e.g., the Internet). The corner cases are illustrative.

- If someone had the only telephone in the world, to whom would that person place a call? A network of one produces no value
- If everyone had a telephone, then all parties are within reach. A network of all produces the greatest value.

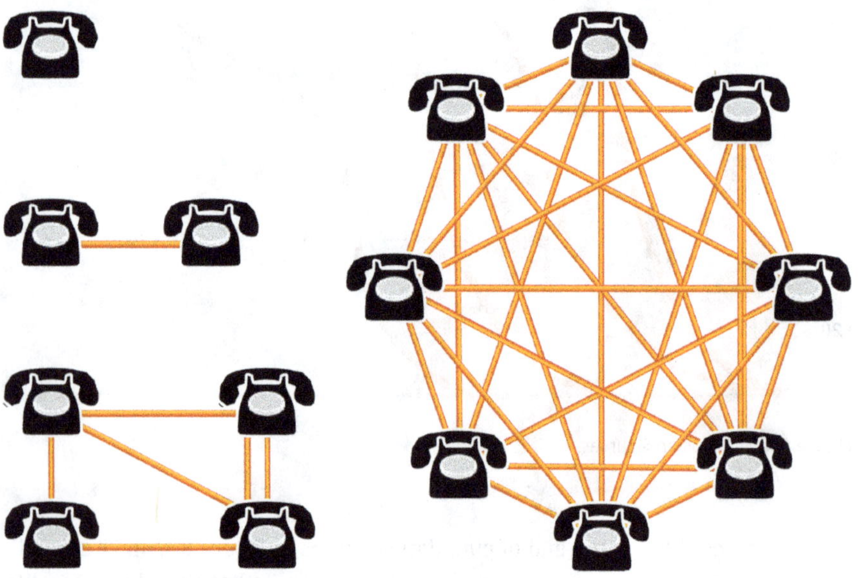

Figure 8.5: The Basis of Metcalfe's Law.
Source: Adapted from Wikipedia, public domain.

Metcalfe's law—the rule that value grows with the square of the number of networked users—is illustrated in Figure 8.5. Interconnections grow as a square of the number of nodes. Metcalfe's law, taken literally, produces a curve that soars to a maximum value as the population of users is exhausted. Figure 8.6 illustrates the curve as value rises to 1,000,000 when networked people increase to 1,000. We say *literally* because there is a debate in the literature as to whether Metcalfe's law is to be taken literally. Metcalfe does not define a metric for value, which is part of the problem, and there is some debate about whether *Value* = $People^2$ is the correct mathematical function.

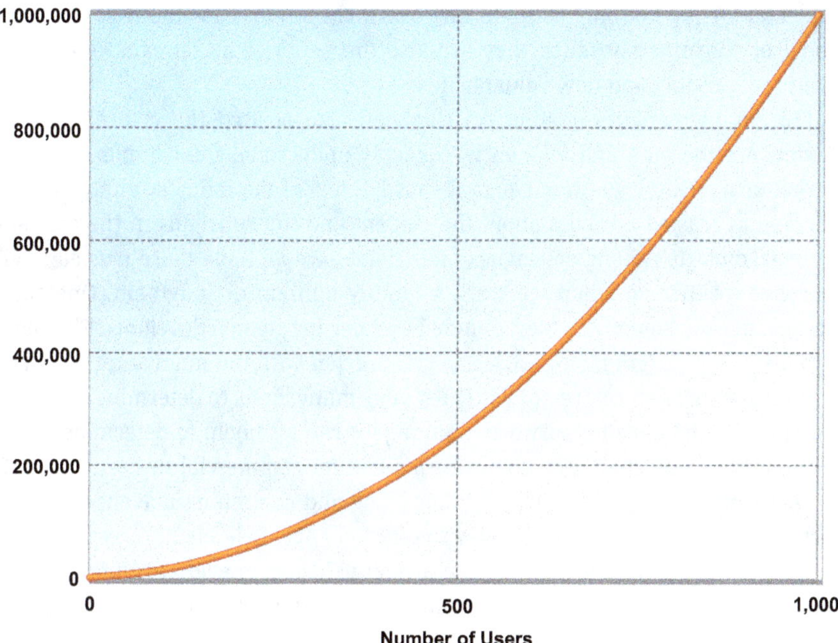

Figure 8.6: Number of People and Value of a Network.
Source: Intel IT.

Gladwell's Tipping Point

> Malcolm Gladwell's studies of diffusion focus on the special roles that some people take as ideas spread through a community and on the explosive nature of change when a critical mass is reached. That critical mass is *The Tipping Point*, which is also the title of Gladwell's first book (Gladwell, 2000).

Connectors and Mavens

Gladwell's thinking begins with his realization that some individuals are able to muster more support for a new idea than others. In a social network, not all people are equally powerful. Using a sociological test, Gladwell identified what he calls *connectors*—individuals with very large social circles. These individuals are especially capable of delivering strong endorsements for new ideas to a large group of people.

In thinking about our own colleagues and friends, we can easily iden- tify connectors. They not only stand in line overnight to purchase the first of a new model of consumer product, they are also the people who let everyone know about that product and how valuable it is.

To complement the connector, Gladwell also posited the role of maven. Mavens are the men and women who deeply understand the complexities of a market or a technology. In our digital world, a few of the industry analysts have emerged as trusted advisors about the current and future trends in the technology marketplace. Among colleagues and friends, we all have those trusted advisors that we turn to when we want a quality opinion or judgment. One such trusted advisor, Gideon Gartner, founded Gartner Inc., which developed The Gartner™ hype cycle methodology. Used in conjunction with the innovation adoption curve, it is a tool you can re-apply to map your innovations to determine commercial viability and gaps for forward planning.[1] It can also help to determine when investment is needed and what must be in place for commercial success.

According to Gladwell, actively identifying and combining mavens and connectors into teams is a powerful way to effect change. Reliable and respected information can be widely broadcast in a relatively short period of time. Mavens guide connectors who are the largest hubs in the social network.

The Tipping Point

It is Gladwell's observation that change, which in our context is the adoption of an innovative capability, begins slowly as word gets out that something better is available. As more and more people adopt a digital innovation, the rate of adoption begins to rise. Much in the spirit of Rogers, Gladwell believes that a tipping point is reached and the adoption of change then occurs very rapidly.

Friedman's Flat World

In 2005, Thomas Friedman published a book about how converging technologies were changing the nature of global business. Friedman's allusion was to a flat, fair playing field where modern countries and emerging ones could begin to do business. Of the ten *flatteners*, four are emerging information technologies. Friedman highlights the browser, workflow software, informing, and personal digital equip-

1 https://en.wikipedia.org/wiki/Hype_cycle

ment. By informing, Friedman means the use of search engines like Google to independently gather information. Underpinning these flatteners is the internet.

These new technologies and the internet together change the way companies work together. These five flatteners are open sourcing, outsourcing, off-shoring, supply chaining, and insourcing. Friedman's example of insourcing is United Parcel Service (UPS), which, in addition to its delivery services, provides repair services for Toshiba computers.

Friedman emphasizes that the world is flat because of the convergence of these technologies and business models. For knowledge-based industries, the relationship between where work is needed and where it is done has vanished. The rapid adoption, in the past few years, of digital team spaces and collaboration tools, such as Zoom, Slack, and Microsoft Teams has accelerated the flat world affect.

Rapid Binary Adoption

Prof. Matt Mullarkey of the University of South Florida has been writing about the phenomenon of 'binary' adoption which occurred during COVID, when normal resistance to innovation barriers was removed and radical digital innovation happened to meet very urgent needs. Matt observed how what we mostly thought about digital transformation, being hard and requiring lots of capital investment, turned out not to be true and that digital transformation could be done much faster and without huge investments of capital. He calls the phenomena "binary" adoption, which is literally extremely fast adoption and the characteristics are described in Figure 8.7.

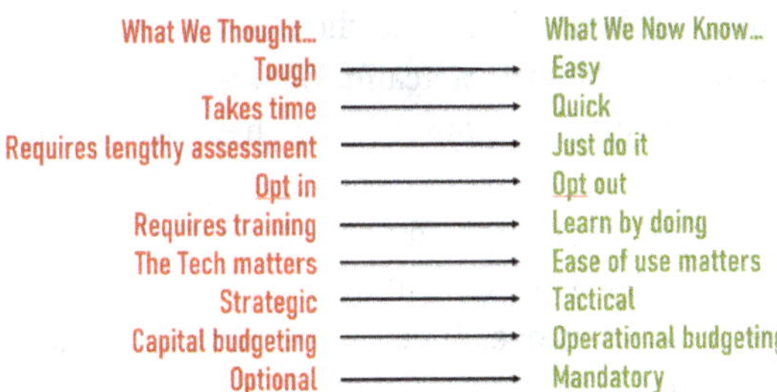

Figure 8.7: Digital Transformation – Lessons from COVID.
Source: Matt Mullarkey.

Matt Mullarkey advocates a ten-step approach to transformative adoption

1. Make a choice, learn, pivot, communicate – repeat.
2. Aim for a peak.

3. Know the first rollout *will be wrong.*
4. Use a guided, emergent *design* doing approach.
5. *Rapid iteration* is better than *slow adoption.*
6. *Customer behaviors* are better than *expert opinion.*
7. *Experiment* with *multiple plausible right solutions.*
8. *Measure* everything – *especially changes in customer behaviors.*
9. *Reward impact, not perfection.*
10. *Execute relentlessly.*

Mullarkey's ten steps start with decisiveness. Make a choice, experiment, learn, pivot if necessary and then communicate and then repeat and iterate quickly. Then aim high. You must shoot for the stars but realize that the first rollout will be wrong. Using an agile approach with quick sprints will allow a measured approach to delivery. A critical recommendation is use a guided, emergent design doing approach. We can no longer wait for the perfect system to be developed and a scaled agile approach allows the right balance to be achieved between risk and progress. Mullarkey advocates for rapid iteration over slow adoption. He prioritizes customer feedback over opinions of experts. Mullarkey advocates generating multiple options and experimenting. As we discussed before, as advocated by Andy Grove, measurement is crucial. Penultimately Mullarkey advocates to reward impact not perfection. And finally execute relentlessly. "Innovate or die."

Diffusion Fundamentals: Lessons Learned

We have offered ideas from six distinguished individuals who have looked at diffusion in slightly different ways; Rogers, Moore, Metcalfe, Gladwell, Friedman and Mullarkey. From our diffusion practitioners' point of view, here are the implications we have drawn for our daily work:

- From Rogers we acquired shared terminology and an under- standing that, over time, diffusion will begin slowly with innovators and early adopters. The concept of tracking multiple S-curves over time has helped us to understand variances in diffusion. Some digital innovation capabilities have a higher velocity uptake, for example, and when looking at an organization as a whole, S-curves top off at different levels.
- Moore's contribution to our thinking centers on the chasm. When organizations develop and field digital innovative capabilities, their first customers are those early adopters who treasure function over simplicity. Listening solely to these customers can lead to a product that is unacceptable to the majority of our customers. The remedy, of course, is to build prototyping and

testing programs that draw on the larger population of customers early in the development process. In this way, the risk of falling into the chasm is lessened.

- From Metcalfe there are two messages. The subtle message is that an expensive network infrastructures will not be cost-effective if usage is low. Economies of scale are an important consideration when building a business case for an innovative digital capability. The bold message is that the benefits of network systems rise sharply as the number of users increases. Linear increases in cost-per-user will quickly be outrun by quadratic increases in accumulated benefits.
- From Gladwell we learned that you can push a rope. Namely, the random diffusion process that describes molecular behavior need not be random when diffusing new digital capabilities. Identifying mavens and connectors is a useful exercise for diffusion managers. Expediting access to innovative products and services for these types of individuals is a viable technique for accelerating adoption of digital innovations and innovations of all kinds.
- Friedman highlights the consequences of a global internet with useful tools such as browsers and workflow systems. For some companies, the work of innovation can be, and is being, brokered and dispatched to contractors and suppliers anywhere on the globe. For diffusion managers, the internet provides a pervasive and inexpensive way to send out new innovation capabilities for testing and, later, for daily use. Friedman also suggests a new world where innovations can be customized for individuals, and in the flat world, diffusion channels can be bi-directional and return information from customers' experience with a new product or service. Mass customization is now a reality made possible by digital innovations in a flat world.
- A new phenomenon of binary adoption has arrived as defined by Mullarkey where extreme conditions such as the COVID pandemic showed that digital transformation may not be as difficult or as expensive as we thought it was. During COVID many organizations were able to rapidly develop and deploy solutions for relatively modest amount of capital. Mullarkey asks why can't this be the norm moving forward.

Diffusion of Innovation

The goal for diffusion is to obtain maximum penetration of the innovation in the desired end-user community with the least amount of investment and optimum value creation. If active efforts to accelerate diffusion are not taken, a valuable innovation will be adopted slowly or, perhaps, not at all. Proactive steps should be taken to develop infrastructure, provide technical support, and actively market the innovation, as shown in Figure 8.8. Well- managed diffusion with discipline enables efficient distribution and faster return on investment.

The mindset for diffusion managers should be one of marketing a product. Technology products often emerge from the engineering department with a host of features. These features need to be transformed into benefits to attract the interest of customers. Similarly, functions fulfill needs and skilled marketeers find ways to fit a new product into the customer's daily life. Usage can be demonstrated in many ways. Live demonstrations, online demonstrations, computer simulations and case studies are four of many ways to reveal the product's value to the customer.

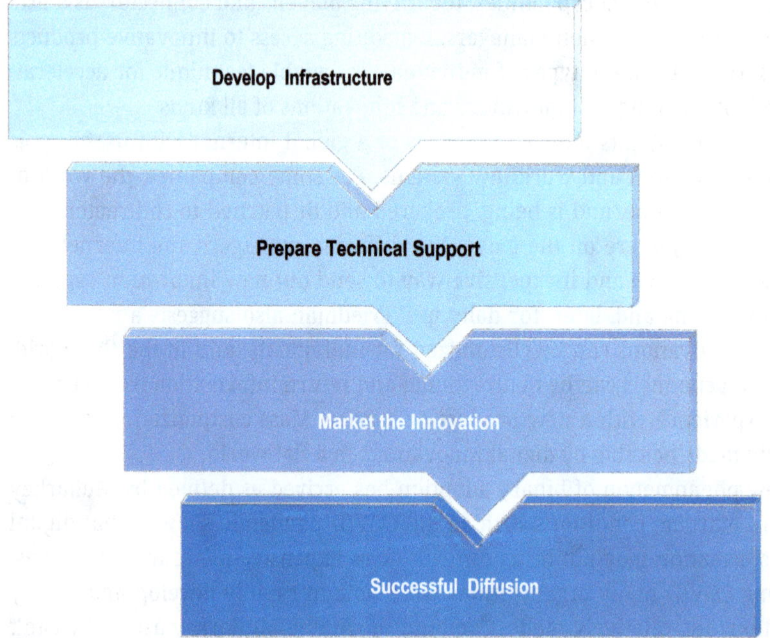

Figure 8.8: Steps in Managing Diffusion.
Source: Intel.

When we think of strengthening our diffusion capabilities, we sort out assets, methods, and skillsets that we have or need. We form a framework, as shown in Table 8.1, and look at their alignment with the diffusion steps from Figure 8.1. We call this a *directed* diffusion framework to underscore the fact that we are actively diffusing innovations, and not simply waiting for the social network to do so.

Develop Infrastructure

The infrastructure that supports directed diffusion draws on assets, methods and skillsets.

Assets

Like any well-run business, the organization needs to think through and develop distribution channels to deliver innovative capabilities. Part of this asset is always in place—its basis is the network that integrates IT systems and is the distribution channel of choice for software.

Table 8.1: The Directed Diffusion Framework.

	Develop Infrastructure	Prepare Technical Support	Market the Innovation
Assets	– Delivery channel – Innovation centers and portals – Content repository	– Toolkits for support – Courseware – User's guide	– Audience analysis – Marketing expertise – Publicity assets
Methods	– Embed innovation into existing systems – Use an intranet innovation portal – Copy-exactly	– Recruit experts – Test the innovation repeatedly during development – Develop training for all stakeholders	– Brand clearly and consistently – Align messages to business goals – Exploit web, virtual and paper media
Skillsets	– IT expertise – Innovation expertise – Diffusion expertise	– Technical writing – Instructional design – Product support personnel	– Marketing and communications – Mavens and connectors – Media developers

Source: Intel IT.

Innovation centers provide focus and the opportunity to demonstrate innovation, both within the company or to the outside world. Innovation portals augment the center and allow remote workers, trading partners, and customers to look in on new ideas, solutions and services.

The innovation portal can also be a one-stop shop that supports innovation at large. The portal can be a gateway to innovation websites, tools, reward and recognition systems, applications and external for funding, and idea-capture sites. Include organizational information related to innovation or assigning roles of innovation champions in the organization to assist with delivering innovation to their organizations.

Methods

Innovative capabilities can often be diffused by building them into existing systems. And many digital innovations manifest themselves as extensions to software that is already in use. Internal customers will find it easier to explore a new feature than to assimilate an entirely new application.

For client-side innovations, it may be possible to fold the new capability into the operating environment. For example, most IT organizations standardize a build for all personal use computers, update it, and upgrade the user community on a regular basis. Digital innovations can ride on the shoulders of this process. For personal computer or device innovations that do not necessarily affect all of IT's customers, a download service or App store is useful. The ergonomic software discussed in Chapter 3 was distributed in this fashion. Some innovations are best offered on a discretionary basis. Users can then choose a quieter time to load them and learn them.

Server-side innovations should exploit the advantages of a web inter- face when at all possible. Browsing is a process customers are familiar with. The more we can make customers comfortable with the digital innovation, the better it will diffuse.

We remind the reader that we believe strongly in the advantages of the copy-exactly process. For customers, and to reduce costs, it is far better to over-invest in developing a high-quality capability and then diffusing exact copies of it far and wide. Conversely, incremental releases of an innovation to different communities, poor quality, and local tinkering lead to unhappy customers and outrageously high maintenance costs.

Skillsets

Three specialties converge when building innovation infrastructure, IT expertise, innovation expertise, and diffusion expertise. Someone is needed who understands the existing IT architectures and standards. Innovation can be built using expert consultants, an innovation curriculum and also includes user-centered design skills, human factors experience, and ethnographic capabilities. In conjunction with these players, the diffusion expert can plan for and build the needed infrastructure.

Prepare Technical Support

The next step is to create technical support for the pool of innovations currently in the pipeline that have been developed to the point of being able to deliver value through communication.

Assets

For most digital innovations, toolkits will be needed for the product support organization. In many ways, this community comprises the early adopters for the innovation. Product support personnel need to understand the use of the innovation and, in addition, they will likely need to know more than the average customer about configuring the innovation and solving typical problems.

Courseware may be required and a user's guide showing the innovation in action is helpful. Investment in these diffusion elements varies with the costs, risks, size of the customer audience, and complexity of the innovation. Courseware developers, like product support personnel, are excellent beta testers as they work to construct an orderly presentation of the innovation's functionality.

Methods

When the innovation prototype is up and running, showing it to content experts is a good idea. If, for example, a new web-based, zero- based budget system is under development, then we recommend demonstrating the system to a web wizard and a zero-based budget wizard. Gaining approval from these experts can be part of the marketing effort. Testing digital innovations must be relentless. The copy-exact mantra, *make the first one perfect*, applies here as well. The IT organization must build a reputation for quality as well as innovation in order to succeed. The rush to be first to market can backfire. Diffusing anything less than a well-tested system puts more than the innovation at risk, it puts the innovation opportunity at risk.

Skillsets

Technical writers, instructional designers, and product support personnel are needed at this stage. Access to the innovation prototype is crucial. We expect the innovation project team to include people with these skills in every case. In other words, we do not send a specification to the technical writing team, we place a technical writer on the innovation team.

Marketing Innovations

It is at the marketing step that the innovation organization looks most like a business. We advertise, we make sure that features are translated into benefits. We offer the digital equivalent of a test drive around the neighborhood.

Assets

While innovation developers are concerned about usage models and user-centered design methods, the marketing group wants to understand the customer as well. Who makes the buying decision for optional innovations? What criteria are most important? A careful analysis of the customer's buying habits is crucial to successful diffusion. Artificial intelligence is playing a growing role in innovation diffusion with the use of preference tracking and recommendation engines. After completing a web search for almost any topic, there is an immediate plethora of similar products or services that will appear on the user's social media feed. Users are now defining diffusion opportunities by their very own queries.

The mature IT organization has a dedicated marketing group. These are professionals who know how to conceptualize and package digital solutions as attractive products and services. They understand the importance of branding and positioning when reaching out to customers, can deliver search engine optimization (SEO) and create publicity assets.

By publicity assets, we mean the capability to put together marketing campaigns and product launches. This can translate into templates for online media assets, posters, organization graphics libraries, technical papers, technical presentations, virtual reality landing zones, networked media displays, videos and booths for demonstrations and road shows.

Methods

Branding is not usually a part of the traditional IT organization's thinking, but it looms large in the minds of customers. Over time, brands deliver the reputation of the product or service offering. Calling the online innovation portal the IT Innovation Engine is a good example. The name itself loads up the features and values of the service being delivered to customers.

Innovative applications should have been aligned with company goals and objectives when the business case was created. These linkages are the basis for another marketing vector. Customers need to know why the company is investing in a particular innovation and what business value benefits are expected.

While it is tempting to use web-based communication exclusively to reach out to customers, we have found that traditional paper-based communication is also important. A eye-catching poster in the employee break room, table tents in the cafeteria, inserts in office carts, the card left on a desk or car, and a full-fledged advertisement will all help accelerate diffusion.

Skillsets

Preparations for the market launch bring two new skillsets to the innovation team. A marketing and communications person is needed to create a brand image, a positioning, and benefits-oriented descriptions of the new innovation capability. The team also needs a media developer to re-express the marketing communication packaging and advertising. For software products that display an interface to the customer, its signage and color should be a part of the marketing plan.

We discussed the roles of Gladwell's mavens and connectors earlier. Well before the product launch, we identify, approach, and invite these individuals to look in on the developing innovative system. When connectors are assured by mavens that the capability will be important, then the word will begin to spread that something interesting is in the works.

One Final Ingredient for Success

Diffusion can be enhanced by the reward and recognition systems that support innovators both in IT and especially in the company at large. This has been an effective part of diffusing innovations in the authors' experience. Contests with rewards and recognition communicate the company's interest in innovation. When winning ideas emerge in different functional areas of the company, employees outside R&D and core business services will participate.

Summary

We have offered five key ideas about diffusion:

- An invention that diffuses rapidly will accrue business value more quickly. From a cash flow point of view, this is a good thing.
- An invention that fails to diffuse cannot deliver business value. Inattention to the diffusion process is a recipe for failure.
- Innovation theorists think about diffusion in different ways, each of which provides insight and guidance.

- Diffusion can be accelerated. We call this *directed diffusion* and we have provided a framework filled with ingredients for building this capability.
- COVID taught us we can do extremely rapid innovation and adoption. Why can't this be the norm moving forward?

And remember, don't defuse innovation, diffuse it.

Chapter 9
Launching Systemic Innovation

Innovation distinguishes between a leader and a follower. — Steve Jobs

This chapter brings together some of the major themes in our book and offers a plan for building an innovation program in an organization. Much of the innovation activity will result in better systems for the company. Some of the innovation activity will support innovation excellence across the company.

Innovation is crucial to meeting the challenge of balancing today's operational excellence with future needs and managing for business value. In order to stay ahead of the competition and contribute to share- holder value, innovation needs to be systemic. It provides the company with a critical ability to adapt to changes in the business environment.

The path to innovation excellence begins with management commitment. Employees need to know that innovation is on that short list of capabilities the company must have. They must perceive that being innovative is the best way to move ahead in the company and the best way to help the company move ahead.

The IT organization is well placed to cultivate innovation capabilities, both internally and across the company. However, the IT organization needs to be executing its core mandate successfully before it can be considered as the host of "Innovation Technology" in the organization. The innovation capabilities are a mixture of courses and workshops, methods and metrics, and systems to manage the innovation process. Over time, investments in innovation enablers will establish innovation as an organizational value and deliver enterprise value.

Gaining Management Commitment

Commitment from management is an absolute necessity when launching a company-wide effort of any kind. It is the responsibility of the company's executives to set forth a strategy and to identify the key capabilities which will enable the company to thrive. Capabilities may include an emphasis on quality, a goal of being first to market with new technologies, or a reputation for using IT in innovative ways throughout the company. Top- down support begins the journey from random and occasional innovation to systemic, methodical innovation.

Managers demonstrate their commitment by sending clear and visible messages that innovation matters. In addition to rhetoric, management commitment

https://doi.org/10.1515/9781501507335-009

includes concrete actions such as allocating resources, putting innovation metrics in place, and paying ongoing attention to the innovation process. When upper management puts innovative excellence on the middle manager's list of objectives, then we can rest assured middle managers will be communicating that same message to line managers and employees. Each workgroup manager is responsible for the day-to-day details of implementing or participating in an innovation program.

Create and Communicate a Vision

A vision is a view of the future that emphasizes what a company intends to accomplish. The vision should include inspirational reach, a unique value proposition, timeframe, and link to the business need. Vision is important because it paints a picture for the entire organization and sets expectations. Moreover, the differences between the state of the company today and the vision of the company in the future translate into a roadmap of accomplishments needed to satisfy the vision. In May 1961 President John F. Kennedy declared to the U.S. Congress and the American people that he intended to send a man to the moon and safely back within the decade. This bold statement galvanized efforts by NASA to engineer a solution to Kennedy's challenge. Kennedy did not say space travel would happen some day and that we would go somewhere. It was a manned flight to the moon and back, we have nine years to do it, and the clock starts now. In July 1969 Neil Armstrong set foot on the moon.

The best visions are concrete, specific, and challenging. They translate well into slogans and are memorable. They electrify emotions and create cohesion in organizations. A well-crafted vision statement sets the company thinking of where they are and where they need to go.

Visions are typically formed on the basis of forecasts. Gordon Moore's 1965 extrapolation of early trends in the density of semiconductor devices provided the semiconductor industry with a yardstick, on the one hand, but more important, with a new set of questions about the future. What if we could create a device with 50 million transistor junctions? What would it do? How would that device fit into a system? What other components will be needed?

To be effective, the company vision must be widely communicated and reinforced over time. The company's employees, customers, and suppliers all know what to expect. A well-communicated vision creates a spotlight of attention. When that spotlight is focused on increased innovation, the stage is set.

Develop an Innovation Strategy

The next step, after creating a vision, in launching an innovation initiative is to develop a strategy. For innovation, or any other cultural transformation objective, the first step is an inventory of relevant current assets and capabilities. Depending on the organization, this step could be complex. Like quality and safety, innovation capabilities can be difficult to identify and quantify. Especially in the case of skillsets, it may take some time and effort to find out who has experience with innovation techniques.

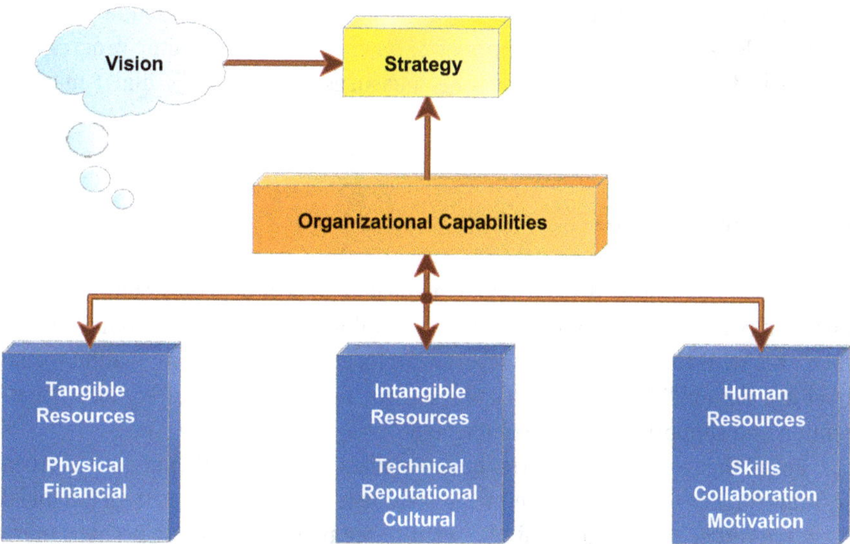

Figure 9.1: Vision, Strategy, and Capabilities.
Source: Adapted from Robert M Grant, Contemporary Strategy Analysis Competency Model, MacDonough School of Business, Georgetown University.

Strategy

A strategy maps the company's or organization's capabilities to the vision, as shown in Figure 9.1. A strategy provides a roadmap that leads from today's capabilities to the capabilities needed to support the vision. The roadmap has a timeline and a sequence of milestones to measure progress. While long-term planning may reach out a decade or more, preparing three-year action plans and revisiting those plans annually is typical.

In Irelands HSE, the Digital Transformation organization defined Stay Left, Shift Left-10X as the Innovation Strategy for a complete healthcare system transformation and immediately established a national masters in Digital Health Transformation to train clinical leaders in the underpinning principles and processes and to establish a critical mass of leaders ready to lead the transformation.

Budgeting intersects with strategy as well. Especially in the IT organization, there are many investment alternatives. Weighing those options and testing how they align with corporate objectives is a key activity. Finding the right balance between innovation and operational efficiency occurs at this juncture.

Outcomes vary up and down the organization. Corporate vision and goals are translated into greater detail until they find their way to specific action plans for each employee. Managers create projects, form teams, and monitor progress. In the case of innovation, new outcome measures (i.e., business dials) may be needed.

Measure Business Value

A sustained commitment from upper management will depend upon measured business results. CEOs are measured by the value they create. Stockholder value increases with the company's measured performance. Thus, if innovation initiatives are not explicitly tied to business results, then they will quickly lose the attention and support of upper management.

Recall that we call our metrics business dials, and a sampling of dials is given in Table 9.1. For each dial, we define how value is going to be measured. Financial dials are rather straightforward. We want to see more revenue, or perhaps more revenue while holding the profit margin constant. We aim for fewer days of inventory and fewer days of receivables. Everything is in monetary units.

Indirect financial dials are a bit more difficult. For example, the simple number of patents should increase when systemic innovation programs are launched. But how much is a patent worth? It is our objective to transform the indirect business dials into monetary units, and that can be a significant challenge.

Developing Innovation Capabilities

The inventory of innovative resources, created as part of the strategy process, provides a foundation for developing additional innovation capabilities. As always, there are interdependencies among the choices. We suggest an incremental and balanced approach, with investments in tangible resources, such as an innovation

Table 9.1: A Selection of Business Value Dials.

Indirect financial dials		Direct financial dials	
Intellectual property	Patents	Revenue	Days of inventory
Standards influence	Product influence	Days of receivables	Headcount
Sales influence	Vendor of choice	Productivity	Turnover
Usage models	Prototypes	Risk management	Scrap reduction
New markets	Business process	Factory uptime	Time to market

Source: Intel IT.

center, along with human resources, such as people trained in user-centered design or innovation science.

Training

In the early phases of an innovation initiative, we typically see the need to invest in training. Large corporate support and IT organizations often have training expertise in place, and can add courses to an existing curriculum. In smaller companies, the organization may choose to budget for outside training, which exists in abundance in the area of innovation.

As innovation skillsets improve and experience accumulates, we recommend that the IT organization provide courses company-wide. Since innovative activities vary in different industries, courses can be tailored to the company's specific needs.

Attending innovation conferences is also helpful at the onset. Conferences accelerate the open innovation process by displaying a number of successful innovations, often in different industries. Conferences also provide a setting for a company's innovation program director to network with other innovation leaders.

How an organization reacts to failure is a good indicator of how successful an innovation program will be. Traditionally, failures are punished, and yet we all recognize that innovation is a risky business. If potential innovators in a company observe bad outcomes when a project founders on unexpected rocks, they will be unlikely to step forward when a new project is launched.

As mentioned, the best failures are those that occur early in the development process and that provide useful information. The authors call this *failing forward.* Ideally, we would like the first-order prototype to reveal as many problems as possible. User-centered design is helpful in this regard. We avoid the temptation to go away and build what we think might be needed. We test early and often, throughout the development and adoption processes.

We recommend that all projects are brought to closure by identifying and archiving lessons learned, both positive and negative. This process brings closure to the team and encourages the fact that all projects provide value. Knowing what does not work, what does not work *yet*, and what does not work for us is valuable information. When the results are archived, we celebrate the achievement.

Celebrating Success

We recommend strong reward and recognition systems to celebrate successful innovation. Robust systems for reward and recognition include a mix of financial and nonfinancial reinforcers, which we also recommend. Reputations matter and recognizing an engineering team for delivering on deadline and to specifications is a powerful reward. Meanwhile, if an innovation can be linked to improvements in business value, then we believe compensation is appropriate.

Innovation and risk-taking often go hand-in-hand. Because we want to reward risk-taking, and especially reapplied innovation and diffusion, consider adopting a reward program the authors worked with and incrementally improved program called the Penguin Awards. The "First Penguin" award rewards the risk takers. The first penguin to jump into the water risks being eaten by the whale. The "Last Penguin" award gains value from the first penguin and adds value by not reinventing the wheel and supporting diffusion.

Rewards need not be substantial in all cases. Offering a trip to a conference for the 100th person to file an idea is a good way to encourage innovative thinking, for example. Providing a convenient parking place for the inventor of the month chosen by election among peers is another modest example.

Innovation Centers

Dedicating a space to support the innovation process raises the visibility of the innovation program. One or two rooms will be needed to support workshops and demonstrations, which are the most common uses for innovation centers. Early on, this "innovation center" may be little more than a setting for evaluating new technologies, demonstrating concept cars and prototypes, and offering workshops and training courses.

Many activities will initially be within the company, but increasingly visits will come from your organization's customers. Figure 9.2 shows the design layout for the IT Innovation center in Ireland and represents the diversity of focus areas that the Intel Ireland IT Innovation center focused on.

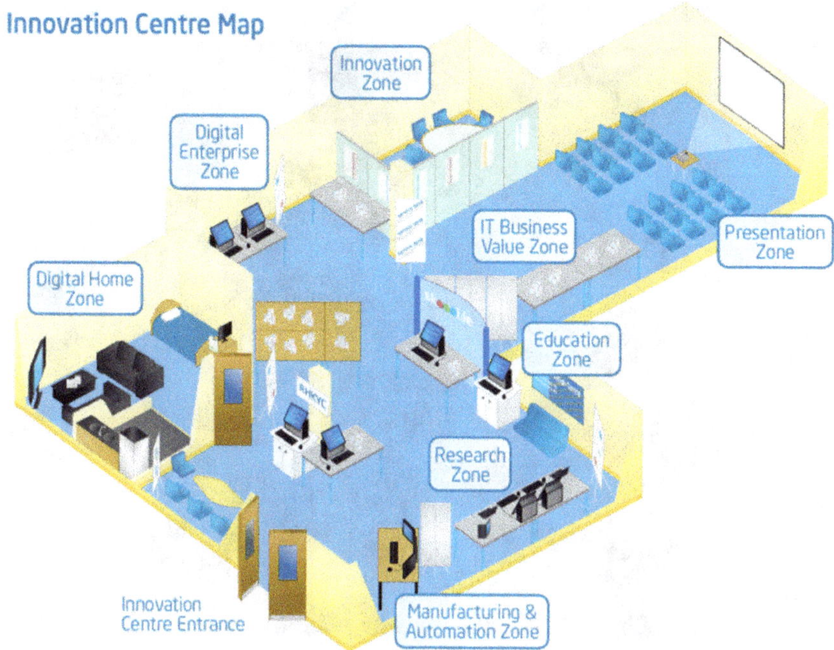

Figure 9.2: Example of Innovation Centre Layout Design.
Source: D. Fleming, Intel.

In conjunction with an innovation center, we recommend an online virtual innovation center be created. In the early days, the virtual innovation center will contain course listings, calendars of events, and links to relevant resources. Later on, the virtual innovation center can become a portal in support of innovation in the large. IT systems within the portal can automate the capture and management of innovative ideas from all around the company. Figure 9.3 shows the virtual innovation center environment we created at Intel.

As momentum increases, innovation centers will likely reach outward to include activities designed for customers, suppliers, and other interested parties. Although they manifest themselves in different ways, these centers make sense for any knowledge-rich industry. Here are three different types of innovation center:

- PricewaterhouseCoopers (PwC), the global business advisory partnership, created a technology center in the mid-1980s. The research center developed practice aids to accelerate the audit process. In addition, the center also served as a destination for visits from CFOs. PwC wanted to demonstrate to its customers and prospects it was committed to streamlining the audit process.

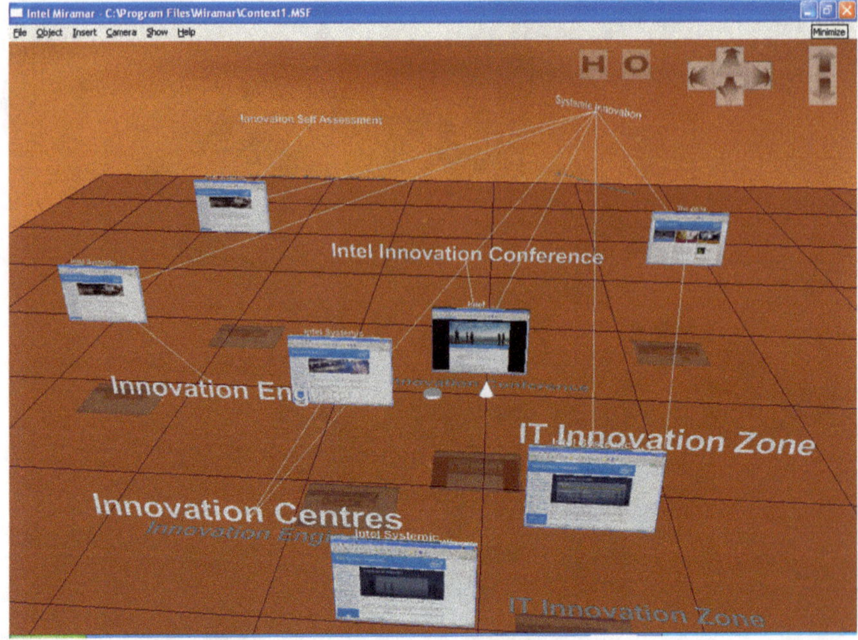

Figure 9.3: Intel Virtual IT Innovation Centre Environment.

- Procter and Gamble (P&G), the consumer products company, added their sixth innovation center in Beckett Ridge in 2000, growing to thirteen by 2022. These centers provide visions of the future for use of home products and packaging, which today includes Holy Grail 2.0, a digital watermark to make recycling fast and accurate. They have a gaming experience "attack of the cavity creeps" and premiered an immersive P&G LifeLab virtual reality experience at the 2021 Consumer Electronics Show. Also, P&G features innovation at its website. Through a program called Connect+Develop, anyone can submit a product or technology idea to the company. (www.pgconnectdevelop.com)
- IMPACT XM, winners of the 2022 Best of CES award, a Silver Stevie winner in the 2021 American Business Awards and in the top 100 2021 IT list, created the BASF Virtual Innovation Center. This center is both physical and virtual. The virtual experience is intended to be a simulation of an actual visit to the center where visitors can place RFID cubes to see individual presentations.
- The St. Vrain Valley School District extended their Innovation Center with a mobile Innovation Lab, contracted from Farber Specialty Vehicles of Ohio, taking its STEM programs on the road. It was inspired by Lockheed Martin's virtual reality Mars Experience Bus. So mobile and virtual can go together hand-in-hand.

These examples show that innovation centers will vary in focus and scope to support different visions in different industries. For PwC, innovation was focused on practice aids whereas for P&G, the focus is product development and became mobile with the advent of virtual reality. We include BASF and the St. Vrain Mobile Innovation Lab to underscore the point that innovation centers can be portable and that there are many opportunities for SMBs, and those who serve SMBs, to be innovative.

Creation and Diffusion

When launching an innovation program, we recommend choosing early projects with special care. While it is tempting to propose a risky idea that might be a smashing success, we suggest the safer bet—a project that reapplies a trusted innovation in a new setting. Costs and risks are lower, providing a much lower hurdle for success.

Criteria for Siting an Innovation Center

When the authors expanded innovation center locations, they formalized criteria for choosing a new site. Here are the primary heuristics:

- Geography—Our objective is to distribute the innovation centers to provide global coverage.
- Company presence—We want our centers located near the majority of our people.
- Customer presence—We want to be near our most important customers.
- Local support—We are influenced by requests from employees, customers, and suppliers who want an innovation center nearer to them. Local government support and funding also play a key role in site selection.
- Innovative culture—We favor sites that are near universities, institutes, and other research and development facilities.
- Optimum cost—We favor locations where we can share costs with other innovation programs, receive contributions from local governments, and put idle resources to use.

Like many collections of heuristics, some of these are at odds with others. Thankfully, our virtual innovation centers do reach every corner of the world.

"A common expression of wishful thinking is to base a grand scheme on a fundamental, unsolved problem," according to Gene Glass (Glass 1978). Wishful thinking and innovation are a dangerous mixture. In IT, start-up ventures often bring grand schemes to the IT organization's attention. Beware of the concept car that is promoted as a prototype, or even worse, as technology ready for deployment.

Partnering and prototyping are the keys to managing risk, as shown dramatically by our case study of Wireless Westminster in Appendix A. This strategy is not just for beginners. The authors have regularly developed cooperative ways to include partners in their innovation projects. Because successful scaling is a well-known challenge for IT systems, we are careful to deploy prototypes in realistic environments.

Getting the diffusion strategy right is equally important. While legacy research on innovation highlights random adoption in a social network, we believe that diffusion can be actively directed and accelerated, especially for IT systems. The incremental cost of supporting additional users is ordinarily low and, as a result, the more rapidly we can deploy innovative IT capabilities, the more rapidly business value will accrue.

Intel's Experience

When Intel IT began to focus on innovation, we had a substantial inventory of resources. This is not surprising, given the nature of our core business. What we envisioned was a day in the future when IT systems would expedite innovation across the enterprise. That is, while building new and better IT capability was one of our primary objectives, we also wanted to build the infrastructure for innovation *writ large*.

Initially our investment in innovation centers was modest compared to other strategic investments in Intel such as the Intel ® Solution centers, but because of the very specific focus on value, they delivered supranormal returns contributing to the extraordinary growth of Intel. The centers were distributed globally and comprised of executive briefing facilities, prototyping capabilities to test emerging technologies, and regular programs in which we share IT best practices with ourselves and with our customers and suppliers. As outlined in the self-assessment, in Chapter 6, management commitment is the most important ingredient for innovation.

The roles of the IT innovation centers were multi-facetted including

- Systemic Innovation
  - Enabling and catalysing innovation
  - Breakthrough Internal Solutions
- Research
  - Relationships with leading Universities, publication and proof points
- Executive Workshops
  - e.g. education, eHealth transformation workshops, IT Business Value, Innovation workshops
- Showcases
  - e.g. Digital Home, Office, School

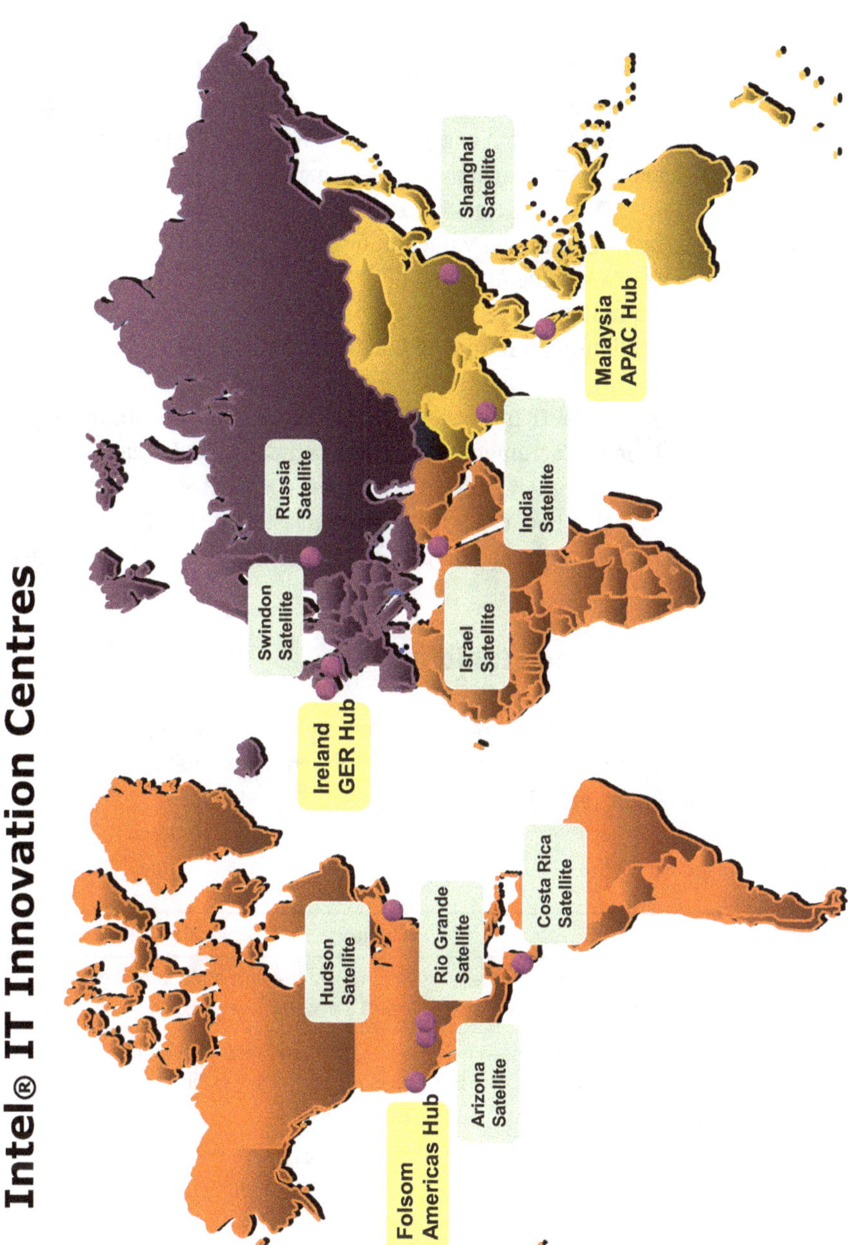

Figure 9.4: Intel IT Innovation Centers, circa 2007 – source Intel.

- Industry Events
  - e.g. Government ICT forum, SGI solutions channel conference
- Catalyst research engagements
  - Transformational research engagements to help develop OGA solutions
- Speakerships and thought leadership influencing
  - Many topics – Mobility, Health, Education, eGovernment, eManufacturing, Enterprise, IT Business Value, Innovation, Machine Learning, etc.
- Chasm Crossing – Managing Adoption
- Open Innovation Initiatives
  - e.g. collaborations with European Commission and others

The architecture of the Intel IT Innovation network was designed with three geographical hubs in Ireland, Sacramento and Kuala Lumpur in Malaysia (as seen in Yellow in figure 9.4). The other small innovation centers acted as satellites but because the centers, which had a relatively small investment, acted as a cohesive network they had a disproportionate impact on the performance of the company.

Innovation Enablers and Inhibitors

The authors conducted a workshop attended by employees from across their company. One result from that workshop was an ordered list of enablers and inhibitors, which is shown in Table 9.2.

Table 9.2: Enablers and Inhibitors of Innovation.

Enablers	Inhibitors
1. Management support—active and positive support for innovation from the top down	1. Bureaucracy—too many approval steps to launch a new initiative or expand on an idea
2. Employee talent—a pool of employees with diverse skills and abilities and the confidence to use them	2. Negative leadership—innovation not supported at a high enough priority to carry projects through
3. Rewards and recognition—ongoing positive reinforcement, including tangible rewards when appropriate	3. Immediate return on investment (ROI)—expectation that an innovation will provide a ROI in too short a period of time
4. Open communication—open-door policies and a community that values the sharing of ideas	4. Risk aversion—simple avoidance of all risk without weighing the opportunity cost of inaction

Table 9.2 (continued)

Enablers	Inhibitors
5. Competitive pressure—the healthy stress of staying ahead of competitors with new and better ideas	5. NIH syndrome—not invented here blocks the adoption of good ideas learned elsewhere
6. Access to resources—sufficient and sustained budget to fuel the innovation process	6. Too little time—day-to-day responsibilities exhaust available bandwidth
7. Risk-taking as a value—the thoughtful balancing of opportunity and risk to maximize benefit	7. Organizational protectionism— barriers within the company that block the sharing of good ideas
8. Policies that support innovation— workshops, release time, mentorships, innovation centers, etc.	8. Lack of funding—lean resourcing of people and funds that reduces the opportunity to innovate
9. Job rotation—the opportunity to gain and share ideas in different settings within the company	9. Lack of vision—no clear picture of where the company will be in the future and thus no path to get there
10. Innovation platforms—systems and repositories for the intermediate results of the innovation process	10. Fear of change—believing that work should be done like we always have, with legacy systems, not innovations

We suggest planning an innovation launch strategy with this table firmly in mind. While it is impossible to eliminate all inhibitors, we believe it is helpful to identify them clearly and construct work-around tactics. For example, if an innovative IT project depends on new enabling tech- nologies and lacks an ironclad diffusion vector, then it may make good sense to argue for a longer return on investment (ROI) payback period. Or, in that same setting, an additional prototype may be needed to verify the expected return.

Systemic Innovation

We recommend the control-loop approach to managing and improving innovation capabilities, which we introduced in Chapter 4. Business- like thinking, a carefully-managed budget, increasing digital innovation capabilities, and assessment of the results are the critical functions, as shown in Chapter 4 (Figure 4.1).

Idea to Reality in China: while leading innovation as the Director of Innovation in the Intel Dalian Factory, Esther set the expectation for leaders using the Capability Maturity Framework (CMF), developed and established an innovation curriculum and collaborated with Human Resources across China to deliver it, re-assess and improve over time. The factory was using an older process that had been improved "as far as it could go" using the "copy-exactly" methodology. Idea to Reality and BHAG campaigns soon resulted in the yield improving beyond anything seen before, and costs were reduced. During one of the "Mathovation" workshops Esther delivered, she taught the "ADD" method. How can you use addition to deliver value and asked, "Why can't we "glue" two test wafers together when they become too thin to reuse?" In 2015 this was laughed at. In 2023 one of her former students sent her a patent showing two wafers "glued" together from his current company. Protecting ideas through intellectual property (IP) management must become part of the systemic innovation process

Using a digital innovation portal can help make sure laughable ideas are not lost, IP is protected and when the time is right ideas can become reality.

Sometimes ideas are "in the air" and multiple people will have the same idea. It is important to acknowledge this and bring all the players along together under the spirit of "great minds think alike." In *The Creative Act: A Way of Being*, Rick Rubin says, "There's a time for certain ideas to arrive and they find a way to express themselves through us."

Systemic innovation will not be an overnight success. It will take several trips around the control loop for innovation managers and the company as a whole to understand the process, its requirements, and its benefits. We suggest that launching an innovation program will take two to three years. In terms of the Innovation CMF, moving up a step each year is a reasonable expectation.

Culture and Innovation

> It is our contention that when innovation is cultivated, it will become systemic, which is equivalent to saying that innovation will become a part of the company's culture. Culture comprises people's shared beliefs and values and the 4Es and 4Cs shared in Chapter 10 point us to practices that can help or hinder innovation. Culture shapes how people normally behave and interact in their daily life and in their work environment. The concept of corporate culture encompasses far more than dress codes and cubicles. The most important part of corporate culture is the shared commitment to company values, for example, to quality, safety, and fearless innovation.

Summary

Launching a systemic innovation program presents interesting challenges. We intended this chapter to identify the paths forward and the potholes to be avoided. Our major advice is as follows:

– Gaining and maintaining management support remains at the top of our list of concerns. We shared our experiences with creating a vision, developing a strategy, and measuring business value.

- We outlined the major elements needed to begin developing innovation capabilities. To ascend the levels in our Innovation CMF, training will be needed and incentives must be in place to reinforce innovative behavior.
- We believe strongly in the value of an innovation center, especially in support of corporate-wide innovation. We also believe that the exact nature of the innovation center's charter will vary by industry and company size.
- We shared a top-ten list of innovation enablers and inhibitors based on our workshop findings.
- We returned to our foundation thinking about systemic innovation to remind and recommend the control loop approach to running IT innovation like a business. We suggest repeatedly attending to innovation business, budget, capability, and impact and making improvements at each turn of the cycle shown in Figure 4.1 in Chapter 4.

We will discuss in Chapter 11 how innovation is moving out of the organization and into the ecosystem and how organizations can the lead in driving ecosystem wide innovation.

Chapter 10
Culture

Culture eats strategy for breakfast. — Peter Drucker

In this book we have explored many aspects of how one should manage innovation in a digital world. However, we must also discuss the importance and criticality of culture. Culture is the synthesis of values, beliefs, norms, assumptions, preferred ways of interacting by an organization's member that influence their performance and behavior. It is of fundamental critical importance to the success and longevity of an organization. Culture can be notoriously intangible, but we can all quickly recognize the difference between a "can do" culture and "can't do, won't do" culture.

Peter Drucker famously said, "Culture eats strategy for breakfast." This point was really illustrated when Martin helped lead a collaborative innovation assessment with Jack Anderson of Chevron for Northrup Grumman. Northrup Grumman is an impressive company that has very diverse businesses, including shipbuilding, building missiles and providing government IT support. As you might expect, they were quite mature in many aspects of their innovation system and had good capability, good strategy, good funding and good systems. However, one remark by a Northrup Grumman employee really landed as Jack and I reported out to eleven CIOs from different divisions. The employee said, "It's ok to take risks at Northrup Grumman, as long as you were spectacularly successful," implying that if you took risks and failed at Northrup Grumman, your career was over.

After vibrant discussion, the CIOs collectively took this away as the major insight and action point from the innovation assessment, to actively work to make the culture at Northrup Grumman more supportive of risk-taking. In contrast, risk-taking was one of the six values at Intel and the repeated demonstrated behavior of Intel leaders in Intel supporting risk taking meant it was truly a lived value.

According to McKinsey (2020), leading cultures can outperform other cultures by over 200%. According to Gustavo Razetti (2023), a strong culture can accelerate business strategy we also believe that a weak culture can completely cripple organizational strategy.

Intel's culture was underpinned by six values but two of the most important were risk taking and "win and have fun." Both of these values enabled a culture which not only supported but actively biased for innovation. Culture is hugely determined by the philosophy AND actions of the CEO. At Intel we were fortunate to have brilliant CEOs such as Andy Grove, Craig Barrett and Paul Otellini who deeply believed and encouraged innovation. The words of Intel founder Robert Noyce were often repeated: "Optimism is an essential ingredient for innovation."

https://doi.org/10.1515/9781501507335-010

Martin often finishes innovation presentations with a picture of Felix Baumgartner beginning his supersonic freefall jump with the words, "It takes courage too." Courage is also important and while Baumgartner's feat is an extreme example of that, courage is required in any innovation endeavor. To recognize this, Wen Hann Wang, then CTO of Intel, introduced a 'first penguin' award to recognize people who take the important first step jumping into the cold water. In real life, it is the first penguin that risks being eaten by a whale when it jumps into the water. Esther paired this award with another one called the last penguin award. This was in recognition of people that re-use and re-apply innovation instead of re-inventing. So many engineers love to innovate and problem solve, but it takes caring about ROI and even humility to re-use or re-apply someone else's idea and achieve results more quickly.

When Bob Swan became CEO of Intel he revised the corporation values to include Fearless Innovation and One Intel. His tenure as CEO, while short, has had lasting impact by eliminating internal competition among innovators and for the first time spelling out innovation as a core value.

A Failure-tolerant Culture

The General Manager of Intel Fab 14 in Ireland, Shlomo Caine made a very important statement on his first day when he relocated to Ireland from Israel. On his whiteboard he wrote: "Reward a failure every day." Every time Martin (automation manager for Fab 14) had a 1:1 with Shlomo, he would see that – as would all other employees. Intel Fab 14 at the time was the largest construction project in Europe, and with a capital budget of $1.4 billion was likely the most complex factory start-up on the planet at that time (circa 2004). Shlomo created a culture where things could be tried but also a culture where we quickly learned from mistakes. A key feature was the inclusive development of strategy by the leadership team. Joint manufacturing manager Pat Hickey told his "building the snowman" story which became a modus operandi for ongoing strategy development and implementation. It doesn't often snow in Ireland, but when it does many people go out and build snowmen. Pat told the story that one day he went out to build a snowman with his two children and he got stuck in right away and started shovelling snow to build the snowman. He got so engrossed that it was only some time after that he noticed his two children had moved elsewhere in the garden to start their own snowman as they had felt left out. The "snowman" story became legendary in Fab 14 and beyond. It is critical when something is being built to use an inclusive approach and act as "one".

Innovation Pacemaker

As we look at culture, any successful large innovation or project needs a pacemaker who sets the cadence of execution. Pat's joint manufacturing manager at Fab 14, Peggy Landers, was such a person who set a fast tempo of execution and led from the front. Everybody could see how committed Peggy was and like the sinoatrial node (or pacemaker) in the heart, Peggy's pace of execution entrained the rest of the organization to execute at this pace.

Cross-functional leadership is an essential element of any successful complex project or innovation. In livings labs it is crucial to include customers and users in the innovation process. In the Fab 14 start-up, Martin co-led the manufacturing ramp segment, with the manufacturing managers Peggy and Pat, which was responsible for starting and ramping the factory. Having joint leadership and accountability meant that the complex information and automation systems required were co-innovated and co-delivered in lock step with the manufacturing plan. Leadership of such a complex start-up is an innovation in itself and required the input and support of leaders such as Joe Kilgannon who led the Fab 14 manufacturing engineering team. The team also recognized the importance of culture and after several design workshops built the mantra of "Learn Fast, Ramp Fast, Do it Right and Make it Last" to describe the macro behaviors and ethos required to deliver outstanding performance and longevity. The $1.4 billion factory started up on time and on budget. Contrast this to Irish National Children's Hospital, which is almost a decade late and whose budget has ballooned from a project of 400 million euros to over 2.2 billion euros, making it the most expensive children's hospital in the world and indeed one of the most expensive buildings in the world. The lack of leadership for a project that had a lot of potential to be very innovative was a critical failure factor, as well as the failure of the multiple parties to coalesce around a shared vision and a shared culture.

Leader Philosophy and Performance

There is a close symbiotic relationship between the philosophy of the leader and the culture of the organization in relation to the performance of the organization. While there are many archetypes of leader philosophy, we identify two contrasting archetypes to illustrate the difference and the critical impact of the leadership espoused and lived philosophy. The most impactful leaders are those who lead by example.

Envision, Enable, Empower to Excel (4E) Leadership Philosophy

A 4E Leadership philosophy is critical to innovation success. This is an approach which allows people to operate at the top of their license, to express their creativity and commit their full energies to innovation. The first requirement is to **envision**. Leaders must have a vision or at least an idea of a vision. President John F. Kennedy is such a supreme example of a leader creating a compelling vision which motivated the alignment and energy of the entire U.S. to "before this decade is out to send a man to the moon, and bring him back safely, not because it is easy but because it is hard." Leaders without vision are almost always found out, but often an entire organization is impacted before this may be discovered.

Lucy Nugent, CEO of Tallaght University Hospital (TUH) in Dublin is an example of a leader who envisions a better future and her vision of a 'hospital without walls' has enabled TUH to expand services into the community and to locations well beyond its headquarter 33 acre site.

High performance leaders **enable**. This is about giving people the means, resources and authority to do something. This is about making something possible. A colleague of ours, David Fleming of Intel Innovation Centres, suggested the following sentence: "Intel, it is not just what we make, it is about what we make possible." This subsequently became the tagline of a significant marketing campaign about Intel "enabling" broader innovation. While ensuring proper processes are in place is key, in our increasingly digital world, enabling means giving employees the latest information and digital tools to allow everyone to be successful.

John Shaw, general manager of Carelon Global Solutions Ireland, is an exemplar of the 4E philosophy while Prof. Eeva Leinonen, President of Maynooth University, is an excellent example in the higher education and public sector.

John Shaw's philosophy is to "think limitless" – this is a key characteristic of Open Innovation 2.0 where there is an important transition from thinking inside the box to thinking outside the box to a scenario where there are no boxes. In less than two years, John grew a team of over two hundred and fifty AI experts in Limerick, Ireland and created a portfolio of over fourteen products which his team are developing and which became highly profitable. One example of a product is an AI tool which quickly summarizes a person's medical history to allow much faster claims processing. Carelon has won multiple national awards in Ireland, including best place to work and a National Invest in Ireland award.

Lucy Nugent in TUH established a core innovation team with full time staff, an innovation centre in the hospital lobby and a budget to enable the full creativity of the TUH staff to be unleashed. The third step is to **empower**, which is to give someone the power or authority to achieve something. A leader cannot be a single point of failure or stage gate in making innovation decisions. By hiring the right people and building trust, an empowered team of innovators can deliver much better performance than a portfolio of innovations carefully managed and stage gated by a central leader.

Steve Jobs famously said at Apple, "We don't hire smart people to tell them what to do, we hire smart people to tell us what to do."

When leaders create a compelling vision and then enable and empower their teams to innovate and deliver against the vision, people and performance **excel** and people are often much happier. Who wants to work for a despot control freak who is looking over your shoulder all the time and approving every step?

Martin's decision to return to Maynooth University in 2023 was prompted by his conversation with Prof. Eeva Leinonen, a full nine months before she moved from Australia to take up her post as the incoming President of Maynooth University. Eeva spoke about her vision of, among other things, the intersection of digital/data and health to drive radical improvement and her inclusive leadership style. When Eeva took up her post as Maynooth University President, she did not immediately impose her vision on the university but instead through an enabling process of strategic workshops, empowered staff across the university to co-develop a new vision and set of strategic priorities for the University. The result was an ambitious, credible and achievable strategic plan which had broad support from university staff.

A key outcome of a 4E leadership philosophy is a workforce who work because of commitment instead of compliance.

Noel Kelly former CEO of Anam who led their turnaround and successful acquisition by Croation Unicorn Infobip, is another exemplar of the 4E leadership philosophy at work. Noel Kelly together with his son Darragh Kelly, acquired Anam, a mobile telecoms company when they were close to bankruptcy and through a process of envisioning, enabling and empowering his team, they were able to excel and turnaround the fortunes of the company. Anam developed technology that filters billions of message on behalf of more than 80 mobile operators across and creates value by increasing the revenue per user by for example by reducing the amount of spam. Noel set a vision of 7 x 24 Innovation for the company and reached out to several external people to help achieve this. Martin had the honour of working with Noel, chairing Anam's Innovation Board whilst a colleague ex UCD Engineering Professor Gerry Byrne chaired the R&D board. Taking a 'platform' approach and also completing an innovation assessment and driving Innovation improvement actions particularly through engaging the full organization of over 50 employees, the fortunes of the company were transformed. In November 2018 Anam won the International Export award in the Deloitte FAST 50 and built strong relationships also across the global ecosystem by taking a leading role in the GSMW Wholesale agreements and Solutions Group (WAS) and particularly in their conferences. In May 2021 the turnaround of the Anam was completed with the announcement that they were acquired by the Croatian Unicorn Infobip. The broader Anam case study is shared in Appendix D of this book.

Martin's personal philosophy is "Dream, Dare, Do" and this also became the mantra of Intel Labs Europe, discussed in the appendices as a case study in our book. This is about envisioning a better future, having the courage to do it and then just doing it. Many organizations have adopted the British SAS motto "Who Dares Wins."

Command, Constrict, Cancel to Control (4C) Leadership Philosophy

In stark contrast to the 4E philosophy there is the 4C philosophy which is all about command and control. We may have all experienced these kinds of environments in our working lives, unless we have been very lucky, and we probably all recognize that these were very unpleasant places to work and that invariably they deliver very sub-par performance. Both Esther and Martin have mostly experienced leaders with 4E philosophies, but unfortunately both also have experienced 4C leaders and because of how difficult this can be, felt it important to discuss this here so readers can recognize it and take action or, more importantly, so leaders of this ilk can too, and change. It should not be confused with the Socratic method of questioning, which, while it can appear argumentative or be uncomfortable for some, is designed to probe more deeply for greater understanding and is especially valuable for difficult concepts or principles.

In Martin's previous workplace, the HSE strategy organization was such one place where the 4C leadership philosophy dominated. HSE or Health Service Executive is the organization responsible for overseeing and providing the national health service to Ireland. Although blessed with many outstanding and passionate clinicians, the HSE was an organization where hierarchy and position power dominated and efforts to drive innovation and change were strongly resisted. For example, in Martin's first strategic meeting with two leaders of the HSE strategy organization, after his organization was transferred into the strategy division, the head of strategy openly declared, "Curley, you should expect plenty of friendly fire from me." and then followed a litany of poor interactions with CEOs of Digital Health SMEs that Martin had invited to present their solutions to the strategy directors. Such an opening gambit is about as far as one can get from a generative 4E culture.

To **command** may mean to dominate from a superior height or to give an authoritative order. We may all have worked in organizations where commands are given and often these are valuable, as someone must give direction for an organization or an ecosystem. However, when those commands come from people who are barely competent, have no vision, or value power above all else, the consequences can be very poor. In Ireland, despite record investment and record addition of headcount, healthcare performance deteriorated spectacularly with average waiting lists almost doubling over a period of 6–7 years and so-called "trolley" headcounts of people waiting in emergency departments also more than doubling. There was a catastrophic failure in strategy, whereby spending was increased by eight billion and fifty thousand employees were added to the health service over a period of eight (2016–2022) years but the net result was just an aggregate composite output increase of 3.5% (Irish Department of Health, 2024). Nobody in business could countenance such an appalling return. While the consequence in business of poor performance may mean reduced profits and revenue or even bankruptcy, the consequences in health are almost certainly increased numbers of deaths and increased suffering. This outcome is a consequence of the 4C leadership philosophy and behaviour exhibited by the two senior directors, who steadfastly refused to approve any new innovations and attempted to dismantle the robust working digital innovation governance that was already in place.

The failure in strategy not only likely resulted in avoidable deaths but also Ireland's poor ranking in Health systems financial performance. A paper published in 2024 by the Irish Department of Public Expenditure stated that health spending per capita in Ireland was 28% higher than the average in the OECD (Organisation for Economic Co-operation and Development) countries despite Ireland having the youngest population (Wall, 2024). The report said that "health spending more closely resembles a country with a much older population" and that twenty one percent of government spending went on Healthcare.

To **constrict** means to make narrower, especially encircling pressure or also to inhibit or restrict. Again, some of you readers may have experienced similar actions in your employment. For example, again in the HSE, the HSE Strategy directors refused to approve any digital health living labs from an available and approved 5 million euro budget, instead choosing to invest an alternative 7.5 million euro into a controversial single application called the high performance visualization platform.

To **cancel** means to neutralize or negate the force or effect of another. Again sadly we draw upon the HSE for an example of this behaviour.

To take a whole new approach to co-designing and co-innovating a new electronic health record for epilepsy patients, a new procurement process was developed and agreed by the HSE Digital Transformation director, the director of procurement and an agile outside legal firm, Philip Lee., Previously the HSE had a very poor record with procuring and delivering EHRs and despite it being official government policy to introduces EHRs since 2004, less than 10% of the country's hospitals had EHRs by 2020.

A new approach was needed. Martin working with Prof. Colin Doherty, a leading epilepsy consultant at one of Ireland's leading hospitals, St. James Hospital, co-led the initiative. Des O'Toole and Aileen Killeen led a design-thinking process which included consultants, nurses, technologists and patients to develop and iterate a specification for a new EHR. A procurement information meeting was held and over 45 expressions of interest were received. Subsequently, seven organizations and consortia presented working prototypes of solutions. The solutions presented were of high quality with three particularly strong solutions presented. Quickly the solutions presented by IBM and Salesforce were selected and co-funded to advance to build a minimum viable product. A joint presentation was shared at the Irish National Digital Health Conference held in Tullamore in 2022 to great acclaim. There was tremendous excitement as this solution could help provide much better care and also replace an old epilepsy EHR system which was creaking at the seams and very expensive to maintain. The co-lead of the project Prof. Colin Doherty, now head of the Trinity College Medical School said the system was 100X better than the incumbent system. And then everything ground to a halt as the HSE strategy directors issued an edict that the project be stopped, with the sole reason that HSE "does not do development." No further progress has been made and epilepsy patient records are still maintained on an old system which is no longer fit for purpose and expensive to maintain. Because of this decision, and blockage of most of the digital innovation portfolio, Martin decided to accelerate his decision to leave the HSE.

To **control** means having the power to direct people's behavior or the course of events. It also is a means of limiting or regulating something or the restriction of an activity.

This desire to control again may have been experienced by some of our readers. Even in organizations which have leaders that exemplify 4E philosophies, there may be pockets of 4C philosophy and behavior. Esther and Martin both agree perhaps the most fundamental requirement for successful leadership is the ability to envision. If you do not know where you are going, how can you get anywhere.

Illinois Governor J.B. Pritzker gave some potential insights into the potential drivers of 4C behaviors in his commencement address at Northwestern University in 2023. The video of his address has been viewed all over the world. He famously said, "to find the idiots, look for the cruellest person in the room." Leaders who are threatened by bright, motivated and often younger employees can resort to bullying and intimidation. Both Esther and Martin agree with Governor Pritzker's opinion, but ask why these leaders cannot adopt the Steve Jobs mindset of looking for new hires to provide direction. It should lead to a win-win situation for all. If you experience behaviors that stem from 4C philosophy, do not be deterred but seek help from 4E leaders. However if 4C leaders predominate, you may have to leave your organization, as Martin ultimately left the HSE as there was an unwillingness at the highest level to tackle continued toxic behaviors. Soon after a 4E leader, Bernard Gloster was appointed as CEO of the HSE and one of his first actions was to shutdown the strategy division and removed the strategy directors from their positions. 4E leaders are action oriented and do not tolerate mediocrity and poor behaviour.

Power or Empower

Perhaps the most critical question that leaders need to ask is whether the motivation for their role having is to have "power" or whether they want to "empower." More developed leaders adopt a "servant leader" approach. Servant leadership is a management philosophy which puts serving others above all priorities and where leaders bring humility and humanity as key characteristics of their leadership style. Rather than a command-and-control style as exemplified by a 4C philosophy, servant leaders focus on creating a high trust environment where their teams can thrive and deliver the highest impact possible. Servant leaders value the intrinsic worth of employees as much as the extrinsic worth of their teams. Leaders that will inevitably fail are those that value the possession and use of power above purpose, progress and people. Servant leaders ask "what can I do to make you successful, what do you need?"

Designing a Culture

In the past, culture has been very much a black box and designing a culture has been very much a black art. Often in organizations, much of the culture is actually hidden and not very explicit. Gustavo Razetti has made an important intervention and breakthrough in publishing his culture design canvas and developing a methodology for co-creating a culture for success. Razetti's culture design canvas includes 10 components aligned with what he calls the ABC of culture, alignment, belonging and collaboration.

1. Values
2. Purpose
3. Priorities

4. Behaviors
5. Decision Making and Governance
6. Meetings
7. Norms and Rules
8. Rituals
9. Feedback
10. Psychological Safety

We could devote most of the book to talking about designing your culture to enable success but instead we recommend that you go to Gustavo's website (Fearlessculture.design) to learn more about how to co-design a culture for innovation success. By way of example Martin has included an example of the culture canvas for his HSE Digital Transformation and Innovation organization.

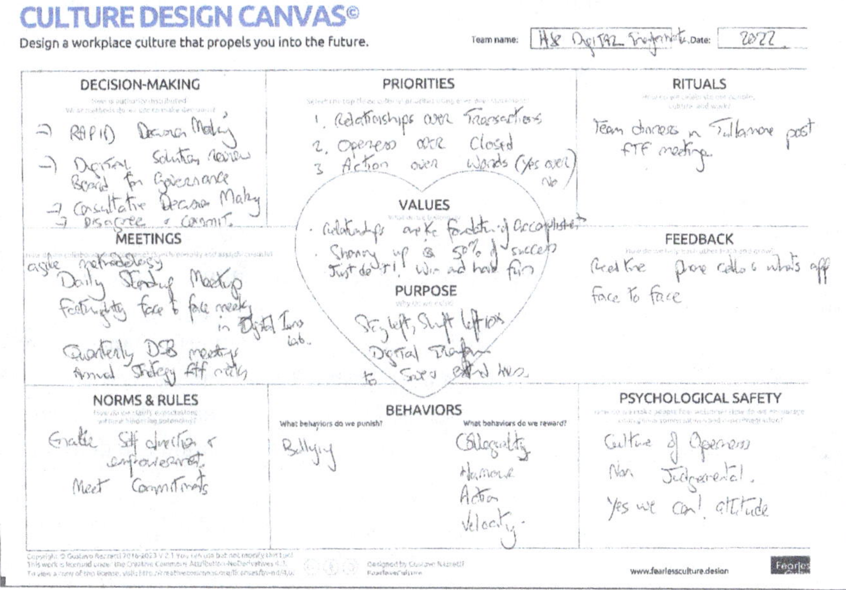

Figure 10.1: Culture Design Canvas – HSE Digital Transformation.

This example (Figure 10.1) shows the critical cultural components that helped make the HSE DTI team very successful despite very significant resistance from senior administrators in the Irish Health Service. The HSE DTI won the ICC/Mind the Bridge Global Public Sector Innovation Award and jointly won a significant amount of Irish Healthcare Awards and Healthtech Ireland awards together with co-collaborators. This example shows that a high performance culture can deliver extraordinary performance. When COVID struck, this high performance culture enabled HSE DTI to deliver significant innovations including remote monitoring solution for COVID patients which kept thousands of patients out of hospital, a real-time respiratory measurement solution which gave up to 12 hours notice of a patient desaturating and was deployed to twenty-three hospitals in four months and an ePrescribing solution which went live after two and a half weeks and transformed how the prescription system worked nationally in response to COVID.

Critical components were shared values and a governance mechanism, a key governance mechanism the digital solutions review board, comprising clinical, technical and administrative leaders which approved the solutions roadmap and a "seek forgiveness" mindset which allowed immediate prototyping to begin once minimum required criteria were met. The use of a daily standup meeting was critical in ensuring a fast tempo of innovation and a bi-weekly face-to-face meeting at the national digital health innovation lab, situated in a working hospital were critical. Additionally, regular team dinners resulted in a high trust, highly connected team.

Summary

Culture is critical to success. We recommend use of the culture canvas to explicitly co-design the culture of your innovation team or broader organization for success. Leadership philosophy is critical to ensuring high performance innovation and we recommend to hire for and to coach for 4E leaders who envision, enable and empower other people to excel. This is servant leadership at its best. Paraphrasing JFK, 4E leaders ask "Ask not what your organization can do for you, but what you can do for your organization".

Chapter 11
Open Innovation 2.0

Innovation is not a sausage machine. You don't get it by a plan imposed by government and you can't measure it just by counting patents or even just spend on R&D. It is all about creative interactions between science and business. —George Osborne, UK Chancellor of the Exchequer, 2012 Speech to the Royal Society

Open Innovation 2.0

Introducing Open Innovation 2.0

Open Innovation 2.0 or OI2 for short, is a natural evolution of open innovation (introduced in Chapter 7), first conceptualized by Henry Chesbrough in his seminal book, *Open Innovation*, in 2003. The definition and codifying of OI2 has been underpinned by a decade of practice and research in a joint collaboration between the European Commission, Intel and the Innovation Value Institute at Maynooth University and many other parties. Anchored by Directorate General (DG) Connect in Brussels, each year an annual Open Innovation 2.0 yearbook was published by the European Commission detailing and showcasing the best of Open Innovation 2.0 practice across the world. The Irish Presidency of European Union (EU) marked the official launch of OI2 as a new paradigm and methodology with a launch conference held at the Dublin Castle Conference Centre featuring contributions from EU Commission President Jose Marie Barroso, EU Research Commissioner Maire Geoghegan Quinn, Intel CTO Justin Rattner, Irish Enterprise Minister Richard Bruton, Drucker Society President Dr. Richard Straub and many others. At the conference, a joint paper by Martin and the EU Commission's Bror Salmelin (Curley and Salmelin, 2013) introduced the new paradigm and the key characteristics of its practice.

OI2 is based on principles of integrated collaboration, co-created shared value, cultivated innovation ecosystems, unleashed exponential technologies, and focus on adoption. An extraordinary feature of OI2, where people and organizations collaborate and co-innovate across an ecosystem, is the potential for exponential returns. This key value proposition of OI2 to have the potential to deliver exponential outcomes, which are multiplicative rather than additive, means it is particularly important and relevant for societal or so called "wicked problems." In this chapter we will discuss the key design patterns that underpin OI2. The book contains a number of case studies where the results achieved were expo-

https://doi.org/10.1515/9781501507335-011

nential using the OI2 approach, the Innovation Value Institute, Intel Labs Europe and HSE Digital Transformation and Innovation.

Three Macro Trends

There are three macro trends that are enabling the emergence of this new Innovation paradigm: Moore's Law, mass collaboration and sustainability

Moore's Law

Moore's Law is the principle that computing power can be expected to double every two years and that this improvement is delivered at less or equal cost. Both Esther and Martin have had the privilege of working for a long time at Intel, the company co-founded by Gordon Moore. It is safe to say that Moore's Law has been fundamental to incredible societal and economic growth – through enabling technology, business and societal innovation – which has been achieved since Gordon Moore's published his seminal paper in 1976.

Mass Collaboration

Mass collaboration is the second macro theme that underpins OI2. The European Internet Foundation (EIF) released an excellent report, "Our World in 2025" (EIF, 2009), saying that although there were many new trends, the macro and dominant trend for society for the new few decades will be mass collaboration. The EIF is a collection of forward-looking Members of the European Parliament, MEP), including Malcolm Harbour, that proposed: "The paradigm we propose is that of a world driven by mass collaboration – enabled by the ubiquitous availability of highspeed, high-capacity digital communications networks, systems, tools and services, connected by the Internet." The EIF talked about the potential of purpose driven online collaboration with the goal of driving economic or social goods and effects. Mass collaboration – the power of platforms.

Sustainability

At the macro level, sustainability is a shared social goal to enable people to coexist on our planet for a very long time. Sustainable development is about using resources to meet human development needs and goals, while also preserving and protecting resources for future generations. Increasingly, it has become a critical political, economic and societal concern and objective. Digital technology is a resource which can enable much more intelligent and sustainable use of natural resources by processes such as automation, substitution and virtualizations.

When the three macro trends intersect, they create the conditions for sustainable intelligent living, a place where humans can realize their optimum potential with efficient and effective use of natural resources, ensuring natural resources are protected by generations to come.

Achieving sustainable intelligent living is the ultimate goal of OI2.

The Evolution of Innovation

The discipline of innovation is constantly evolving and we are now at a strategic inflection point where a new mode of innovation has emerged, which transcends innovation at an organization level where innovation is achieved through mass collaboration often on a mass scale. We call this paradigm, Open Innovation 2.0 as introduced above. As Newton said, “If I can see so clearly, it is because I stand on the shoulder of giants” and so we acknowledge the seminal work by Henry Chesbrough and his seminal book, *Open Innovation*, published in 2003. Martin’s book, co-authored with Bror Salmelin, presents Open Innovation 2.0 or OI2 for short as the new paradigm for prosperity and sustainability. OI2 also had a broader goal to achieve sustainable intelligent living, progressing society while respecting and preserving natural and other resources for future generations.

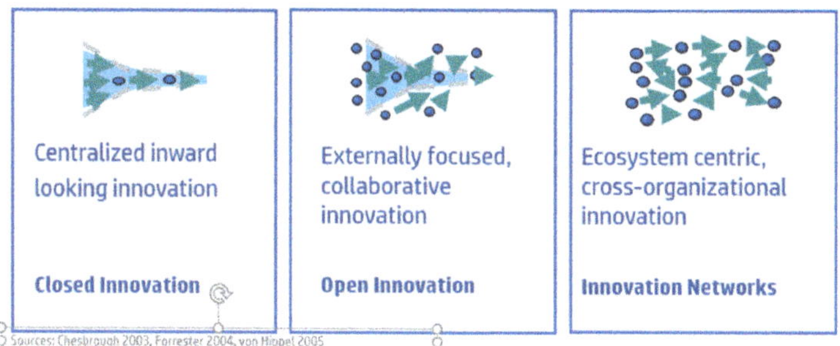

Figure 11.1: The Evolution of Innovation.

Figure 11.1 shows how Innovation has evolved and how the center of gravity for innovation is now in innovation networks. In the past it may have been a long innovator in a Bell Labs that drove a new innovation. Then the phenomenon of co-innovation became increasingly important and Intel Labs Europe, for example, created co-labs with companies like BT, Nokia and SAP. The collaboration between BT and Intel has been very helpful in advancing the paradigm of software defined network whereby by standard Intel or other servers replaced custom silicon in routers and other networking equipment.

However, increasingly the unit of performance and competition is moving to the ecosystem. These ecosystems are often underpinned by platforms, with the most valuable companies in the world now being platform companies such as Microsoft, Google and Meta (formerly Facebook).

Open Innovation 2.0 at the Meta Level

At the core of OI2 is an ecosystem. We define an ecosystem as "a network or coalition of resources, competencies, potential, energy, commitments and promises to realize a shared profitable and sustainable future" (Andersson, Curley and Formica, 2010). We can do so much more when we work together towards a shared purpose. OI2 is about driving structural changes in an industry or ecosystem which are far beyond the scope of what any one organization or person could achieve on their own.

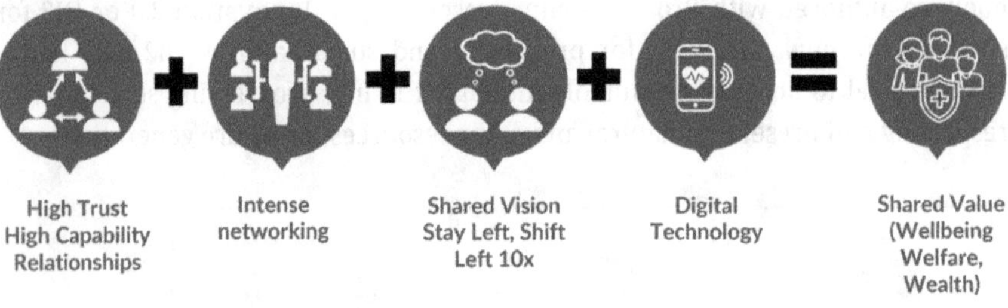

Figure 11.2: Design Characteristics of Open Innovation.
Source: M. Curley.

There are four meta level design characteristics of open innovation 2.0 as shown in figure 11.2.

High Trust, High Capability Relationships

Kark Leric Sveiby famously said, "Trust is the bandwidth of communication" and Stephen M.R. Covey relates this to how quickly teams can respond and deliver results since "change moves as the speed of trust" (Covey 2006). People give and receive trust differently sometimes depending on their life experiences. Some give trust immediately and others build trust over time through observation and experience. When people with high capability and trust come together, they move quickly to overcome barriers, solve problems and innovate together to deliver value.

Intense Networking

At the core of open innovation, intense networking is a socioeconomic process where people interact and share information and ideas to recognize, create, and indeed act upon business or societal opportunities. OI2 creates synergies and indeed network effects.

While working in China for the first time, Esther was asked by the factory leadership team to develop a workshop on networking. This was a big surprise since her perception was that the culture in China was one of outstanding networked relationships and she didn't think she had anything valuable to teach. However, her colleagues in Shanghai had observed her rapid inclusion, as a latecomer to the assembly and test factory start-up team, and noticed networking behaviors that they admired and wanted to know what else she could offer them. So, based on her experience as an introvert that knew how key it is to be connected, she delivered a workshop that changed people's behavior. To give some examples: "Never sit with someone you already know in the factory cafeteria. Sit at a different table every day. Introduce yourself and learn about new people every day." Intense networking and knowing who to reach out to when needed always shrinks the time to value and "many hands" do "make light work."

Shared Vision and Share Values

When mutually interdependent actors work together towards a common goal, extraordinary things can be accomplished. Anthropologist Margaret Mead said, "Never doubt that a small group of committed citizens can change the world, in fact it is the only thing that ever has." Big changes often happen at the edges. While organizations such as the United Nations or the World Health Organization or even governments are great organizations, they are designed for stability and incremental innovation, so we should not expect the source of breakthrough innovations that change the world to come from them. The big changes and innovations will come from groups of committed, passionate and capable individuals.

Digital Technology

The fourth essential ingredient for OI2 is **digital technology**. Digital is the catalyst, the raw material and often the glue and material which is the finished product of a new innovation.

Digital is about the use of intelligent computing, communications and storage technologies to deliver new solutions. Digital is also a mindset, about using core enabling technologies to transform customer and user services, about redesigning organizations or industries and about trying to deliver nonlinear outcomes from new solutions. We are at a really unique point in history where we have multiple disruptive technologies all showing up at the same time. Cloud computing, 5G Networks, artificial intelligence, blockchain, and social media, etc. are all fusing to create a chain reaction of change. This is a perfect storm.

The output of OI2 is **shared value**. We define shared value as improved **welfare, wellbeing and wealth** and these are key characteristics of the destination of sustainable intelligent living. The concept of shared value was initially espoused by Porter and Kramer (2011) and it is about reconceiving the intersection between society and corporate performance and contribution, seeking win-win outcomes, and being profitable through solving big, wicked problems.

We define welfare as the health, happiness and fortunes of an individual, groups or indeed a society. We define wellbeing as the state of being healthy, comfortable and/or happy.

We define wealth as an abundance of valuable possessions or money or having plentiful supplies of a particular resource. It is having enough to share with others.

In OI2 we seek to deliver solutions which not only generate profit but materially deliver improved welfare and wellbeing of people and organizations. This is not only desirable but very achievable. A digital health solution, for example, which prolongs healthy life expectancy, and which is also very profitable for the innovation provider is a great win-win result for all.

Six Key Design Patterns for OI2

A design pattern is a general reusable solution to a commonly occurring problem (Vaishnavi and Kuechler, 2007) and it is often manifested as a description or template for how to solve a problem that can be used in many different situations.

There are six core3 design patterns which underpin OI2 which are shown in Figure 11.3. The platform provides the foundation for the OI2 initiative. Platforms exist at several levels. A software or clinical platform is a foundation upon which other parties can build complimentary products and services. To drive a structural change in an industry, we also need an industry platform with a shared vocabulary where ecosystems players can network and exchange and advance ideas. This function is increasingly being called "systems convening" and it is a role that Martin and others, such as New Zealand's Ryl Jensen and Dr. John Sheehan of Blackrock Health in Ireland, have been using in the digital healthcare industry.

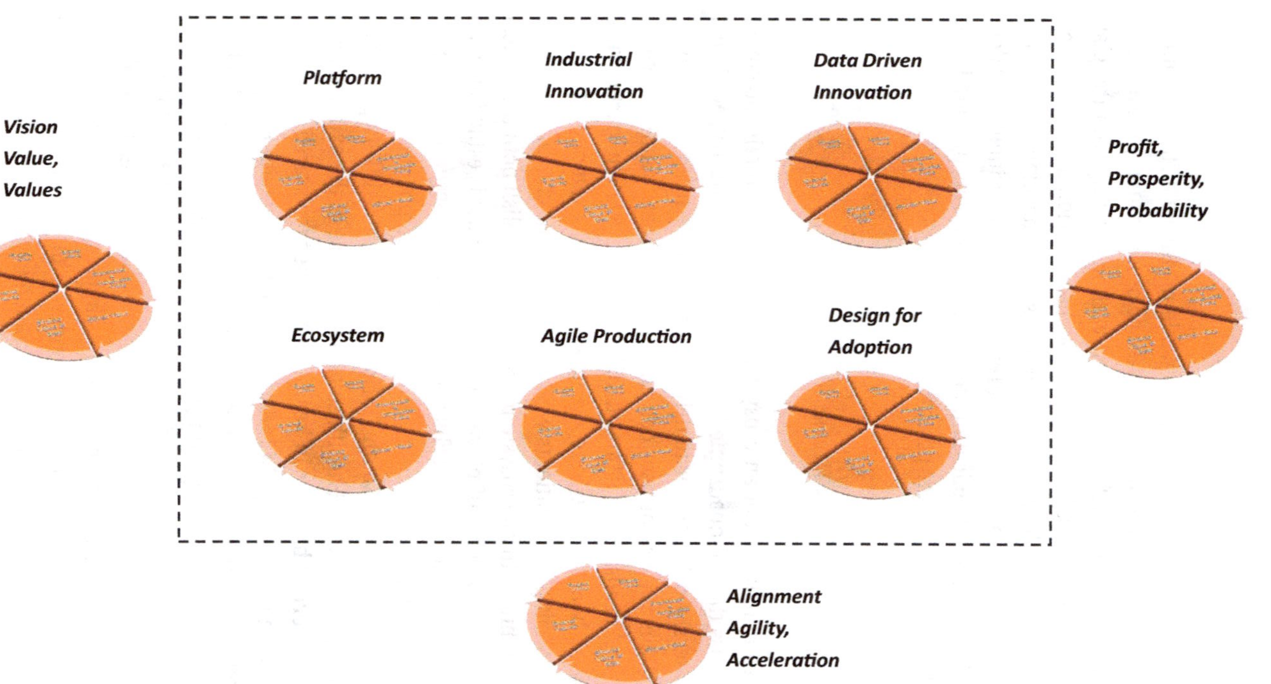

Figure 11.3: OI2 Design Patterns.
Source: Martin Curley.

Platforms

According to Amrit Tiwana (2014), "Platforms enable massively distributed innovation on a scale that exceeds conventional service or product supply chains" and they share risk and costs and benefits associated with innovating with the platform with all ecosystem partners. When there is a shared vision and shared values, the process of emergence leads to new solutions being developed in a common direction using a mixture of self and shared interest among interdependent partners. For small players and application developers, platforms provide lower entry barriers and also create a larger potential customer pool.

Ecosystem

We have introduced a definition of an ecosystem earlier where the involvement of players from across the full quadruple helix (government, industry, academia and citizens/customers) work together to drive seismic change in an orderly way. A key feature of OI2 is the use of user-driven design to create solutions which meet or exceed users' needs. "Digital" has democratized innovation, particularly in industries such as healthcare where we now see many examples of digital health innovations coming from patients with unmet needs or clinicians who see better ways of doing things. In an ecosystem we need to establish both the critical connections and the critical mass of players. Once critical mass is established, an autocatalytic or network effect can be achieved with adoption occurring very rapidly. Professor Matt Mullarkey has been teaching about the phenomenon of binary adoption at the University of South Florida. During the COVID-19 pandemic we saw big bang adoption of digital health solutions because of the extreme need and also because the normal blockers in health were either too scared to come to work or distracted with other things. In Ireland, Martin worked with Eamon Costello of PatientMpower to introduce a remote monitoring solution for COVID-19 patients, using Bluetooth-enabled pulse oximeters; the first working prototype was available with 48 hours of COVID-19 arriving in Ireland. Within five days the solution was being prescribed by two major hospitals in Dublin and was available all over Ireland within a few weeks of the pandemic happening. This solution kept many thousands of Irish patients with mild-to-moderate COVID symptoms out of Ireland's hospitals, keeping scarce hospital beds available for the sickest patients.

Emergence is such a crucial concept for successful OI2. Emergence is a self-organizing, ecosystem-wide order that arises both from a master vision and plan (such as Stay Left, Shift Left-10X in Healthcare) AND the interdependent actions of players, acting from both shared interest and self-interest, continuously adapting to new technology innovations and to what others are doing in the ecosystem (adapted from Dougherty and Dunne, 2011 and Chiles et al., 2004)

Industrializing Innovation

The third key design pattern is industrializing the innovation process. This is essentially building a manufacturing process for managing the innovation pipeline and the adoption of innovations across an industry. This is likely driven by the keystone player who acts both as the innovation pacemaker and the ecosystem orchestrator. In the Irish health system, the HSE, the national health provider acted as the pacemaker and the orchestrator. Each quarter Martin would host a cross ecosystem Digital Academy Forum (DAF) where the latest strategy and update were presented and leading innovators in the digital health ecosystem would present new solutions and updates to educate and excite the ecosystem and establish new connections. Multiple new connections and options were created in a series of physical and virtual DAFs. The use of a standard living lab charter template and a four-stage process for managing innovations through the pipeline was an important step in professionalizing and industrializing the innovation process. Working with John Joyce's agile development team in the Irish midlands, a novel innovation pipeline manager product was developed so all innovations being developed and trialled across a network of living labs could be managed and reported on. Having visibility of all the innovations in a single place was very helpful in deciding what innovations should be prioritized and accelerated.

Agile

The use of Agile methods is the fourth design pattern of OI2. Agile is an integrated set of practice which has come to the fore since the launch of the Agile Manifesto in 2011 and its goal is to improve the efficiency and particularly the effectiveness of software development to provide solutions which have lower risk and better meet the needs of users and customers. Agile is about iteration and incrementalization that focuses on delivering a working product quickly. At the core of Agile is the OI2 concept of user-centered design where close and frequent collaboration with users and customers helps ensure solutions meet needs better and seize on opportunities that developers may have blind spots to. The emergence of low-code and no-code solutions means that solutions can be developed much faster and often more cheaply than using conventional programming approaches.

Designing for Adoption

Michael Schrage of MIT famously said, "Innovation is not innovators innovating, it is customers adopting." According to the OECD, 20% of the value of innovation comes in the creation process, but 80% of the value comes from the adoption process. The authors have found that adoption part of the innovation equation is often the most difficult as discussed in Chapter 5. In OI2 there is a pattern which looks at different aspects of an innovation to maximize the chance of adoption. If an innovation is compellingly better than an existing solution, then the chance of adoption become much higher.

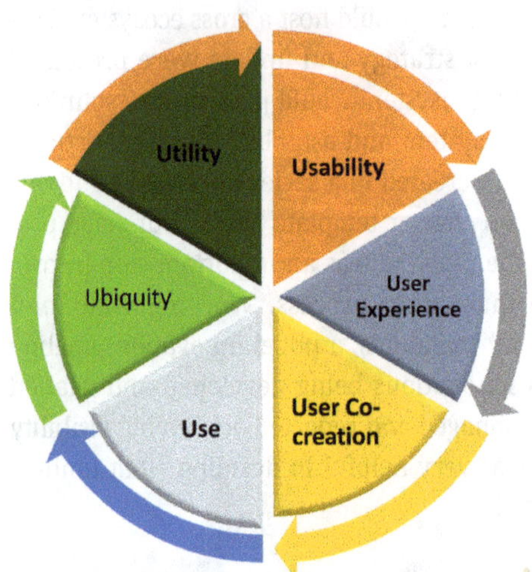

Figure 11.4: Designing for Adoption.
Source: M. Curley.

You can find more details on the pattern designing for adoption in Martin and Bror Salmelin's book on OI2, but the simple idea is to look at six different, but important, aspects of adoption (see Figure 11.4).

The first is utility – what is the usefulness of the solution and what value will it bring? Second, how useable is the solution? An innovation might provide a great solution but if it is too difficult to use then it will not be adopted. What is the user experience like? This is critical. Involving users in the innovation process to co-create the solution will ensure a solution that better meets their needs.

The Norden Bombsight introduced during the second world war by the U.S. Air Force produced much better accuracy and replace a lengthy manual procedure for airmen, so it was rapidly adopted to help deliver more accurate bombing.

What is the need or use of the solution? A very complex problem may be being solved, but if there is just a small total available market (TAM) then it is unlikely to be viable to drive development or adoption. Finally, what is the potential for ubiquity of the solution? The Hoover vacuum cleaner became so ubiquitous that the name Hoover became part of the English language. With the internet as the distribution channel, products from companies like Meta, Microsoft and Google have become ubiquitous.

Data-Driven Innovation

Perhaps the most valuable of all the design patterns is that of data-driven innovations, but this is likely the last pattern to be adopted as all of the other patterns are in place and fully functional. When products or services are digitized, the opportunity to create a digital twin of the product and services exists and even to create a digital twin of the entire ecosystem. In some industries such as healthcare, which are so information-intensive, data-driven innovation creates the opportunity to find and reverse disease early and to build learning health systems. The financial services industry has long been a great exponent of data-driven innovation, generating great profits but sometimes to the detriment of the economy and society, by burying risk, sight unseen in products, and aggressively marketed to uneducated consumers. When data-driven innovation is used on an industry-wide scale in the name of a noble purpose, such as extending health life expectancy in healthcare, the results can be extraordinary.

Ultimately, when these six design patterns are used in unison, the assets and resources in an ecosystem are aligned, amplified and accelerated to deliver the shared purpose of the ecosystem with faster progress, higher profits and higher probability of success.

Open Innovation 2.0 and Directed/Guided Open Collaborative Ecosystem

An open collaborative ecosystem (OCE) is a new form of business structure and collaboration about which Gastaldi et al. (2015) wrote, "a deep mutation in the competitive landscape occurred with the birth of the open collaborative ecosystems (OCEs)." The authors and others, such as Eric van Hippel (Baldwin and von Hippel, 2011), of MIT have been discussing OCEs for the past decade or so.

OCEs are based on principles of integrated collaboration, co-created shared value, cultivated innovation ecosystems, unleashed exponential technologies, and extraordinarily rapid adoption (Curley and Salmelin, 2013). In an OCE there is continual realignment of synergistic relationships of people, knowledge and resources for both incremental and transformational value co-creation (Ramaswamy and

Gouillart, 2010). Gastaldi et al. make the case for academics as orchestrators of continuous innovation ecosystems, and at the Innovation Value Institute in Ireland we have created a **Directed** OCE with an overarching innovation agenda **"Stay Left, Shift Left – 10X"** (Curley et al., 2020) as the shared vision. When an OCE is innovating in the same direction the alignment drives acceleration and amplification of results with multiplicative rather than additive outcomes.

OCEs encapsulate a new form of primordial soup as depicted in Figure 11.5, whereby in healthcare for example, multiple actors from policymakers to politicians to practitioners to patients to physicians and pharmacists all work together to envision, innovation and create a better future. The coordinated and cohesive actions of multiple different players across an ecosystem can create a metamorphosis of the entire ecosystem.

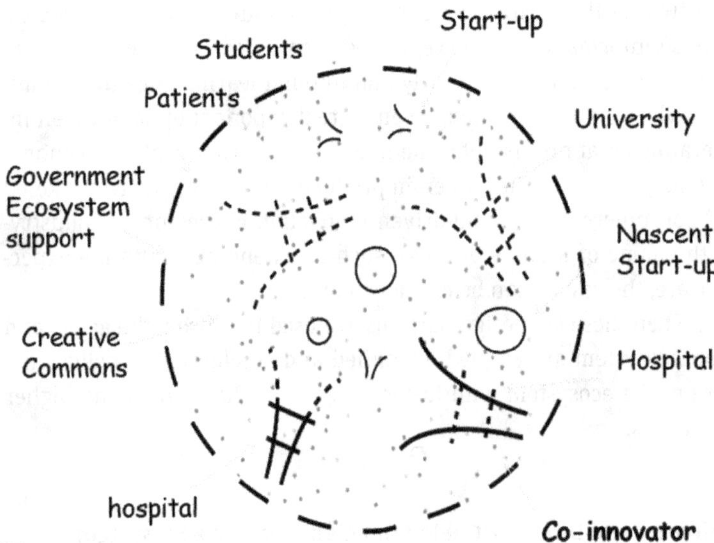

Figure 11.5: Open Collaborative Ecosystem.
Source: M Curley/B Salmelin

The promise and potential of OCEs is that they can and do deliver exponential results. In the appendices we share several case studies illuminating how and what exponential results have resulted in real-world settings such as Intel Labs Europe, Ireland's Health Service and the Innovation Value Institute at Maynooth University.

Exponential and Non-Linear Output

OI2 ecosystems are all about strategy, synthesis and synergy. First, having a strategy that is linked to achieving a shared vision and creating shared value. Second, a synthesis process leveraging the collective intelligence of all the players in the ecosystem. And lastly, achieving synergies whereby the interaction of multiple organizations gives rise to an output far greater than the sum of the parts. The combination of these three S's can lead to extraordinary success.

Rivira Yuana and Eko Praesatio and team (2021) from the Bandung Institute of Technology in Indonesia have done a remarkable study on the characteristics of innovation in an OI2 ecosystem and created a comprehensive simulation model to study the effects and benefits. They found the more parties involved in an open innovation collaboration; the less risk capital needed. They found in their simulation that companies involved in OI2 had significantly higher revenues as shown Figure 11.6 and achieved faster product development. In a top-notch paper, they discuss how relationships, network effects, ecosystem culture and technology all combine to help deliver mutual accelerated shared value. They share that IT and digital investment is a must for revitalizing companies. They conclude that open innovation is important to a company's growth engine and after two years of participation in open innovation activities, it contributes substantially to a company's revenue growth.

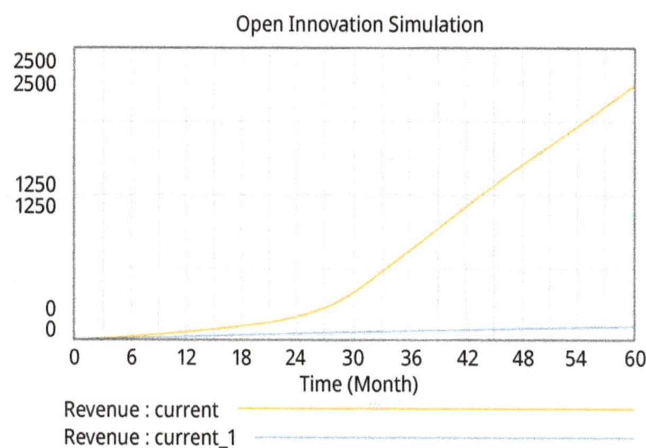

Figure 11.6: Exponential Revenues from OI2 Simulation source Yuana et al. (2021).

Yuana et al. have created a comprehensive model of an open innovation ecosystem, and we recommend a comprehensive investigation of their seminal 2021 paper as you seek to design your future OI2 ecosystem.

Living Labs

An essential part of OI2 initiatives is often the use of living labs. The use of living labs is a methodology for co-creating and introducing radical innovation in a way that is non-threatening, reduces risk and creates innovation using an agile incremental approach, living labs are constructs where research and innovation in real-life environments is performed using iterative and Agile processes where users and customers are put as the focus of the innovation efforts and help co-design evolving solutions to ensure solutions deliver real benefit and are sustainable. In healthcare, a living lab could be located in a hospital, primary care center, a home or even in an ambulance. Living labs often involve the four dimensions of the quadruple helix (government, industry, academia and citizens/ users.) as depicted in Figure 11.7. Living labs often use design thinking and are focused on co-creation, rapid prototyping, testing and iteration and provide a roadmap for scaling and diffusing innovations to create value for all stakeholders involved. In IVI there are five phases to the living lab process – exploration, proof of concept, demonstrator, broad adoption, international adoption. While living labs can be considered a testbed, a real differentiator is that users are not considered observed subjects in the testing process, but are co-innovators contributing to exploring and shaping of emerging ideas and solutions and radical concepts and breakthrough solutions.

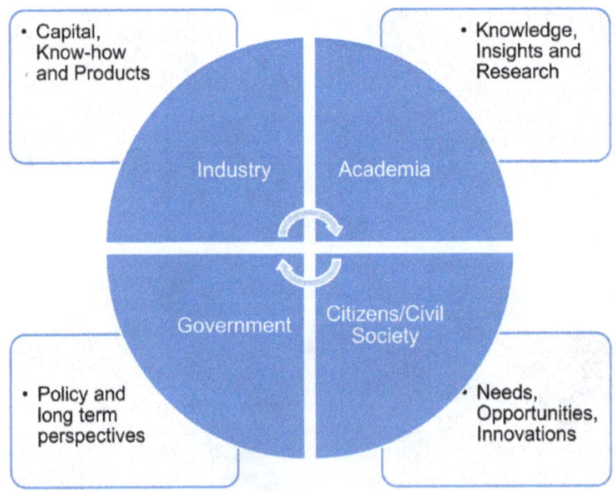

Figure 11.7: Living Lab Components Source Salmelin and Curley.

AI as an Innovation Partner

The emergence of ChatGPT creates a whole new opportunity for dramatically enhancing the productivity and creativity of Innovation initiatives. ChatGPT and other AI chatbots such as Microsoft's Copilot enable human like cerebral interactions based on large language models.

The ability to synthesize, analyze and summarize large volumes of information in seconds is a formidable capability which will change the pace and productivity of innovation engagements. An innovation workshop for the American Irish Medical Summit in August 2024 at Microsoft's Garage in Dublin used Copilot as an active innovation partner to help co-create an actionable digital health innovation plan using the collective intelligence of all participants.

Microsoft Copilot itself says that it can amplify Human ingenuity, such a clever statement.

Generative AI (Gen AI) is another gamechanger for Innovation. Gen AI creates original content in response to prompts, based on learning from patterns and structures in the relevant training data. Gen AI can produce new text, videos, images and software code. This game changing capability is enabled by breakthroughs in transformed based deep neural networks and we are just at the beginning of an amazing era of AI enabled innovation.

Summary

We posit that Open Innovation 2.0 or OI2 is both a designed and natural evolution of the innovation process, whereby mass collaboration driven by a shared vision and shared values can deliver exponential results. We discussed the six key design patterns that underpin OI2 and the importance of a shared vision to drive structural change in an industry. The rapid adoption of AI in Innovation will turbocharge Innovation efforts and rapidly accelerate progress. In the appendices we share three examples of successful OI2 initiatives which have driven structural change and extraordinary results. We can help shape a sustainable and prosperous future and OI2 provides a paradigm and core design patterns which can help us achieve that, together!

As we wrap up this final chapter in what we hope will be a valuable collection for the reader's innovation journey, we point to Intel founder, Robert Noyce, who often said, "Go out and do something wonderful." Let's do that!

Appendix A
Case Studies in Innovation

Innovate and integrate to work smarter, not harder. Dan Etheridge, Intel corporation

There are few reports of the challenges faced when identifying, developing, and diffusing innovative IT capabilities. At the same time, there is an abundant supply of white papers and news releases that report on successful IT innovations. Thus we know where to go, but not always how to get there.

We offer two case studies focused on the process of delivering innovative IT capabilities that, tracked over time, show the path from vision to reality with incremental innovation adoption leading to better and better services. Sometimes it is important to look back and track from the origin how we arrived at the innovative and groundbreaking services of today.

- The City of Westminster is a borough in the heart of London and its governing authority has for many years been intent on providing excellent public sector services. Could IT innovation be used to better support mobile service providers such as parking enforcement officers? Security and policing and other public services could realize a significant digital innovation investment payoff.
- At most large companies, significant resources are dedicated to supporting IT systems and often the support is provided by help desk personnel. Could some of the support features be expedited by IT systems and, if so, what are the candidate' support functions?

Wireless Westminster, Part 1

"I believe that it is time for us to push our service excellence to the next higher level," Peter Rogers stated. Rogers, Chief Executive of the City of Westminster was discussing strategy with the leader of the council, Sir Simon Milton in early 2003. Sir Simon Milton was clear that the council needed to develop a vision for the city that delivered world class services efficiently and effectively on a 24/7 basis and needed to embrace the many constituent communities – residents, businesses, and visitors. This later became enshrined in the Council's "one City" vision.

The City of Westminster

The City of Westminster is a borough in the heart of London. It is home to over 200,000 residents and also to the seat of government for the United Kingdom. Embedded immigration under metropolis of 17 million people, The city supports a diverse population far greater than it's resident population. Over a million people join the city's resident's on a daily basis. Commuters flood into

https://doi.org/10.1515/9781501507335-012

the city to work in its many businesses. Theaters and concerts bring many more, the visitors to London seek out destinations in the city such as Hyde Park, Piccadilly Circus, and Buckingham Palace and the right spots of the West End.

Vision

Rogers asked for input from two of his staff, Vic Baylis and Graham Ellis. "To be aligned with the council's agenda we should seriously consider a vision for actions that will reduce crime," they all suggested. "We know it's the problem, most often caused by criminals who are not residents of our city and also by the opportunities created with the many late night activities in London's West-End. And, we must work to coordinate our needs with the police force that is London -wide."

"With fewer police on the beat, we have a scarce resource that is not capable of being everywhere." Rogers added. "We need to find ways to support the policing resource and to increase its efficient use. And, the police are one of several street based resources. We have parking wardens, noise monitoring personnel, and people who inspect and provide permits for various functions of the City."

"Mobility is a common element, isn't it?" Baylis observed. "We should focus our thinking about how we can reach out to our mobile workforce. Direct them to where they are needed, and provide them with access to information when we are on the streets of the City. We have an opportunity here to allow them to work more smartly and to enable them to spend more productive time out and about in the City rather than wasting time traveling back and forth to the office."

Innovative Uses of Information Technology

One of Westminster's elected Councilors, Ian Wilder, was first to see the potential benefits of using wireless technology to support the council's vision. It was Wilder who saw wireless technology in its infancy in the United States and introduced Rogers and his team to the pioneering work being done by Intel at the time.

"When mobility is an issue, wireless networking comes to mind," Vic Baylis said. "The demonstration systems we observed at Intel certainly suggest that this technology is robust and ready to deploy. And, industry analysts agree that wireless TechNet work technologies will be increasingly important in the future."

"Imagine what we could do if we could deploy our camera capabilities without cabling," Ellis suggested. "The sheer cost of cabling is an inhibitor to that effort. With the wireless network, we could deploy cameras to an event or to the street within hours. That would be a massive improvement on the months it was taken to redeploy cameras on the existing fixed line network. This would result in far more dynamic and flexible enforcement model across the City not only for the council but with its key enforcement partners, notably the police."

"If we plan for sufficient bandwidth and work with the right partners to construct a truly citywide network, then we might also be able to 'piggyback' other applications and other access to our City's residents and businesses," Baylis added.

"A Wireless Westminster," Rogers concluded. "Please take this vision and build it out further. We'll need a small proof-of-concept prototype system. We will need to examine two primary benefits, one for improving security with wireless cameras and the other to optimize the mobility and productivity of our staff on the streets. And, our Council will certainly want to see a robust business case."

The Prototype

One way to test a technology's maturity is to see what others have learned. Westminster City capitalized on Intel's investment in an IT Innovation Centre in Dublin, Ireland. A visit to the center provided Rogers and his team the opportunity to see wireless technologies in use. Intel had recently developed and delivered a campus-wide wireless infrastructure and it was adopted rapidly. Intel studies of the business benefits of mobile computing enabled by wireless networks showed significant paybacks in monetary terms.

"Our experience with mobile systems enabled by wireless networking leads us to believe that the technology is robust and ready for deployment. We began our prototyping about two years ago. Uptake by operating groups at Intel has been quite rapid." said Martin Curley, Intel's Director of IT innovation.

Usage Models for the City of Westminster

"The visit to Intel's Innovation Center was helpful." Peter Rogers noted. "It's time to think more specifically about our mobile workforce. We want to avoid the tendency to create solutions looking for problems. What we need is a winning application an application for which there is a compelling business case."

For Westminster one winning application might be the administration of parking in the City. There were approximately 250 street wardens walking beats in the City. The blend of wireless cameras that could be moved around without any fuss and more intelligent deployment of the street wardens offered a new parking enforcement model across the City. It meant the number of street wardens could be reduced because camera surveillance allowed monitoring from a central site and with the right technology provided this prospect of streamlined administration and reduced handling costs of all the *back office* processes.

The flexibility of wireless technology also offered new opportunities to relocate the administration center to cheaper parts of the country. Baylis saw the main benefit being a very different model for City management, moving away from traditional *beats* or inspection regimes to one which facilitated intelligent deployment of street-based resources across all public services.

"Let's assume we have an incident at Leicester Square," Vic Baylis said. "With our cameras, our street based staff can receive real-time streamed images on their hand-held device, assess the situation in dispatch appropriate resources – City guardians, wardens, or the police. We can see whether weapons are involved and whether anyone is injured."

Prototype Phase 1. This thinking led to a first prototype, designated phase 1A by the innovators. The single key component of the overall vision, wireless camera technology, was deployed at Soho Square and tested for 30 days. To reduce risk and to begin building strategic partners the City of Westminster teamed with Vertex, an outsource provider of IT services. Intel Corporation, Cisco Systems, Telindus, and Capgemini also joined the team. By December 2003 the first prototype had delivered a technical success. The City could reliably monitor activities with cameras supported by a wireless network. And the functionality was so useful that the system was not turned off.

Prototype Phase 1B. Following the successful technology proof of concept experiment, the City of Westminster launched a more complex second prototype, which was designated phase 1B. Phase 1B was a three-month experiment that extended beyond camera technology to see how well other applications could be supported for different City workers and services. These other applications were aimed at suppressing crime and anti-social behavior, monitoring noise, supporting mobile devices for parking wardens and food and licensing officers. Vic Baylis and the Council's IT organization proposed to expand the system to include a wider Soho area, and importantly, two large housing estates, Lisson Green and Churchill gardens. Both were under the management of the Council's arms-length housing company called City West Homes.

Westminster and Vertex IT strategists also wanted to move to understand the integration of camera technology and mobile devices to provide an integrated street management system. And, most importantly Westminster needed to generate empirical benefit estimates to support a business case for full deployment. The phase 1B prototype investigates benefits for mobile workers as well as the wireless cameras. Would an investment in citywide wireless networks improve the City's ability to serve its residents businesses and visitors?

The Business Case

For the City of Westminster, the outcome metrics of interest are not the typical business value indicators such as profitability or market share growth. Along with cost reduction, a significant improvement in the quality of public services was paramount to enhance its reputation as a world-class city. At the top of the list of concerns was safety. In late 2004 the City Council considered an expenditure of £1.293M to fund the phase 1B prototype period to justify the investment benefits were identified in four areas:

- Improved public security and safer street environments. Remote monitoring cameras would target anti-social crimes such as flyposting, refuse dumping, and illegal parking.
- Increased productivity and efficiency of mobile workers. Licensing inspections could be recorded electronically and transmitted to the City's IT systems instantly.
- More intelligent deployment of street-based staff leading to new models for integrated street management across a broader range of services. Scarce resources could be directed to areas of need with information gained from the camera network and transmitted to the mobile staff.
- Opportunities for residents. The same network that supports City services would also be available to residents to move to online transactions with the council particularly in the area of *payments*.

The £1.293M would be the City's contribution to a total cost of £ 2.527M. The City had stakeholder contributions and government innovation grant totaling £ 1.527M. Vertex offered to contribute half the cost of developing the new applications and City West Homes contributed funds to extend the phase 1B to include some of its properties.

What should the City of Westminster do?

Wireless Westminster, Part 2

Following council approval, phase 1B was launched within 12 months. As hoped, British Telecom (BT) joined the collaboration, which reduced the cost further.

BT's interest was in piloting for-fee Wi-Fi services and the phase 1B experiment was a perfect test bed.

"We're seeing some challenges," Vic Baylis told Graham Ellis as they monitored deployment of the system. "Development of the mobile applications for food and licensing offices is lagging, and we won't have findings in phase 1B. Camera liability is another concern. And how different functions share the camera resources is more difficult than expected."

"Remember that we are the first City in the world to experiment on this scale," Ellis replied. "And the problems that are emerging are surmountable. Our phased approach to prototyping covers these snags."

Phase 1B went into operation in between December 2005 and March 2006, the projects team monitored the indicators previously selected against pre-determined baselines. That is, the team compared *before and after* surveys of residents and local businesses.

Business Process Changes

"Many of our expectations are being realized," Peter Rogers told Vic Baylis and Graham Ellis as they poured over the empirical data. "Look at this. For parking, the blended *camera-and-street warden* model resulted in less wardens on the street being more productive than before. One side benefit which had not been anticipated was markedly less violence against the wardens from aggrieved motorists. Sound monitoring, while not fully deployed is also showing potential to help in the enforcement of our licensing conditions for restaurants, pubs, and clubs."

"Experiments on our housing estates through City West Homes were quite revealing," Baylis pointed out. "City West has concluded that the wireless technology, per se, does not positively impact their ability to respond for needs for repair. They found the cameras useful, and expect them to be a substantial means of combating crime and disorder at their housing estates." This was endorsed by the residents of Lisson Green estate, who noticed a big improvement in their quality of life.

City West and other parts of the Council also concluded that they would need to change their business processes to gain more benefits from the wireless systems. This has been a common finding over the years when new technologies and existing business processes come together.

Organizational Changes

The UK Home Office recommended that phase 1B findings requirement disorder reduction be anecdotal, rather than statistical because three months does not provide enough data to uncover robust trends. Meanwhile, the effects of the wireless capability did change the way in which the policing agencies did that. First responders were more able to move to trouble spots and the wireless camera capability was directly associated with 58 incident responses, 15 arrests, 5 victims taken to the hospital, and 20 police stops where police question suspects at the scene.

Societal Customer Changes

In April of 2006, Peter Rogers looked over survey results for residents in the phase 1B areas. "Residents reported that they were pleased to see more parking attendants," he noted. "And, in fact we have reduced the number of attendants during that time. Our efficiency in this domain increased in the visible way. Our service was also seen as fairer– a good result when paying fines is never going to be popular."

"Residents also report that they feel safer with more cameras in place," Graham Ellis added. "More residents are noticing the cameras and also noticing that we have more of them. Except for some early concerns with health risks and wireless networks, acceptance in the community has been positive."

"While residents see the cameras, they don't know that the Wi-Fi is there." Observed Vick Baylis. "In one way this is a good thing because they shouldn't have to care about what technology is based on, but in another way we have a really exciting opportunity to engage our residents and communities about what else this technology can do and what other applications we can run over a wireless network."

Vision Revisited

"The results of our 1B prototype are quite encouraging," Peter Rogers declared. "And, with these experiments, we have a much sharper vision of how wireless and available technologies fit our needs."

The updated vision served four different stakeholders, business, community, visitors and importantly the council itself. The vision was broad ranging covering many topics including economic development, digital inclusion, safety, efficiency and reputation.

Based on the success of 1B, in November of 2006 the council approved a plan to build a wireless network across Westminster in collaboration with Vertex, Capgemini, BTM, and Telindus. Westminster was the lead UK City in BT's Wireless Cities Programme and in the Autumn of 2007, BT completed a square mile of wireless coverage cross the West End of London.

The first wave of Westminster's private network was completed and the City of Westminster successfully using wireless CCTV for wider enforcement including parking. Other mobile wireless applications quickly followed on the back of a pioneer competition that was launched to engage residents, neighborhoods, businesses, schools and visitors in coming up with additional ideas.

Fast-forward to 2024 and we can see the Wireless City of Westminster has grown from the vision of Sir Peter Rogers into one that has now expanded beyond the City proper, into peripheral residential areas and then across the UK, with BT coverage now reaching 97% of UK citizens. Digital cities have become ubiquitous across the globe and digital modernization plays a role in attracting investment. It has become cities competing against cities to attract the likes of Intel when in the past it was countries competing for investment. The latest wave of digital innovation in cities has arrived with technology like NB-IOT being deployed and AI being used for a variety of value-added activities including:

- Image recognition for license plate numbers
- Facial recognition to: alert for security breaches in safe enclaves, identify at-risk individuals or track missing children, identify repeat offenders and proactively dispatch police presence
- Identify tampering with City equipment
- Track and coach PPE compliance by City workers – alert for accidents or "man-down" incidents
- Alert for security incidents – luggage left in public or on public transportation
- Alert for street flooding and events requiring utility personnel intervention
- Water leak detection in infrastructure
- Fire prevention

With the 2024 BT launch of their NB-IOT Network there is further promise for innovation and optimization in many sectors including the City processes that still rely on people's intervention, utilities, construction, event management, and even agriculture.

Digital innovation has led to dramatic changes in cities across the world.

Innovative eSupport at Intel, Part 1

"These projects, however clever, are just not lasting over time," Dan Etheredge reflected as his next assignment was on the horizon in 2003. In his role as an IT support engineer, Etheredge had built a half-dozen or more software tools to expedite product support. Scripts, help files, FAQ's – a collection of useful information for IT's customers and for IT support personnel. However, as assignments shift these homespun materials and tools fall into disrepair and disuse.

"Let's do some thinking about how support systems could be improved," Etheredge said to Mark Storace, then the technical manager of the IT group's call tracking system. "We need an overall framework to understand how support systems fit together. Independent point systems simply aren't effective."

In reviewing the literature in search of new ideas stories, Storace and Etheredge came across a Forrester Research (1999) model that offered both a view of the state-of-the-art in eSupport systems and also a view toward the future. That diagram is shown in Figure A.1. Influenced by internet-working Forrester analyst, Paul Hagen postulated that a new and more efficient tier would soon appear in customer support systems.

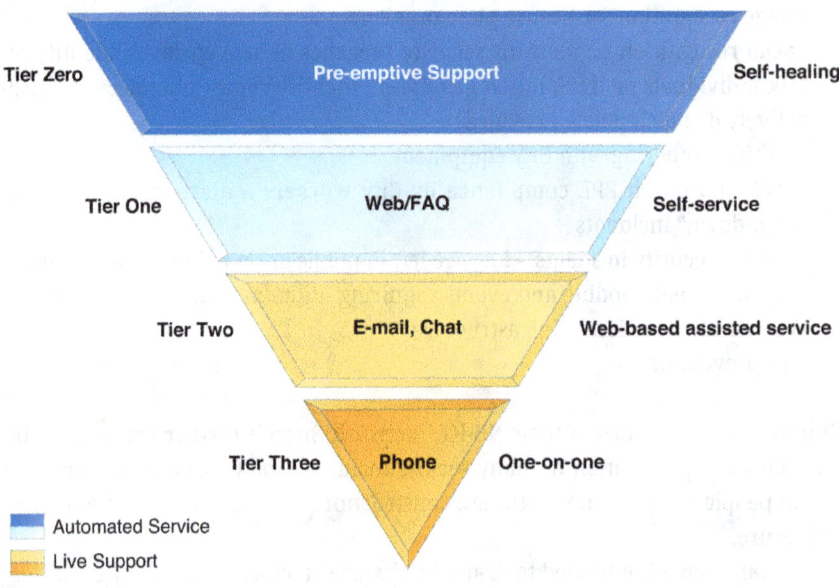

Figure A.1: Four tiers of support.
Source: Forrester group 1999.

A Vision is Born

"This Forrester model makes a lot of sense," Etheredge said to Storace. "The Tier 3 method for helping customers is a one-to-one contact between a support person and the customer, and this tier identifies the most expensive way to provide support. Tier 2 solutions are web-based and allow a support person to address the needs of several people at once using e-mail or chat capabilities. Tier 1 solutions provide FAQ and knowledge bases so that customers can find solutions for themselves. And to these three layers Forrester has added a fourth; Tier 0 methods preempt the need for support by automatically healing the problem, perhaps without the customer's knowledge."

"Forrester's inverted triangle highlights two important issues," Storace pointed out. "First, progress up the layers demands increasingly sophisticated technology and a deeper understanding of potential support needs. However with each step upward the cost of support decreases dramatically. This is most clear with Tier 0. When we broadcast updates across a wide audience of customers, we are preempting a multitude of recurring problems."

"There are two other important lessons here." Etheredge added. "These support systems have broad applicability. If we were to develop a well-engineered infrastructure for our IT support needs, that infrastructure would be available to others at Intel who provides support of different kinds. HR has a multitude of needs, for example, that are primarily inside Intel. Purchasing has another set of needs, both within Intel and including Intel's trading partners.

"The second lesson is that vendors in the packaged software market are gaining maturity. We have been building point solutions because we had to. It's time to consider whether we can buy and configure systems rather than building custom solutions. While the content of our support systems will be unique, the requirements for storing, retrieving, and delivering support are likely to be very similar to other enterprises."

Formalizing the Effort

Polly Herron joined the effort in 2004 and took responsibility for evaluating the business implications of the technology alternatives. She worked with Dean Wehsels, who focused on the technology itself. Intel IT is methodical about its traces of software products and Herren and Wehsels applied their methods to available support system solutions.

"We focused on the functionality currently available in the products we evaluated," Herren explained. "What might be available in the future was set aside.

We also examined the ability of products to integrate with existing Intel systems, for example, our ActiveDirectory and our personnel databases. The goal is to find a software platform that was ready to be configured to our needs and to avoid software platforms that would need to be customized."

"We also asked for reference accounts and spoke with other IT organizations in larger companies like ours. Then, when we narrowed the field to two companies, we invited them to spend a week with our support organization and demonstrate how their products would be configured to our needs."

"We performed a careful analysis of how an eSupport system would be deployed at Intel and what business benefits we could expect to counterbalance the costs of development and support. We needed to consider how the system aligned with the companies overall strategy as well," Herren concluded.

All of this work culminated in a business case for an investment in a third-party software product providing innovative tools to automate customer support. The business case looked at gains in efficiency as tasks are migrated higher in the Forrester's four-tier model.

"The bottom line of our business case was that, over time, we could increase the quality of support while at the same time reducing head count," Herren explained. "Moreover, again over time, we could re-invest some of the resources freed up by our more efficient eSupport systems, and with technology improvements, we could strive to move our support procedures higher in the Forrester tier model."

Calling for the Question

In 2003, the eSupport project sponsor, Ron Hurle, took the teams plans before Intel IT's Business Process Steering Committee and to Doug Busch, Intel IT's CIO. As Hurle explained it, "When it comes to providing customer support, we are currently in a stovepipe mode. What we need is a single solid eSupport strategy." eSupport was positioned as part of a larger Intel IT goal: to reduce the unit cost of delivering current IT services by 50 percent and to free people and dollars for investments in new competitive capabilities.

The eSupport team forecast a 35% reduction in the cost of support achieved in the second year.

Should Intel IT invest in eSupport?

Innovative eSupport at Intel, Part 2

With endorsements from management oversight committees and from IT's CIO Doug Bush, the eSupport project was approved and the project kicked off in early 2004

"We involved our customers early in the process," Herren explained. "We knew that user acceptance of new support systems would be a critical factor. We put measures in place to track system usage and to locate areas where support was weak or unsuccessful. We built marketing material to inform our customers what we plan to do and when to expect changes."

Initial Development

To plan an order of attack, the eSupport team inventoried existing support technologies and identified which new capabilities would make the most difference early on. The vendor providing the packaged software, *SupportSoft* also provided advice on which capabilities to launch first.

ServiceDesk "In the initial deployment the ServiceDesk capability was called *Ask-Tech*, and that was a mistake." Herren explained. "It was a hard word to say and to hear. A lot of people thought the system was *Aztec* and so early on we renamed the overall eSupport system to be ServiceDesk, and that worked much better. *ServiceDesk* is a multi-channel user portal that is the gateway to our eSupport capabilities."

Tier 1 *KnowledgeCentre* was the first capability delivered by way of ServiceDesk. This capability provides IT customers with ways to help themselves via *tell me, show and do it for me* scripts. They were created in the format of FAQs with the "do it form me" scripts also having embedded links to solutions that customers could directly execute to resolve known issues on their PC's themselves.

Tier 2 LiveAssist (or CHAT, as it was initially named) was deployed next and provided real-time access to service personnel using a web-based instant messenger interface as an alternative to phone support. In the Forrester model, this capability is at Tier 2. With both parties online, service personnel could show the customer where to find necessary information or provide it directly. More importantly, one support person might well be helping two or three people at the same time, which is a gain over the one-on-one characteristic of telephone support.

Tier 0 The third capability deployed was *PC Health Check*. This capability was a Tier 0 application capable of preemptive, automated support. As the day implies the system was capable of identifying and repairing problems with personal computers. "Since the potential leverage was so great for this service," Herren said, "we spent extra time thinking about how we might best deploy it."

Diffusing PC HealthCheck

In 2006, the eSupport team prepared to launch *PC HealthCheck.* To make sure that their customers were aware of the new offering, the team planned a series of roadshows. eSupport teams visited Intel sites in Chandler, Arizona; Beaverton, Oregon; Swindon, UK; Dublin, Ireland; and Chengdu, China.

"We provided demonstrations of *PC HealthCheck* and supplied our customers with fact sheets and a success story white paper," Herren said. "We also listened carefully to what our customers had to say about *PC HealthCheck* in particular, and about IT support resources in general. Several customers had ideas about how we might improve *PC HealthCheck.* Adding the capability to verify security settings with one of those ideas."

Effects on Work

"eSupport improved employee career paths for our group," Herren reported. "We still utilize people delivering advice by phone, but now those people can move upward to provide Live Assist Chat. With more information being captured about support requirements, there are now positions for support analysts – people who study the support process and seek out incremental innovations."

Also, as a global company, Intel has a multitude of employees for whom English is a second language. Providing self-help in a written form and interactive help as a chat session actually eases the way for the non-English speaker. This applies to both support personnel and the IT customers that they serve.

Customer Consequences

"As we continue to study our customers' satisfaction, we found that our self-help systems are empowering. When we provide the right information and the ability to search for what is needed, people are able to serve themselves. This is the Tier 1 approach." Herren explained. "In fact, I have a report from a customer:

> *ServiceDesk is an awesome resource! I was having an issue and I typed in a few words and performed a search. I scanned the returned results of voila! Your tool provided the info I needed! Saved me much time! Love this tool! Thanks!*

Business Value Consequences

Measured results in 2007 show that the eSupport functions require 14% fewer people – a direct cost avoidance benefit. What is more difficult to measure is the time saved for IT customers who can more quickly, proactively, and efficiently maintain their PCs and remain on task with their daily work.

An Evolving Vision

As eSupport capabilities continued to roll out, Etheredge and Herren revisited the original Forrester figure that had jumpstarted their thinking.

Most importantly, as Figure A.2 shows, they added a tier on top: Tier −1. This tier reminds us that higher quality IT solutions will have fewer support needs. Now, there are three tiers that represent automated solutions in the six-level model. At the bottom of the funnel, Etheredge and Herron added a layer they called *Tier 4, 5, 6*. "We realized that there were other more highly paid people in the support organization and beyond. From time to time, we need engineering or vendor consultants to help us solve a support problem," Etheredge explained.

Layers and Dollars

"Our eSupport vision has a direct relationship to the cost of handling support incidences," Herren pointed out. "It could easily cost $50.00 to $100 or more for resources in Tiers 4, 5, and 6. This would be a resource we might put to the task of writing or updating a script for our self-help library. With phone support, the cost drops to perhaps $15 to $20 per incident. By leveraging support staff with e-mail and web technologies we might be able to reduce the cost of an incident to $1.00 to $5."

"What's dramatic is that the lifecycle costs of automated systems may be a nickel or a dime per support incidents. Providing our customers with ways to take care of themselves results in enormous cost avoidance," Herren concluded.

Epilogue

One of the goals for the eSupport project was to make a robust customer support system available to others at Intel, and it took hold. Intel product groups reused the eSupport infrastructure, primarily to store and develop their knowledge bases. Etheredge and Herron's vision that the eSupport technology platform would be useful for other activities at Intel turned out to be true.

As we fast forward to 2024, we can note that the scripts and knowledge bases that were created for the eSupport system became enablers in order to move into

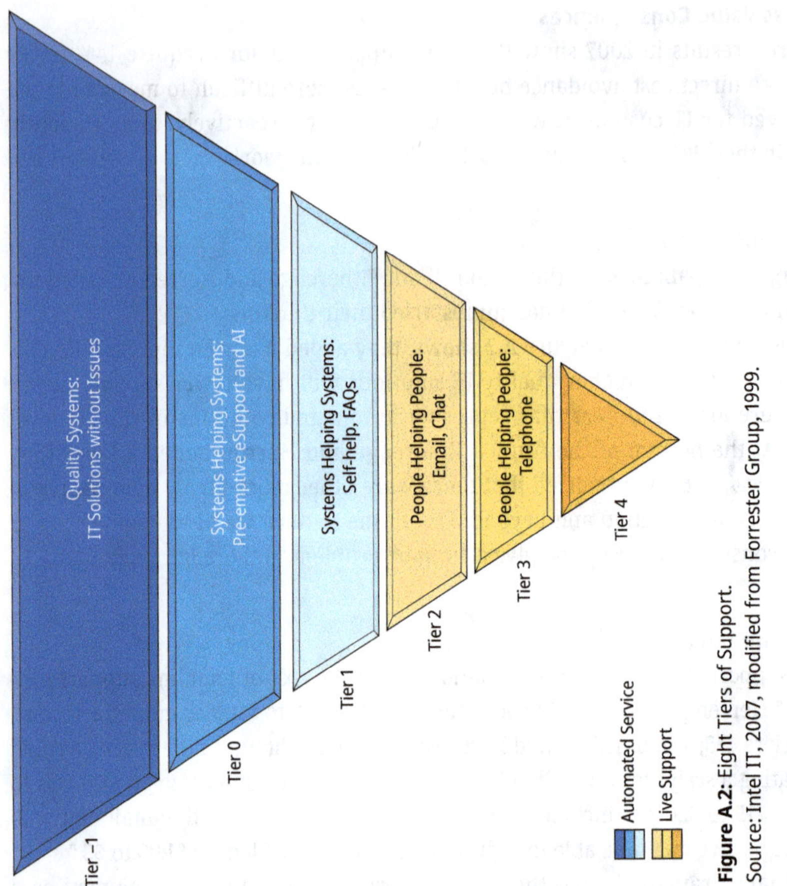

Figure A.2: Eight Tiers of Support.
Source: Intel IT, 2007, modified from Forrester Group, 1999.

AI-based solutions for chat. With the advent of AI large language models, and natural language processing, it has become standard to allow chat bots to be the first line of service for eSupport. Often solving problems or dispositioning the next line of support when needed, all while the user may not know they are not chatting with a human. The cost for incident support has now approached $0. This fits in to the Tier 0 model shown in Figure A.2. Moreover preventative or self-healing systems have become routine in the background, both preventing and solving problems for the IT user invisibly. Tier −1 has become the norm.

Appendix B
Innovation Assessment Tools

This appendix contains a modified version of Intel's innovation self- assessment tool. We removed some Intel-specific language in the interest of making the tool more useful to a general audience and more easily adaptable to the reader's situation.

A thorough discussion of the self-assessment process, guidelines for scoring within the categories the tool evaluates, and how to develop action plans based on its results can be found in Chapter 6.

Also included at the end of this appendix is a matrix that provides an example of how to incorporate innovation capability maturity in individual performance appraisals.

Self-Assessment Tool

Section 1: Management Commitment

1.1 **Management Involvement** **50 points**	**Examples**
– Evidence of management involvement in innovation	– An innovation strategy has been defined – Our manager discusses and values innovation – Innovation assessment is conducted annually – Team innovation is recognized and rewarded
– Areas of potential improvement	– Management could encourage measured risk taking – Management could set forth an innovation vision – The enterprise could set a corporate innovation goal – Managers and innovators could share decisions
1.2 Communication of Priorities **50 points**	**Examples**
– Evidence of communicating that innovation is equal to other business priorities	– Innovation is mentioned in status meetings – Innovation is on the regular staff agenda – Innovation initiatives and projects are widely reported – Innovation is a part of informal conversations
– Areas of potential improvement	– Include innovation in management walkarounds – Innovation goals could be in department plans – Innovation articles a part of corporate publications – Include innovation activities in progress reports

https://doi.org/10.1515/9781501507335-013

(continued)

1.3 Upward Communications 20 points	Examples
– Evidence that the importance of innovation is being communicated to the team's management	– Innovation is mentioned at every status meeting – Innovation is called out in work plans – Managers endorse the team's innovation plans
– Areas of potential improvement	– More time could be spent on innovation planning – More budget could be allocated to innovation
1.4 Working Innovation Policy **30 points**	**Examples**
– Evidence of the existence of an innovation policy or an innovation strategic objective	– Management is accountable for delivering innovative solutions – Team performance is measured against the innovation policy – Policy is reviewed and updated to a defined schedule
– Areas of potential improvement	– Policy could be used on a day-by-day basis – Additional policies could be useful for new disciplines
1.5 Innovation as a Value **30 points**	**Examples**
– Evidence indicating that innovation is valued by the organization	– We have examples of how innovation is valued – Leaders communicated the value of innovation
– Areas of potential improvement	– Stronger ties are needed between innovation and corporate values – Sharper understanding of benefits is needed
1.6 Resource Allocation **30 points**	**Examples**
– Evidence that shows that resources are allocated for innovation and how they are allocated.	– Three of the team's seven projects involve innovation – One-third of the team's budget and manpower is dedicated to innovation – The team has a roadmap showing future innovation investment areas
– Areas of potential improvement	– More space is needed for innovation prototype testing

(continued)

1.7 Key Innovation Assets Identified 30 points	Examples
– Evidence that key innovation assets are identified and described	– Our team regularly prepares invention disclosures – We systematically review patent options for innovations – Team members have experience with innovation techniques and tools – Our innovation expertise is documented – Innovation tools and equipment are available
– Areas of potential improvement	– A central repository for intellectual property could be helpful – Innovation prototyping tools could be more robust – Online access to innovations resources needed – We could use a dedicated lab for experimenting

Section 2: Business Responsibility

2.1 Organize Staff to Improve Innovation 50 points	Examples
– Evidence that the team is organized to support innovation	– We have a defined process for investigating novel solutions
– Areas of potential improvement	– We measure and track the business value of innovations quarterly – Innovation is an informal process at best – We don't know whether our innovative systems are returning on our investment – Investments are sometimes pet projects and are chosen without proper analysis
2.2 Make Innovative Actions and Results Accountable 50 points	**Examples**
– Evidence of accountability for innovation results	– Innovative projects are managed with standard methods, milestones, and checkpoints
– Areas of potential improvement	– Our innovative projects meet their deadlines – Some projects are cancelled and set aside without review for lessons learned – We often miss milestones for innovative projects

(continued)

2.3 Adhere to Enterprise Standards for Innovation 50 points	Examples
– Evidence that enterprise standards for innovation are used	– We measure ourselves as a level three on our Competency Maturity Framework – We prototype and benchmark to estimate value and determine investment levels
– Areas of potential improvement	– Investment decisions are primarily made in the organization – We need to adapt a Competency Maturity Framework for innovation
2.4 Routinely Assess Innovative Initiatives 30 points	**Examples**
– Evidence that assessment activities for innovation initiatives are routinely assessed	– We report assessment activities on a monthly basis
– Areas of potential improvement	– Our action plans include innovation objectives – Our assessments are informal and irregular – We need guidance to understand how to increase the quality of our innovation skills
2.5 Involve Employees in Innovation Planning 30 points	**Examples**
– Evidence that employees are involved in innovation planning	– We include all employees in "map day" where we plan areas of research and investment – Employee work plans are based on shared organizational objectives
– Areas of potential improvement	– We sometimes assign staff members to projects with little or no input from the employee – We don't leverage employees' areas of special interest
2.6 Plan for IT Innovation Improvements 30 points	**Examples**
– Evidence that improvement plans for innovation are used	– We use gap analysis and link findings to action plans
– Areas of potential improvement	– We seek out customer opinion for our goals and plans – We spend much of our time putting out fires, rather than being strategic and planful – Our plans lack well-defined business value indicators

(continued)

2.7 Discuss Innovation in Meetings and Communications 20 points	**Examples**
– Evidence that innovation activities are being promoted in meetings and communications	– We consult with a marketing and communication person when developing communication – Innovation is on the agenda for most of our meetings – We maintain a website telling customers what's new and next from our organization
– Areas of potential improvement	– We should bring more innovations into the company from other industries and enterprises – We could contribute to the corporate newsletter more frequently

Section 3: Innovation Competency

3.1 Innovation Training and Learning Programs 40 points	**Examples**
– Evidence that innovation training and learning are available and built into HR and OD systems	– Awareness training for innovation is available – Our team can access job-specific training – Innovation is part of IT development plans – Capturing intellectual property is part of our job – Innovation is listed as a competency in job training
– Areas of potential improvement	– Innovation not a part of new hire orientation – We lack an explicit innovation curriculum – There are too few workshops on innovation – Manager training on innovation is lacking
3.2 Innovation Training Improvement Process 20 points	**Examples**
– Evidence of ongoing improvements in innovation training	– Innovation training is updated on an annual – basis – New ideas are folded into the curriculum regularly – Evaluations provide a basis for improvement – Level 1–4 Kirkpatrick evaluations are planned and conducted

(continued)

– Areas of potential improvement	– The scope of innovation training should be broader – We have no measures of effectiveness of training – We should provide feedback on training courses so that instructors can improve them
3.3 Employee Development and Improvement Systems 10 points	**Examples**
– Evidence that demonstrates OD improvement	– We link innovation to our focus on quality skills training is widely advertised and available. – Surveys are used to evaluate employee development systems and for management performance – Innovation training is available 24 x 7 to all shifts and locations
– Areas of potential improvement	– Employee development plans do not include – innovation – Our completion rates are low for innovation training – We should provide feedback on training courses so that instructors can improve them

Section 4: Enterprise Values

4.1 Communicate Enterprise Values 20 points	**Examples**
– Evidence of communication that corporate values include innovation	– We have a clear mission statement that includes innovation – Our corporate values highlight being innovative
– Areas of potential improvement	– We don't have an explicit business vision – While innovation is an enterprise value, it is not integrated with other values
4.2 Seek Customer Input to Products and Services 20 points	**Examples**
– Evidence that customer input is being sought and captured	– We have a web site for capturing customer ideas – Our database of customer ideas is growing rapidly – We include customers in milestone decisions – Our customers know where and how to give input

(continued)

– Areas of potential improvement	– We don't have a consistent evaluation methodology – A small percentage of customers provide most of the input – Assistance center information is not used as an input source
4.3 Utilize Customer Input to Products and Services 20 points	**Examples**
– Evidence that customer input is being used	– A third of our innovations were driven by customers – We maintain a database of customer comments – Ethnographic surveys – We conduct observations of customers to see what is needed
– Areas of potential improvement	– We don't feed complaints into the innovation – process – Many customers are unaware of our interest in input – We could learn more from the use of help systems
4.4 Measure Customer Input to Products and Services 20 points	**Examples**
– Evidence that customer input is being tracked and measured	– We track and report the frequency of customer – input – We proactively seek out input on a semi-annual basis
– Areas of potential improvement	– Response rate for our surveys is only 50% – We focus our customers on services and not products – No point of use input is consistently captured
4.5 Include Innovation in Performance Appraisals 20 points	**Examples**
– Evidence that individual performance appraisals includes innovative accomplishments	– Our appraisal process explicitly identifies innovation – The appraisal process accepts innovation failures
– Areas of potential improvement	– Digital innovation is subordinated to efficiency mostly – Criteria for evaluating innovation are vague
4.6 Track Innovation Systematically 20 points	**Examples**
– Evidence of systematic monitoring of innovation projects	– We monitor innovative projects separately – Innovative experiments precede deployment – We publish an innovation portfolio that includes business dial indicators of success

(continued)

– Areas of potential improvement	– Our efforts are primarily undirected skunkworks – We often fail to reuse an innovation in other situations – We lack a reuse program to reapply assets
4.7 Provide awards for innovation excellence 10 points	**Examples**
– Evidence that awards are used to reinforce innovative performance	– We have an annual award for the best innovation – Excellent innovations are highlighted on our web site – Individuals can nominate others for recognition
– Areas of potential improvement	– Successes are occasionally rewarded within the group – Senior managers are often unaware of our good work – There are gaps in the award process across the organization
4.8 Apply Innovation to the Margin of the Core Business 10 points	**Examples**
– Evidence that innovative projects address more than core business needs	– We allocate resources to non-core innovation – Our management values the importance of innovation throughout the enterprise – We have time and a place to experiment with innovation
– Areas of potential improvement	– Only core business investments are made in innovation – Our teams are territorial and rarely share innovations – Our organization is 100% focused on keeping the business running
4.9 Manage Change and Risk Systematically 10 points	**Examples**
– Evidence that systems are used to expedite change and reduce risk in innovative projects	– It is a corporate value that the status quo is not – good enough – We identify risks for innovative projects and manage those risks – We use pipeline management processes.
– Areas of potential improvement	– Our team often encounters problems we should have anticipated – Some senior managers avoid risk whenever possible – We need a risk management process for innovative IT projects

(continued)

4.10 Conduct Post-Project Reviews 10 points	**Examples**
– Evidence that reviews are used to draw out lessons learned	– Post-mortem review is a part of our methodology – We pay special attention to expected risks, to see whether our forecasts were correct – We revisit previous project reviews prior to launching new projects
– Areas of potential improvement	– We rarely look back at an innovative project – Post-project reviews are more frequent for successful projects – Although we file project reviews, we never put them to use
4.11 Track Ideas, Needs, and Challenges Systematically 20 points	**Examples**
– Systems that are in place and are used to track emerging requirements	– We use a web-based system to capture ideas, – problems, and needs – We observe our customers doing their work on a regular basis – We often host campaigns on specific business process topics to seek out needs and challenges
– Areas of potential improvement	– We have no regular contact with some of our customers – Most of our customer comments are useless complaints – We collect ideas, but rarely take action to use them
4.12 Adopt a Failure Management Policy 20 points	**Examples**
– Evidence that methods are used to extract value from totally and partially failed projects	– Our management demands useful analysis of projects that encounter problems – Our motto is "Don't reinvent the wheel, and also don't reinvent the flat tire." – Our projects are archived for potential re-use
– Areas of potential improvement	– We rarely dwell on failures – There is no policy regarding projects that go astray – We keep legacy systems longer than we should

(continued)

4.13 Encourage Open Participation in Innovation 20 points	Examples
– Specific methods that are used to encourage and entice customers to participate in innovation projects	– We have quartlery contests seeking out new ideas from customers – Line-of-business colleagues are part of our innovation process – We have a watching brief for innovation at other companies
– Areas of potential improvement	– New ideas for innovation are the responsibility of an R&D group
4.14 Recognize and Reward Innovation Systematically 20 points	**Examples**
– Specific systems that are in place to recognize and reward innovation	– Innovation leads to promotions and, sometimes, bonuses – Our customers rate innovative services and we recognize those who created them
– Areas of potential improvement	– We have no regular predictable recognition – process – Management recognizes efficiency, not innovation – Cash and non-cash reward methods are not in place
4.15 Maintain and Share Goals for Innovation 10 points	**Examples**
– Evidence of shared goals for innovation	– Providing innovative solutions is part of our mission statement
– Areas of potential improvement	– Being “fast followers” is a specialty of our team – We put innovation objectives in our work plans – We need to develop a shared definition of innovation – We have not updated our thinking about innovation for 10 years

Section 5: Innovation Support

5.1 Processes for Innovation 70 points	**Examples**
– Evidence that processes are used for managing innovation	– We have an innovation prototyping laboratory – Our team knows how to obtain funds for innovative projects – We have templates for thinking through our diffusion strategy
– Areas of potential improvement	– Innovation, for us, is ad hoc skunkworks – It is difficult to find time or funds for innovative projects – We should plan more workshops on innovation fundamentals
5.2 Use of Innovation Experts 30 points	**Examples**
– Evidence that experts are available and utilized to encourage innovation	– We consult with innovation experts quarterly – Mentors of different types are available on an as-needed basis
– Areas of potential improvement	– Experts are hoarded and are difficult to access – Innovation expertise as a skill set has not been considered in our organization
5.3 Use of IT Systems to Support Innovation 20 points	**Examples**
– Evidence that IT systems in support of innovation are available and are being used	– Our on-line tools for sharing ideas and requirements are available with 24 x 7 access – We use content storage technologies to seek re-use opportunities for innovations
– Areas of potential improvement	– Most of the good ideas are in the heads of IT personnel – Email notes store our ideas, which is a weak approach
5.4 Business Planning and Innovation 20 points	**Examples**
– Evidence that our business plans include innovation	– Our strategic plans identify areas where breakthrough information technologies are expected – Innovation is central to our changing business models

(continued)

– Areas of potential improvement	– Business planning and innovation are not coordinated activities – We generally minimize spend to improve business profitability

Section 6: Impact of Innovation

6.1 Inventory of Innovations 120 points	**Examples**
– Evidences that goals for innovation success are explicitly stated	– We use a business value index to measure the potential results of an innovation – Our vision statement maps to objective criteria indicating success
– Areas of potential improvement	– We often fail to take baseline measures before deploying new systems – For some deployments, we have no measured results
6.2 Business Value of Innovations 120 points	**Examples**
– Evidence that business value of innovations is being measured	– We maintain a library of standard business value dials and use them consistently – We run experiments to determine productivity improvements and inform investment decisions
– Areas of potential improvement	– Finance prepares investment analyses without our input – Some projects are launched without a thoughtful business case

Appraising Innovation Performance

Table B.1: Performance Appraisal Matrix for Innovation.

Improvement Required	Below Expectations	Successful	Above Expectations	Outstanding
ABSENCE	**BEGINNING**	**DOING**	**EXCELLENCE**	**ROLE MODEL**
– Does not participate in Innovation activities	– Demonstrates support for innovation activities – Able to locate corporate and IT innovation on the web.	– Plans or participates on teams that plan innovation Activities – Contributes to Innovation COP	– Leads teams that are delivering innovation activities	– Role model for routinely coaching others and leading innovation activities at the division or industry level
– Unable to locate or describe innovation web sites or tools	– Able to locate innovation tools, systems, and resources	– Provides feedback for improving the innovation system	– Shares innovation BKMs and routinely offers improvement suggestions – May deliver innovation content	– Role models innovation practices, tools and solutions by using and sharing them with others – Participates in assessment teams and formally and informally recognizes innovative performance

– Fails to attend innovation training classes	– Attends innovation training classes and begins applying skills	– Attends training classes and consistently applies training skills in the workplace	– Takes responsibility for maintaining and growing innovation skills and coaching of others	– Instructs innovation classes and/or shares innovation expertise
– Uses anti-innovation language, e.g., “this can't be done” and “we've done this before”	– Corrects anti-innovation behavior after being coached	– Recognizes correct innovation behavior and corrects without being coached	– Coaches others in innovative behaviors and acts as a gatekeeper for anti-innovation behavior	– Proactively works with the Innovation and Research teams to raise the bar to achieve a world class systemic innovation system
Does not complete business value forecast for projects	Completes business value forecast behaviors after	Completes business value forecast and corrects it without being coached	Coaches others in completing business value forecasts and consistently delivers BV	– Proactively works on developing business Value – Teaches business value classes and/or leads innovation evaluations and assessments – Ensures systems are in place

Appendix C

This appendix shares three different case studies where Open Innovation 2.0 (OI2) has been successfully used to drive radical transformation and non-linear outcomes.

Case Study 1 – Intel Labs Europe

Transforming Intel Research and Innovation in Europe

In 2009 Intel research investments in Europe were in decline and also the relationship between Intel and the European commission was problematic and somewhat antagonistic. With the sponsorship of the global Intel CTO, Justin Rattner and other Intel executives, CIO Diane Bryant and EMEA VP Christian Morales, Martin and his team created a strategic initiative and vision for Intel Labs in Europe to act as a network and to build a collaborative open ecosystem in Europe and to dramatically transform Intel's relationship with the European Commission. The network would be called Intel Labs Europe and the initiative using OI2 as the paradigm, worked spectacularly with Intel Labs Europe becoming one of the most dynamic forces in European innovation and research in a very short period of time.

Shared Vision

At the core of any successful OI2 initiative is a vision that is clear, compelling and concise. At the beginning of the Intel Labs Europe (ILE) journey, Martin proposed a vision of a digital Europe which would be enabled by computer hardware, mobile broadband, a broad set of digital services and a digitally literate society. The goal was to create usage models and then design patterns which could fundamentally transform important aspects of European industry and society such as education, health, government and indeed the home.

The vision was initially shared and tested with key fellow travelers to a strong response. A key test was to share the vision with the European Commission and the first engagement was to share it with Khalil Rouhana, then a key executive with DG Connect, in the European Commission. Martin and his ILE network manager, Brian Quinn, travelled to Brussels to meet Khalil and the meeting went very well. Martin then directly approached EU Research Commissioner Potocnik

https://doi.org/10.1515/9781501507335-014

about his support and feedback for such a Vision with positive feedback. With assistance from Irish MEP Brian Crowley, Intel Labs Europe was launched in the European parliament with the President of the European Parliament, two Commissioners and the Intel CEO, CTO and CIO as well as top executives representing key parts of the triple helix including Prof. Dr. Lutz Heuser, Andrew Parrish and Professor John Hughes representing SAP, Wavebob and the National University of Ireland, Maynooth respectively.

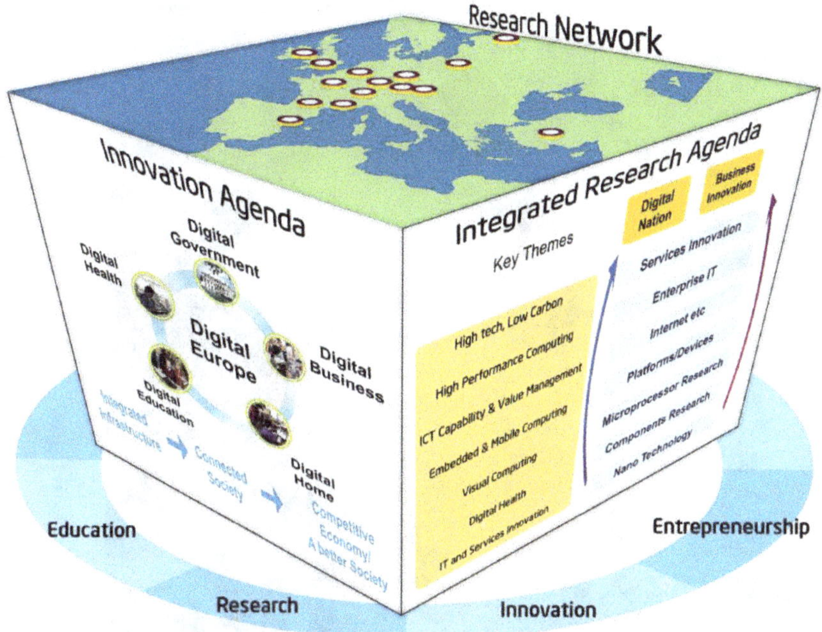

Figure C1.1: Intel Labs Europe Value Proposition Source: Intel (Curley/Koehl).

The central mission of ILE Labs Europe was to simultaneously advance Intel architecture innovation AND European competitiveness as depicted in figure c1.1. Leveraging the deep history of Intel innovations, the goal was to drive for closer collaborations with European researchers and policymakers with a core innovation agenda focused on digital Europe, which would drive the adoption of Intel architecture in new usage models and a research agenda which would create a pipeline of new technologies for future Intel products.

This involved creating the network and building and orchestrating an ecosystem of partners who would research and co-innovate to make accelerated collective progress towards a digital Europe. This mission was fully complimentary to

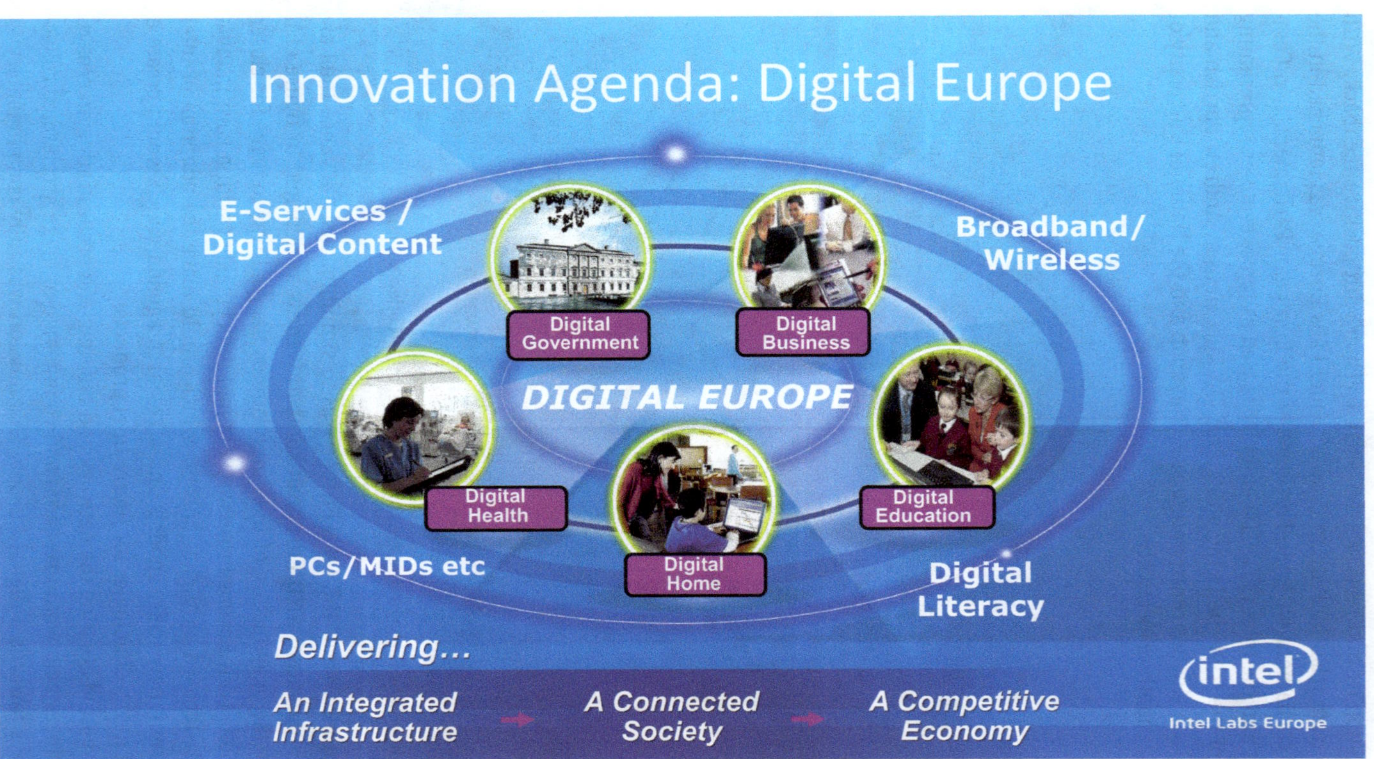

Figure C1.2: Shared Vision – Source: Intel Labs Europe, Curley/Fleming.

the Intel vision of developing and advancing computing technology to "connect and enrich the lives of everyone on the planet" but also the European Commission's ambition and policies for a more competitive and research-intensive Europe. A core observation was that most of the global tech giants were headquartered in Silicon Valley and with the exception of SAP and handful of other companies (Nokia, Ericsson) there was limited success scaling tech giants from Europe.

Using the OI2 core design patterns such as ecosystem orchestration, industrializing the innovation process and agile development a number of engagement vectors were prioritized including

- Establishment of ILE Network with open labs in Leixlip, Munich and Istanbul as depicted in figure C1.3.
- Increased participation in the Seventh Framework Programme for Research and Technological Development (FP7) and Open Innovation
- Joint innovation programs with leading European companies
- Strategic research centers with European universities
- Joint innovation with high-potential start-ups

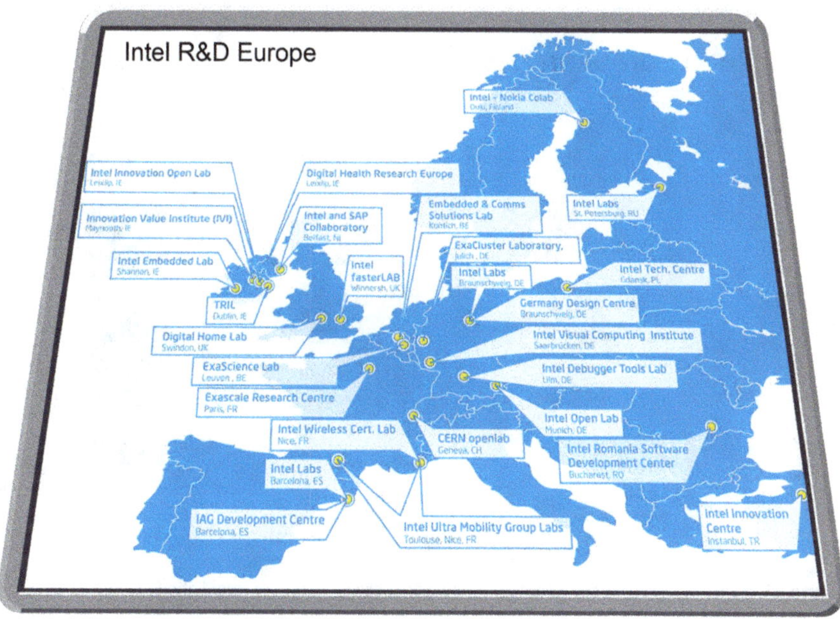

Figure C1.3: ILE Network – circa 2010 Source: Intel.

Research Management Infrastructure

A small central research infrastructure team was put in place (three people) led by Finian Rogers, with great legal support from Intel lawyer Andrew Bush, to coordinate European Framework projects submission and execution and well as developing a software application to manage project governance and approvals as well as an Open Source Customer Relationship Management (CRM) system. The first European Framework project that Intel became involved in was the Genius Project in FP5 with the University of Reading, led by Prof. Vassil Alexandrov as the coordinator (with Martin as the Intel technical lead). The project delivered a pan-European eLearning delivery system and curriculum and perhaps the first streamed lecture across multiple universities in Europe. The first lecture was delivered from Carlos the III University in Madrid to students at Trinity College Dublin and the University of Reading in the presence of then Irish Minister, the late Brian Lenihan. Martin and his team realized that as well as building outstanding technical proposals, establishing relationships with key European Commission policymakers and fellow traveler executives was key, so there were many trips to

Figure C1.4: Intel Labs Europe Research Framework Success – Source: Intel Labs Europe/Curley.

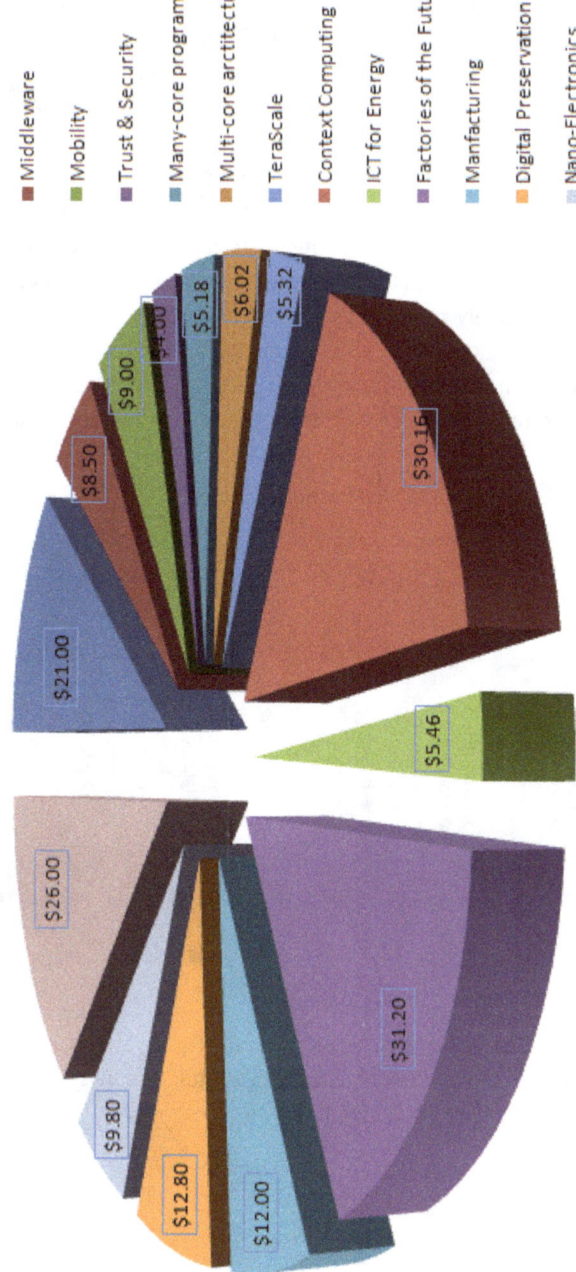

Figure C1.5: ILE Research Portfolio (circa 2012) Source: Intel Labs Europe.

Brussels and other locations such as Munich, Waldorf and Espoo. Through a concerted effort, Intel's participation leapt from just two projects each in FP5 and FP6 to seventy-seven (77) in FP7 as shown in Figure C1.4.

By any measure, this was an extraordinary non-linear result. Intel's participation moved from a portfolio of a handful of million euros to a shared research investment approaching almost a billion euros of co-funded research and innovation. The research projects we applied for were not picked on a random basis but were and prioritized and aligned with a "From Sand to Silicon to Circuits and Society" research agenda aligned with Intel business groups. This resulted in a targeted and high potential of future technologies which Intel could adopt. On an ongoing basis the portfolio was actively managed and Figure C1.5 shows a snapshot of the portfolio at a point in time showing the co-investments in the different technology areas.

We actively benchmarked ourselves against peer companies and were delighted that we often outperformed our peers (and sometimes collaborators) by a

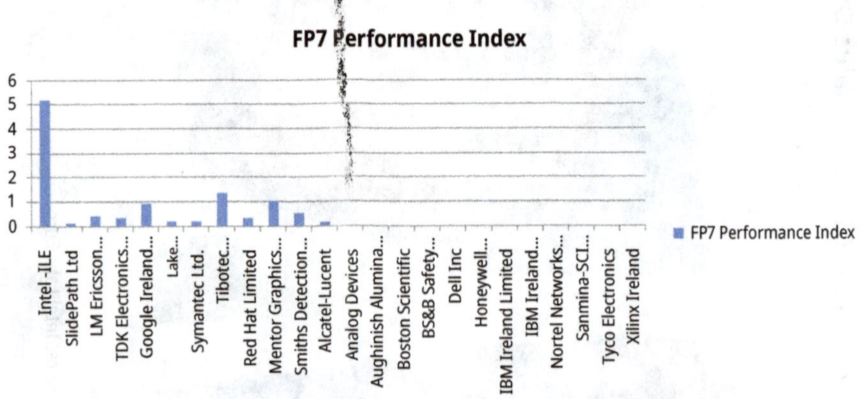

Figure C1.6: Snapshot – ILE success performance versus peer labs/companies Source: EU FP7/Intel Labs Europe.

factor of 5X as shown in Figure C1.6. The use of OI2, the establishment and nurturing of high trust, high capability relationships and, of course, excellent research proposals led to repeated out-performance.

Impact and Growth

There were many successes in multiple output domains, including technology architecture and adoption, new spin-outs and increased Intel revenue. The SLA@SOI project produced key insights and technologies to enable multi-cloud and cloud-bursting solutions. A key European project involving Intel, NXP and IMEC ultimately led to the development of the Intel secure enclave technology based on PUFs (Physically Unclonable Functions). PUFs provide a digital fingerprint that serves as a unique identifier and are often based on unique physical variations occurring naturally in the semiconductor manufacturing process.

The N4C project which developed delay tolerant networks in association with the University of Lulea in Sweden led to the creation of a new company, Tolerant Networks led by ex-Intel researcher Kerry Hartnett. Health research led by Seamus Small and Barry Green led to a spin-out, Kinesis, which developed remarkable falls prevention and prediction software, and which has now been acquired by Canadian Linus Health.

The SDN co-lab established with BT in Ad Astral Park, UK helped accelerate the adoption of software-defined networks and the replacement of customer silicon in networking equipment with standard Intel servers. Initially skeptical US executives, such as Steve Pawlowski, then CTO of the Server product group, ultimately moved eighty percent of Intel's exascale research to Europe in collaboration with organizations such as the French Atomic Agency (CEA) which had computing loads and future needs which would need exascale platforms.

A key part of the ILE OI2 strategy was to build a robust and extensive ecosystem with Intel architecture affinity and capability. At peak, ILE had an ecosystem of over seven hundred research and innovation partners.

In five years, the ILE network grew non-linearly from eighteen (18) labs to fifty-five (55) labs and the number of Intel researchers and innovators in Europe grew from eight hundred (800) to five thousand five hundred (5,500). Intel's relationship with the European Commission improved dramatically and from a place where the initial goal was "they don't hate us" to at least a trusted partner, if not more. European Commissioners Geoghegan- Quinn and Kroes came to speak at the ILE European Research Innovation Conference (ERIC) in Dublin in successive years. The ERIC conference, which moved around to various European locations where Intel had labs such as Nice, Barcelona, Braunschweig and Dublin, became the core vector and instrument used to orchestrate the ecosystem where Intel and ILE strategy were shared, progress updates were given, and new relationships were forged and strengthened and new co-innovation ideas were hatched and further developed.

Case Study 2 – Irish Health System

In 2018 the Irish health system was a laggard in digital health with the OECD ranking Ireland last for technical and operational readiness for eHealth. In Ireland, the

Health Service Executive (HSE) is the public organization responsible for delivering healthcare. It is by far the largest employer in Ireland with over one hundred and thirty thousand employees. The HSE had a very dedicated clinical workforce but unfortunately this work was hampered by the lack of digital health tools.

In order to address this deficit, an OI2 inspired digital transformation strategy and vision was developed to deliver new digital health solutions to the Irish health system. At the National Health Summit in May 2018, Martin introduced a new strategy (Stay Left, Shift Left) to direct innovation efforts toward building a new kind of health system enabled through digital technology and eight digital health companies presented how their solutions could enable a shift toward preventative care and more remote care and home care. There was a terrific reaction from many including the then COO of the HSE, John Connaghan with six companies demonstrating how their solutions could help achieve this shift to the left.

In early 2019 a new digital transformation and innovation function was established to accelerate efforts to develop and adopt digital health solutions. Using the OI2 design patterns an open collaborative ecosystem was established, and a quarterly Digital Academy Forum (DAF) was established to orchestrate and connect the ecosystem. Each DAF began with an update on the SL2-10X strategy and progress made since the prior DAF, which were then followed by 6–8 TED-style keynotes which were designed to stimulate the ecosystem and align, accelerate and amplify collective digital health innovation efforts.

A new digital transformation strategy was presented to and approved by the board of the HSE in April 2020 and one core element of the strategy was the development of a network of living labs to advance the Stay Left Shift Left -10X (SL2-10X) strategy in a coordinated way as shown in figure C2.1. Great progress was made in establishing a network of living labs and clinicians and patients enthusiastically embraced living labs both because of the pressures they faced but also because of the hope for a better future that they brought. Each of the living labs had an agreed one-page charter which documented the problem to be solved, the solution, key participants and the critical success factors.

In order to proactively and properly manage the network of living labs an innovation governance mechanism, the digital solutions board was put in place and a clearly defined stage process with a four-stages idea, proof of concept, demonstrator and finally broad adoption was established. This provided an effective and clear mechanism for managing ideas through the pipeline through to implementation as shown in figure C2.2.

An informal digital health collaborative ecosystem was created in Ireland with organizations which subscribed to the Stay Left, Shift Left strategy. There was no formal commitment required to be part of the ecosystem, but many organizations and leaders volunteered to be part of the ecosystem, as it was providing hope to a

Figure C2.1: Network of Living Labs c. 2022: Source: HSE Curley/Cullen.

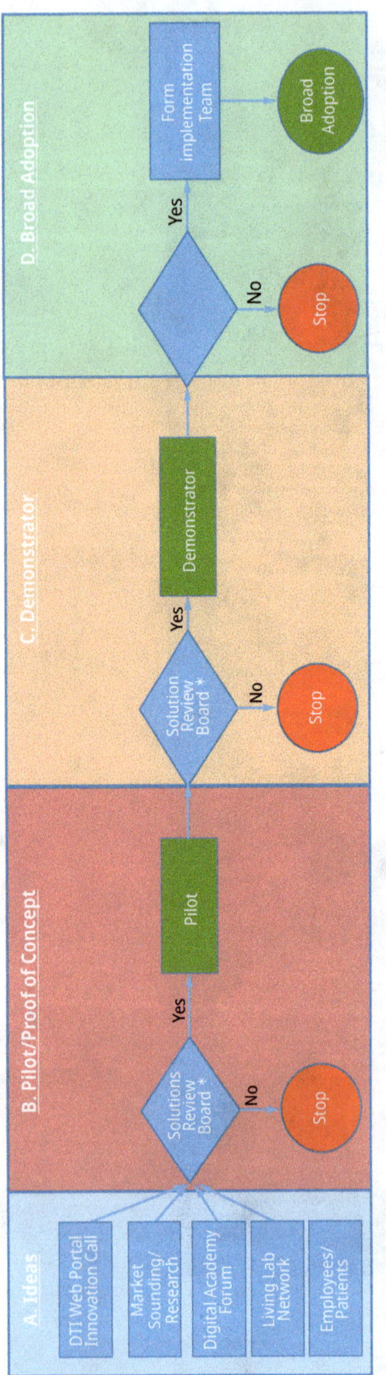

Figure C2.2: Innovation Governance and Pipeline Management Source: HSE Curley/Cullen.

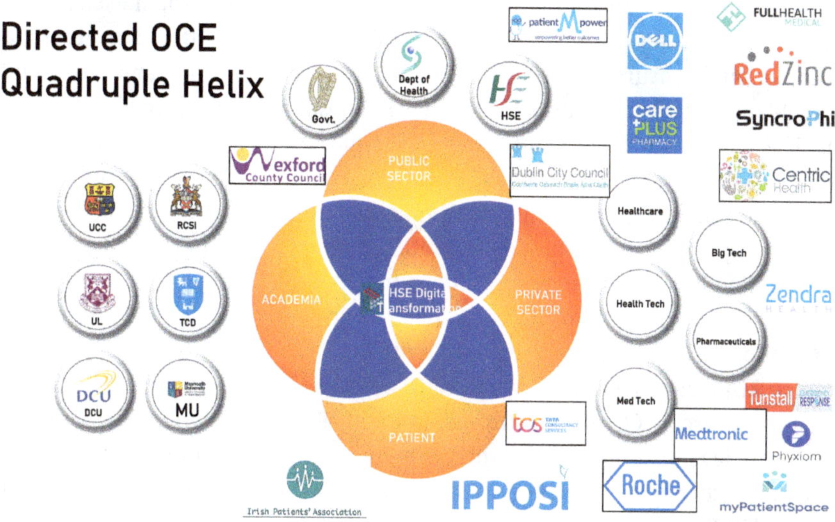

Figure C2.3: A sample of participants in the Directed Open Collaborative Ecosystem orchestrated by HSE Digital Transformation, source Curley/Sheehan.

health system which was very clearly digital-deficient and had a track record of abject failure in delivering digital solutions, with the one exception of a national radiology imaging system provided by ChangeHealth. Figure C2.3 shows a snapshot of organizations from across the quadruple helix (government, industry, academic and patients/citizens) which participated in the open collaborative ecosystem.

The OI2 living labs proved to be a very good mechanism for introducing radical change in an incremental, non-threatening way. Unfortunately, the Digital Transformation initiative experienced extreme resistance from leaders in the HSE Strategy organization with attempts made to dismantle the innovation governance and stop all funding of the living labs. It is remarkable that such blocking behavior existed and was openly tolerated in the organization chartered to deliver care to the citizens of Ireland. Despite attempts to bully and intimidate the HSE Digital Transformation team they persevered with their efforts and with huge support and partnering from clinical leaders and the ecosystem many new digital health solutions were delivered. A national automated respiratory rate measurement system (Respirasense) was deployed in a living lab in Beaumont Hospital with Professor Richard Costello as an immediate response to COVID and was quickly iterated to a production system and deployed across twenty-three hospitals across the country of Ireland in four months. The system provided up to twelve hours' notice of a patient desaturating and helped modernize respiratory rate measurement in Irish hospitals.

A vital signs automation(VSA) living lab developed by Syncrophi Systems Ltd was deployed in a Cavan General Hospital Living Lab and after its success, a rapid national procurement process was run, catalyzed by Covid and a contract to deploy VSA to twenty wards in twenty Irish hospitals was awarded to Syncrophi. The VSA solution fully automated collection of patient observations eliminated high error rates on patient early-warning scores, significantly reduced cognitive load for nurses and giving them time back to spend with patients as well as, most importantly, detecting deteriorating patients more quickly, saving lives and avoiding ICU admissions. The VSA solution is a hugely important first step in modernizing wards in Irish hospitals., Before deployment of the solution Martin and vendor Syncrophi led by their excellent CEO, David Toohey, had performed a detailed ROI analysis which showed an ROI of 1,100% on deploying the solution.

In response to COVID, Martin worked with PatientMPower's CEO Eamonn Costello to develop a remote monitoring solution for COVID using Bluetooth pulse oximeters which was developed within forty-eight hours of COVID hitting Irish shores. HSE Digital Transformation Comms lead, Lorraine Smyth, then drove the deployment of the solution across the country and within weeks there were over thirty major sites prescribing the solution which was then subsequently extended to GP practices across the country. Lorraine, who drove the project as part of her masters in digital health transformation won "student project of the year" at the Irish Healthcare Awards in 2021.

A mobile X-ray living lab with mobile medical diagnostics, which was motivated by founding CEO Mary Jones's experience of spending many hours waiting in A&E two weekends in a row with elderly parents and parents-in-law waiting for X-rays after falls. This motivated her to say there has to be a better way, and she sourced a mobile X-ray machine and began bringing the X-ray to older peoples' homes to trial the solution. Assisted by Dr. John Sheehan, the fledgling living lab was very successful with the study showing that 90% of callouts did not require transfers to hospitals. Again, this solution was sadly resisted by administrators. However, MMD persevered and under a new CEO, Paul Flynn, continued to push and in February 2024 the solution was ultimately announced as available nationwide. There were many other examples of innovations in living labs which faced stiff, even extreme resistance.

However, the strength of the ecosystem persevered and in September 2022, Leo Clancy, CEO of Enterprise Ireland and Martin were able to announce at the UNGA Digital Health Symposium in New York the "First 25," a cohort of twenty-five Irish Digital Health SMEs whose solutions were being used by the Irish Health Service, despite the corporate HSE strategy division blocking all funding. The

Figure C2.4: First 25 Digital Health Companies Source: HSE Digital Transformation/Enterprise Ireland.

logos of the companies are shown in Figure C2.4 and the companies have made remarkable contributions to improved health for patients in Ireland and abroad, improved tools and working conditions for clinicians, and improved efficiency and effectiveness of the overall health system.

The case shows the effectiveness of the OI2 approach in effecting radical change in an environment where there was extreme resistance to Innovation. The case shows OI2 living labs as an extremely effective mechanism for introducing radical change and the strength of a high-trust and committed open collaborative ecosystem in persevering in delivering critical innovations which helped save and extend lives. In this case there were just a handful of main blockers who created such difficulty for progress, all who exhibited the 4C leadership philosophy discussed in chapter 10.

Based on inspiration from Gastaldi et al (2015) paper on “Academics as Orchestrators of Continuous Innovation Ecosystems” and Martins conversation with the incoming President of Maynooth University Prof Eeva Leinonen in 2022 who talked about health and digital being key future priorities, Martin made the decision to return to Maynooth University and to shift the open collaborative ecosystem orchestration to the Innovation Value Institute (IVI) at the University. With a small period of discontinuity, the ecosystem regrouped and began to grow and thrive again. An example was the announcement of a Digital Health Living lab for pulmonary arterial hypertension (PAH) patients at Dublin’s Mater Living Lab co-funded by Johnson and Johnson and Science Foundation Ireland. However, the jewel in the crown was the announcement of a Digital Living lab with an open source electronic health record OpenEMR in partnership with the Social Inclusion division of the HSE supporting 15,000 patients with complex needs, at the 2nd International Digital Health Summer School hosted by IVI in June 2024. This was a dramatic breakthrough for a country which had failed for almost two decades to make any real progress on EHRs, so much so the announcement was a main news story on the national public service broadcaster RTE. As is often the case for radical innovations this kind of breakthrough depends on just one or two key individuals. Maxine Radcliffe, an ex NHS nurse and leader was the main clinical driver and Pete Boyd, CEO of Brighton based OpenPlanIT was the main technical architect of the platform supported by a Danish ED consultant Halfdan Kolasa. Weeks after Martin left the HSE, a new CEO joined the HSE and one of his early actions was to shut down the HSE Strategy organization.

In the national Digital Transformation awards in July 2024 the work of the Maynooth University led ecosystem was awarded the best Irish digital health transformation of the year award and the best overall Irish Digital Transformation of the year.

Case Study 3 – Innovation Value Institute (IVI)

IVI is a multidisciplinary research institute focused on digital transformation and technology adoption based at Maynooth University, Ireland. Founded in 2006 by Martin and then President of Maynooth University Professor John Hughes as a collaboration between Intel and Maynooth University, it has built a strong track record of academic-industry collaboration globally. IVI was established around a shared problem that the pace of technology development was seriously outpacing the development of management practices for delivering value from information technology. An expression of interest meeting in 2005 attracted over fifty global leaders who committed to a shared vision of creating an IT capability maturity framework based on founding IP from Intel and Martin who had successfully developed and used an early version of an IT-CMF to improve Intel's IT Value performance (Curley and Kenneally, 2011).

Of critical importance was creating an open collaborative ecosystem which had memberships from different stakeholders in the industry as shown in figure C3.1.

IVI's mission was agreed to be to research, develop and disseminate empirically proven and industry validated best practice for Digital Transformation using a capability maturity framework approach. Inspired by what the Software Engineering Institute achieved with the development of the Software CMM model, IVI aspired to develop a similar impact in professionalizing enterprise IT management. Boston Consulting Group (BCG) agreed to join IVI as a steering pa-

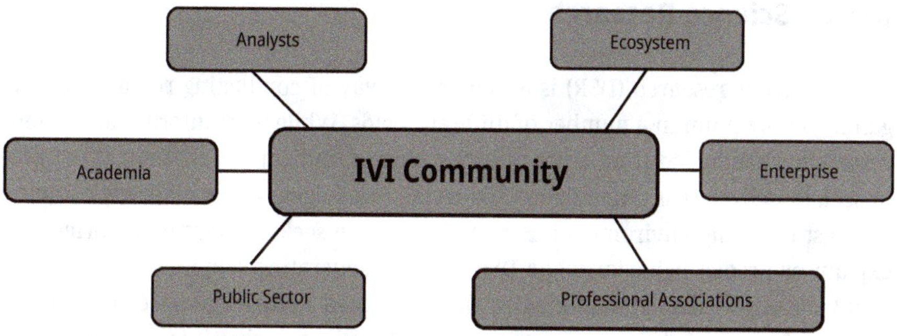

Figure C3.1: Key Stakeholders in IVI Community, Source: Curley.

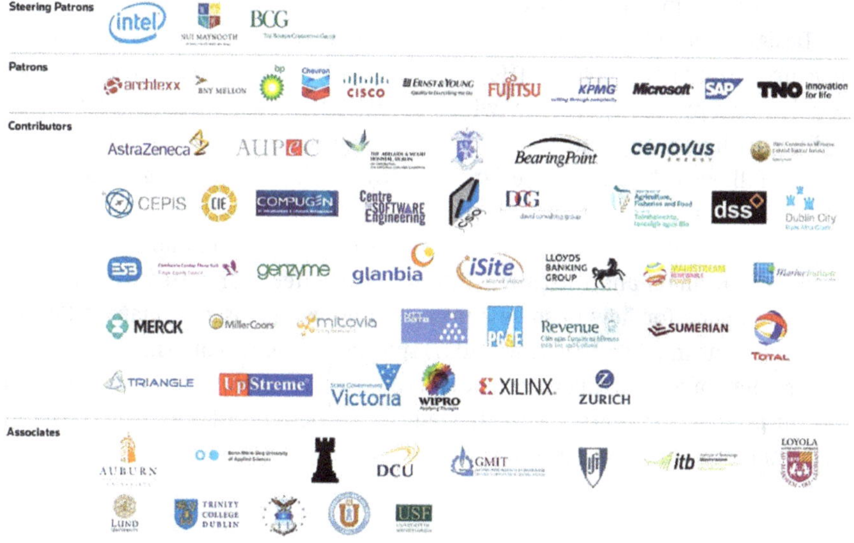

Figure C3.2: IVI OCE Members Source: Innovation Value Institute.

tron with Intel and Maynooth University and a world class set of organizations (shown in the figure C3.2) to develop the IT-CMF using a design science research approach and an engaged scholarship where industry executives contributed to the research in working groups led by academic researchers.

Design Science Research

Design science research (DSR) is an emerging way of conducting research that is gaining momentum in a number of different fields. While most information system research is conducted from a behavioral science paradigm, IVI chose to adopt DSR to seek to deliver real solutions to CIOs trying to navigate an increasingly complex and fast changing environment. Behavioral science seeks to develop theories that explain or predict behavior while DSR is about generating solutions to real world problems while also contributing to the associated knowledge base. The distinguishing feature of the typical output of a DSR activity is that it is prescriptive or normative and that it often takes the form of a solution concept, which is a general prescription which can be used by a practitioner to help develop a solution to a specific problem in a particular domain.

Design Science Research (DSR) "creates and evaluates IT artifacts intended to solve organizational problems" (Hevner et al., 2004). This research approach is an iterative step-by-step process by which artifacts and theory are generated and verified, with both an inductive and a deductive process being used. The research process followed the general design cycle (GDC) adapted for design science research (Vaishnavi and Kuechler, 2007)

A design pattern is a general reusable solution to a commonly occurring problem (Vaishnavi and Kuechler, 2007) and it is often manifested as a description or template for how to solve a problem that can be used in many different situations. Vaishnavi and Kuechler (2007) specifically define patterns as a solution to a problem in a recurring context and as a general technique for approaching a class of problems that are abstractly similar. The output of IVI was primarily in the format of codified Design Patterns.

Engaged Scholarship

Engaged Scholarship (Van de Ven, 2006) is a new kind of research whereby academics and industry professionals worked together to research, innovate and co-create knowledge and new artifacts manifested as new solutions to real world problems and opportunities. Engaged scholarship, a movement that has been growing steadily since 1996, offers a new way of bridging gaps between the university and civil society and the economy. IVI is a leading exponent of engaged scholarship with over 200 global industry professionals having contributed to the development of the IT-CMF. This engaged scholarship approach brought bleeding edge IT management practice to the IVI ecosystem and also significantly amplified the research capability of IVI.

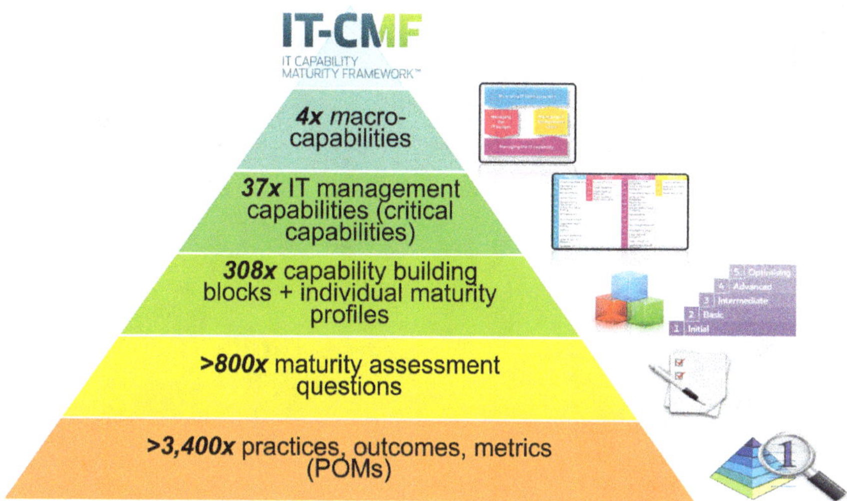

Figure C3.3: IVI Capability Maturity Framework Source: Innovation Value Institute.

Non Linear Results

Over a short period of years the IVI ecosystem developed and delivered the IT capability maturity framework (Curley, Kenneally and Carcary, 2015; Curley and Kenneally, 2011) which was a vast repository of organized knowledge available to help assess and improve organizations' IT capability and their ability to translate IT investment into value. Over 300 capability building blocks were created and over 3,000 practices, outcomes and metrics (POMs) were documented as shown in Figure C3.3.

Over 150,000 research hours were contributed by industry executives and through this approach the IT capability maturity framework was developed with an approximate budget of 5 million euros which compared favorably to the $0.5 billion invested in development of Software CMM. Over seven hundred organizations globally have used the IT-CMF assessment tool and, according to BCG, adoption of the IT-CMF was five times faster than initial adoption of the Software CMM model.

The Innovation Value Institute continues to thrive and now hosts the definitive repository of Open Innovation 2.0 research with a decade of research and innovation contained in the annual European Commission yearbooks curated by Bror Salmelin, assisted by Martin. You can access this repository at the following link www.ivi/publication/openinnovation2-0.

References

While all publications cited in the book are listed here, please note that this list of references also includes the authors' suggested readings in the foremost literature on innovation.

Agarwal, R., and Sambamurthy,V. 2002. Principles and Models for Organizing the IT Function, *MIS Quarterly Executive*, Volume 1 (1), March: 1–16.

Alter, A. 2003. Do You Have Any Faith in Your ROI Numbers? www.cioinsight.com, March.

Alter, A. 2006. The Bitter Truth About ROI. www.cioinsight.com, August 4.

Altshuller, G. 1994. *And Suddenly the Inventor Appeared*. Translated by Lev Shulyak. Worcester, MA: Technical Innovation Center.

Altshuller, G. 1996. And Suddenly the Inventor Appeared: TRIZ, the Theory of Inventive Problem Solving.

Anderson, J., Gimenez, L., Nunley, D., Baldwin, E. 2007. Developing Systemic Innovation in an IT Organization, *Premier IT Magazine*, CXO Media CIDGMA. USA Winter.

Andreessen, M. 2002. Sidestepping the New IT Crisis. Tech News/CNET.com, December.

Andersson T, Curley M and Formica P (2010). Knowledge Driven Entrepreneurship, The Key to Social and Economic Transformation, Springer.

Baldwin, C., von Hippel, E.,(2011) Modeling a Paradigm Shift: From Producer Innovation to User and Open Collaborative Innovation. *Organization Science* 22(6): 1399–1417.

Baldwin, E. 2004. Innovation in Industry and Academia. In B. Fitzgerald and E. Wynn (Eds.) *IT Innovation for Adaptability and Competitiveness*. IFIP TC8/WG8.6 Seventh Working Conference Proceedings, Leixlip, Ireland: Kluwer Academic Publishers.

Baldwin, E. Building Sustainable Economic Development using IT Innovation. Eisenhower Fellowship Symposium Hu Bei, Beijing PRC 2004.

Baldwin, E. and Parchef, S. 2005. "Inside Innovation", Intel Innovation Centre whitepaper. USA/Israel.

Baldwin, E., Gene, M. and Kahn, K. 2007. "Innovation as a Science" Computex.

Baldwin E. MIT Sloan School – "Innovation is a Discipline" http://sloanreview.mit.edu/article/it-innovation-baldwin-article/-April, 2010.

Baldwin, E., D'Hooge, H., Intel Technology Journal-Essential Computing, *Architect*. Vol. 14 Issue 1 Apr 2010.

Baldwin, E. 2019. Inside Big Data, "HPC and AI Convergence Enables AI Workload Innovation" https://insidebigdata.com/2019/07/22/converged-hpc-clusters/

Barney, J.B. 1991. Firm Resources and Sustained Competitive Advantage. *Journal of Management*, 17 (1): 99–120.

Baldwin, E., and Curley, M. 2007 *Managing IT Innovation for Business Value*, Intel Press.

Bartend, D.A. 2004. Reaping the Business Value of IT: Focus on Usage, Not Just Deployment, to Optimize Payback. IMDb publication number 114, November.

Boyer, E.L. The scholarship of engagement.Sustained Competitive Advantage. *Journal of Public Service & Outreach*. 1996; 1(1):11–20. Management, 17 (1): 99–120.

Busch, D. 2006. Personal communication.

Byrne, G. and Kelly, N. Achieving Excellence in R&D in Irish SMEs. A Case Study ANAM Technologies Ltd. Workshop on R&D in Industry. Nova Centre UCD, 2018.

Chesbrough, H.W. 2003. *Open Innovation: The New Imperative for Creating and Profiting from Technology*. Boston, MA: Harvard Business School Press.

https://doi.org/10.1515/9781501507335-015

Carty, M. and Lansford, R. 2009. Using an IT Business Value Program to Measure Benefits to the Enterprise, IT@Intel Whitepaper.

Chiles, T.H., A. D. School PressMeyer, and Hench, T.J. 2004. Organizational emergence: The origin and transformation of Branson, Missouri's musical theaters. *Organ. Sci.* 15 (5) 499–519.

Christensen, C. M. 1997. *The Inventor's Dilemma: When New Technologies Cause Great Firms to Fail.* Boston, MA: Harvard Business School Press.

Christensen, C.M. Competing Against Luck: The Story of Innovation and Customer Choice.

Covey, S. 2006. *The Speed of Trust: The One Thing that Changes Everything.* Simon & Schuster.

Covey, S.R., 2020. *The 7 Habits of Highly Effective People*, 30th Anniversary Edition. Simon & Schuster.

Crosby, P.B. 1979. *Quality is free: The Art of Making Quality Certain.* New York, NY: McGraw Hill.

Curley, M. (2024) Operationalizing Open Innovation 2.0 to deliver breakthrough Digital Innovations and superior performance across a National Health Ecosystem, R&D Management Conference, Stockholm.

Curley, M. and Kenneally, J. 2011. *Using the IT Capability Maturity Framework to Improve IT Capability and Value Creation: An Intel IT Case Study, IEEE.*

Curley, M and McElligott, A (2024) A Novel Masters in Digital Health Transformation driving cohesive systemic digital change. Advances in Higher Education Proceedings, Valencia.

Curley, M. and Salmelin, B. 2018 Open Innovation 2.0, the New Mode of Digital Innovation for Prosperity and Sustainability, Springer.

Curley, M. 2016. Twelve Principles for Open Innovation 2.0, Nature.

Curley, M. 2015. The Evolution of Open Innovation, *The Journal of Innovation Management.*

Curley, M. and Formica, P. 2013. The Experimental Nature of New Venture Creation. Capitalizing on Open Innovation 2.0, Springer.

Curley, M. and Salmelin, B. 2013. Open Innovation 2.0, A New Paradigm, European Commission.

Curley, M. and Donnellan, B. 2012. The Application of Open Innovation 2.0, engaged scholarship and design science research in the Innovation Value Institute, Open Innovation 2012, European Commission.

Curley, M. et al. 2020 The Digital Transition of Healthcare – Stay Left, Shift Left-10X. UNGA 76 Digital Health Symposium.

Curley, M. 2004. *Managing Information Technology for Business Value: Practical Strategies for IT and Business Managers.* Hillsboro, OR: Intel Press.

Curley, M. 2006. *A Value Based IT Capability Maturity Framework.* Ireland: Intel EMEA Academic Forum.

Curley, M. 2006. IT Innovation, A New Era. Proceedings of the International Conference of Computational Science, Reading, UK.

Curley, M. 2006. The IT Transformation at Intel. *MIS Quarterly Executive*, Volume 5, Issue 4 (1), December. pp. 109–122.

Curley, M. 2007. Introducing the IT Capability Maturity Framework. Proceedings of the International Conference on Enterprise Information Systems, Portugal, June.

de Bono, E. 1986. *Six Thinking Hats.* London: Penguin Books.

de Geus, A. 1997. *The Living Company: Habits of Survival in a Turbulent Business Environment.* Boston, MA: Harvard Business School Press.

Dedrick, J., Gurbaxani, V., and Kraemer, K.L. 2002. *Information Technology and Economic Performance: A Critical Review of the Empirical Evidence.* University of California, Irvine, Center for Research in IT and Organizations (CRITO), November.

Department of Health, Ireland (2024) An Examination of Trends in Activity, Expenditure and Workforce in Publicly Funded Acute Hospitals in Ireland. Irish Government Publications.

Doughtery, D., and Dunne, D. 2011 Organizing ecologies of complex innovation. *Organ. Sci.* 22.

Devane, C., 2021 HSE Board Minutes 28th of April, 2021, Health Service Executive.
Drucker, P.F. 1985. *Innovation and Entrepreneurship*. New York, NY: Harper and Row.
Earl M.J. and Sampler, J.L. 1998. Market Management to Transform the IT Organization. *MIT Sloan Management Review*, Summer.
Everett, M.R., 2003. *Diffusion of Innovations*, Washington D.C.: Free Press.
Eckert, A. 2002. Maximizing ROI Through User Proficiency. Insiders' View, SAS.com, June.
Eleanor, W. August 2015. *Adapting Enterprise White Paper, ResearchGate*, Berlin, Germany.
Friedman, T. 2005. *The World is Flat*. New York, NY: Farrar Straus, and Giroux.
European Internet Foundation. 2009. The Digital World in 2025 Indicators for European Action EIF.
Gastaldi, L., Appio, L.P., Martini, A. and Corso, M. 2015. Academics as orchestrators of continuous innovation ecosystems: towards a fourth generation of CI initiatives. *Int. J. Technol. Manag.* 68.
Gladwell, M. 2000. *The Tipping Point: How Little Things Can Make a Big Difference*. Bsoton, MA: Little, Brown and Company.
Glass, G. 1978. Standards and Criteria. *Journal of Educational Measurement* (Special Issue on Standard Setting): 15, (4) pp. 237–261.
Geoffrey, A.M., 1991. *Harper Business Essentials. NY, NY.*
Gurbaxani, V. and Kemerer, C.F. 1990. An Agency Theory View of the Management of Information Systems. Proceedings of the International Conference on Information Systems, pp. 279–288.
Hevner, A. and Chatterjee, S. 2004. DESIGN SCIENCE Research IN INFORMATION SYSTEMS, Springer.
Humphrey, W. 1989. *Managing the Software Process*. Software Engineering Institute, Pittsburgh.
Intel Corporation. 2003. Effects of Wireless Mobile Technology on Employee Productivity: Wireless Mobility Changes the Way Employees Work. Santa Clara: Intel Corporation. IT@Intel white paper, November. www.intel.com/it/alpha.htm.
Intel Corporation. 2004. Business Benefits of Wireless Computing: How Wireless Improves Productivity and Return on Investment. Santa Clara: Intel Corporation. IT@Intel white paper, September.
Intel Corporation. Intel Communicates Globally through Instant Messaging. Santa Clara: Intel Corporation. IT@Intel white paper, May. www.intel.com/it/alpha.htm.
Intel Corporation. 2004. The Workplace Hits the Road: Intel IT Finds its Field Employees Save Time, Improve Productivity Using Intel Centrino Mobile Technology. Santa Clara: Intel Corporation. IT@Intel brief, February. www.intel.com/it/alpha.htm.
Intel Corporation. 2005. St. Vincent's Hospital Enhances Patient Throughput with RFID and Greater Visibility of Patient Flow. Santa Clara: Intel Corporation. IT@Intel white paper.
Keely, L., Walters, H., Pikkel, R., Quinn, B. (2013) *Ten Types of Innovation*. NY: John Wiley.
Kelly, N., Curley, M., Byrne, G. And Darcy, A. (2022) Anam Innovation Growth Case Study, ISPIM Conference, Berlin.
Kohli, R., and Deveraj. 2004. Realizing the Business Value of IT Investments: An Organizational Process. *MIS Quarterly Executive*, Vol. 3 (1), March: 53–68.
Kotter, J.P. 2012. *Cotter from Harvard Business Review Press*. Brighton, MA.
Livitov, P., and Petrov, V. TRIZ: Innovation and Inventive Problem Solving. Handbook Paperback – October 19, 2019.
Kotter, J.P. 2014. *Accelerate – XLR8 by from Harvard Business Review Press*. Brighton, MA.
Marchand, D.A. 2004. *Reaping the Business Value of IT: Focus on Usage, Not Just Deployment, zo Optimize Payback*. IMD publication No. 114, November.
Markus, M.L., and Soh, C. 1993. Banking on Information Technology: Converting IT Spending into Firm Performance. In R.D Banker, R.J. Kauffman and M.A. Mahmood (Eds.), *Strategic Information*

Technology Management: Perspectives on Organizational growth and Competitive Advantage. Harrisburg, Pennsylvania: Idea Group Publishing, pp. 405–444.

Markus, M.L. and Soh, C. 1995. How IT Creates Value, a Process Theory Synthesis. Proceedings of the 16th International Conference of Information Systems, Amsterdam, The Netherlands.

McKinsey. 2020. https://www.mckinsey.com/solutions/orgsolutions/overview/organizational-health-

McNichol, T. 2007. A Startup's Best Friend? Failure from Dogster to Google, Web Companies are Finding that Mistakes Can be Shortcuts to Success. April 4, 2007. CNNMoney.com.

Meadows, C.J. 2020. Innovation Through Fusion: Combining Innovative Ideas to Create New Soltuions.

Mooney, J. G., Gurbaxani, V., and Kraemer, K. 1995. A Process Oriented Framework for Assessing the Business Value of Information Technology. CRITO paper, UC Irvine.

Moore, G. 2002. *Crossing the Chasm: Marketing and Selling High-tech Products to Mainstream Customers*. HarperCollins.

Moore, G. 2003. *Diffusion of Innovations*, 5th Edition. August 16, 2003.

Moore, G. 1965. "Cramming More Components onto Integrated Circuits," *Electronics*, pp. 114–117.

Mulholland, T., Kurchina, P., and Thomas, C. 2006. *Mash up Corporations, The End of Business as Usual*. Evolve Technology Press.

Osborne, G. 2012. Speech by the Chancellor of the Exchequer, Rt Hon George Osborne MP, to the Royal Society – GOV.UK (www.gov.uk)

Paulk, M.C., Curtis, B., Chrissis, M. B. and Weber, C. 1993. Capability Maturity Model for Software, Version 1.1. Software Engineering Institute, CMU/SEI-93-TR-24, DTIC Numbe r ADA263403, February.

Peppard, J. and Ward, J. 2004. Beyond Strategic Information Systems: Towards An IS Capability. *The Journal of Strategic Information Systems*, 13 (2), July: pp. 167–194.

Porter, M. and Kramer, M. 2011. Creating Shared Value, How to reinvent capitalism—and unleash a wave of innovation and growth. Harvard Business Review.

Ramaswamy, V. and Gouillart, F. 2010. Building the co-creative enterprise. Harvard Business Review.

Razetti, G. 2023. https://gustavorazzetti.substack.com/p/the-four-types-of-organizational-cultures

Rocco. 2019. SMS Firewall vendor performance, https://www.roccoresearch.com/2019/05/22/a2p-sms-messaging-vendor-performance-reports-2019/

Rocco. 2020. SMS Firewall vendor performance, https://www.roccoresearch.com/2020/02/13/sms-firewall-vendor-performance-2020/

Rogers, E.M. 2003. *Diffusion of Innovations*, Fifth Edition. New York, NY: Free Press.

Ross, J.W., Beath, C.M. and Goodhue, D.L. 1996. Developing Long-term Competitiveness Through Information Technology Assets. *Sloan Management Review*, Vol. 38, Fall.

Ross, J.W., Weill, P. and Robertson, D. C. 2006. *Enterprise Architecture as Strategy: Creating a Foundation for Business Execution*. Boston, MA: Harvard Business School Press.

Rubin, R. 2023. *The Creative Act a Way of Being*, Penguin Press.

Salman, R. and Younis, N. 2005. Lessons to Management from the Control Loop Phenomenon. *Transactions on Engineering, Computing and Technology*.

Sambamurthy, V. and Zmud, R.W. IT Management Competency Assessment: A Tool for Creating Business Value Through IT. Working Paper, Financial Executives Research Foundation.

Susman, G. I. and Evered, R.D. 1978. "An Assessment of the Scientific Merits of Action Research." *Administrative Science Quarterly* 23: 582–603.

Sveiby, K.-E., Gripenberg, P. and Segercrantz, B. 2015. Challenging the Innovation Paradigm, ISBN: 9781138959880, Taylor & Francis.

Sward, D. 2006. *Measuring the Business Value of Information Technology: Practical Strategies for IT and Business Managers*. Hillsboro, OR: Intel Press.

Sward, D. 2007. Gaining a Competitive Advantage through User Experience Design. Santa Clara: Intel Corporation. IT@Intel white paper, January. www.intel.com/it/alpha.htm

Tallon, P., et al. 2000. Executives' Perspectives on the Business Value of Information Technology. A Process-Oriented Approach. *Journal of Management Information Systems*, 16 (4): 145–173.

Thompson, C. 2007. *What a Great Idea 2.0*. New York, NY: Sterling Press.

Thomson, D. 2006. *Blueprint to a Billion*. Hoboken, NJ: John Wiley.

Teece, D.J.; Pisano, G. and Shuen, A. 1997. "Dynamic capabilities and strategic management". *Strategic Management Journal*. 18 (7): 509–533.

Tiernan, C., and Peppard, J. 2004. Information Technology: Of Value or a Vulture. *European* Management Journal 22 (6): 609–623.

Tiwana, A. 2014. Platform Ecosystems, Aligning Architecture, Governance and Strategy, Morgan Kaufman.Details. ISBN. 978-0-12-408066-9

How Big Data Keeps Planes In The Air (forbes.com)

Van de Ven AH, Johnson PE. Knowledge for science and practice. Academy of Management Review. 2006; 31(4):822–829.

Venkatraman, N. 1997. Beyond Outsourcing: Managing IT Resources as a Value Center. *MIT Sloan Management Review*, Spring.

Vaishnavi, V. and Kuehler, W. 2007. Design Science Research Methods and Patterns, Taylor Francis.

Vial, G. 2019. "Understanding digital transformation: A review and a research agenda." *J. Strateg. Inf. Syst.* 28: 118–144.

Wall, M (2024) Productivity and Efficiency must be core to debate on health service spending. Irish Times 2 July 2024.

Weill, P. 1992. "The Relationship between Investment in Information Technology and Firm Performance: A Study of the Value Manufacturing Sector." *Information Systems Review*, Vol 3, Number 4: 307–333.

Weill, P. 2004. Don't Just Lead, Govern. How Top-performing Firms Govern IT. *MIS Quarterly Executive*, Volume 3 (1), March.

Weill, P., and Ross, J. 2004. *How Top Performers Manage IT Decisions Rights for Superior Results*. Boston, MA: Harvard Business School Press.

Weill, P., and Ross, J. 2004. IT Governance in One Page. MIT CISR Working Paper #349.

Weill, P., and Woodham. 2002. Don't Just Lead, Govern: Implementing Effective IT Governance. MIT Sloan CISR Working Paper #326, April.

Yuana, R., Prasetio, E.A., Syarief, R., Arkeman, Y., and Suroso, A.I. 2021. System Dynamic and Simulation of Business Model Innovation in Digital Companies: An Open Innovation Approach. *J. Open Innov. Technol.*

List of Figures

https://doi.org/10.1515/9781501507335-016

List of Tables

https://doi.org/10.1515/9781501507335-017

About the Authors

Esther Baldwin is a Solutions Architect and Artificial Intelligence Strategist at Intel Corporation. She is an Eisenhower Fellow from Liverpool, U.K. Esther has enjoyed leadership and technical roles including three assignments to China and has built data centers in the UK, Japan and USA. She has served as technical assistant to the Vice President of Intel Research and Future Technologies Research and Director of Innovation for Intel Semiconductor Dalian, China and was responsible for building an innovation culture, taking ideas to prototype in months, and conceived and led the first factory machine learning for predictive maintenance project. Esther designs workshops on Innovation and AI helping companies identify relevant AI uses and "get started". She was an Executive Committee member for the American Chamber of Commerce NE China where she lectured on Innovation Science to local members and universities. Esther served on the National Advisory Council for Innovation and Entrepreneurship (NACIE 3.0) for two United States Secretaries of Commerce and was an Economic Advisor for the Jieyang, Guangdong government. She obtained an MSc in International Management (International MBA) with Mandarin from the Thunderbird School of Global Management, and has aa BSc double major in Design Engineering Technology (College of Engineering), and Design (College of Fine Arts), Brigham Young University. The authors can be reached for consultation at innov8n@live.com.

Martin Curley is Professor of Innovation at Maynooth University and Director of the Digital Health Ecosystem at the Innovation Value Institute at Maynooth University, Ireland. Most recently Martin was Chief Information Officer and Director of Digital Transformation for Ireland's National Health Service (HSE) and previously was Senior Vice President at Mastercard and head of Global Digital Practice. As Chair of the European Commission Open Innovation Strategy and Policy Group he co-created the breakthrough Open Innovation 2.0 paradigm. He has previously been Vice President, Senior Principal Engineer and Director of Intel Labs Europe as well as Global Director of IT Innovation at Intel Corporation. He is the author of eight books on innovation, digital and entrepreneurship. Recognized as a transcendental innovation leader, he has delivered digital and innovation executive education across the world. He is the co-founder of the Innovation Value Institute and the creator of the IT Capability Maturity Framework used by hundreds of firms globally to improve the value they create from IT. He has a BE in Electronic Engineering and a Masters in Business Studies from University College Dublin and a PhD in Information Technology from Maynooth University. The authors can be reached for consultation at innov8n@live.com.

https://doi.org/10.1515/9781501507335-018

About the Authors

Index

https://doi.org/10.1515/9781501507335-019

www.ingramcontent.com/pod-product-compliance
Lightning Source LLC
Chambersburg PA
CBHW061239220326
41599CB00028B/5482

* 9 7 8 1 5 0 1 5 1 5 7 8 1 *